# Abandoned Families

# Abandoned Families

## Social Isolation in the Twenty-First Century

✍

Kristin S. Seefeldt

Russell Sage Foundation
New York

# The Russell Sage Foundation

The Russell Sage Foundation, one of the oldest of America's general purpose foundations, was established in 1907 by Mrs. Margaret Olivia Sage for "the improvement of social and living conditions in the United States." The foundation seeks to fulfill this mandate by fostering the development and dissemination of knowledge about the country's political, social, and economic problems. While the foundation endeavors to assure the accuracy and objectivity of each book it publishes, the conclusions and interpretations in Russell Sage Foundation publications are those of the authors and not of the foundation, its trustees, or its staff. Publication by Russell Sage, therefore, does not imply foundation endorsement.

**Library of Congress Cataloging-in-Publication Data**

Names: Seefeldt, Kristin S., author.
Title: Abandoned families : social isolation in the twenty-first century / Kristin S. Seefeldt.
Description: New York : Russell Sage Foundation, 2016. | Includes bibliographical references and index.
Identifiers: LCCN 2016023826 (print) | LCCN 2016036423 (ebook) | ISBN 9780871547835 (pbk. : alk. paper) | ISBN 9781610448628 (ebook)
Subjects: LCSH: Families—United States. | Poor families—United States. | Marginality, Social—United States. | Family services—United States.
Classification: LCC HQ536 .S3989 2016 (print) | LCC HQ536 (ebook) | DDC 306.850973—dc23
LC record available at https://lccn.loc.gov/2016023826

Text design by Suzanne Nichols.

RUSSELL SAGE FOUNDATION
112 East 64th Street, New York, New York 10065
10  9  8  7  6  5  4  3  2  1

*In memory of Ned Gramlich*

# CONTENTS

# LIST OF TABLES

# About the Author

Kristin S. Seefeldt is assistant professor at the School of Social Work and the Gerald R. Ford School of Public Policy at the University of Michigan.

# ACKNOWLEDGMENTS

Many people helped me on this project in so many different ways. At the very beginning, Helen Levy (University of Michigan) and I developed the pilot interview guide and oversaw data collection of the pilot interviews. I am extremely grateful to Dr. Malverne Winborne, director of the Charter Schools Office at Eastern Michigan University, for his very early support of the project. He introduced me to the principals at a number of charter schools in southeastern Michigan who agreed to allow me to send home study recruitment flyers with their students. Dr. Cullian Hill of Commonwealth Academy in Detroit was particularly helpful in publicizing the study to parents. Michael Barr of the University of Michigan then graciously gave me access to participants in his Detroit Area Study on Financial Services, which allowed the study to really take off. Conversations with him over the years gave me much greater insight into the financial services system, an area in which I had little background when I started this project.

Because this project spanned many years, quite a few undergraduates, master's students, and doctoral students worked on it as they passed through the University of Michigan. Maria Johnson, Margaret Hudson, Benecia Cousins, Matthew Alemu, L'Heureux Lewis-McCoy, Jessica Wyse, Lloyd Grieger, Ashley Reid Brown, and Jessica Wiederspan helped conduct interviews from 2006 to 2009. Casey Parrotte transcribed many of the interviews in the first several years of the project. Other students who transcribed were Melisa March, Mark Strayer, Justin Sanders, Carly Johnson, Emily Bantz, Megan O'Rourke, and Meredith Horowski.

Sascha Demerjian was instrumental to this project in its early years, conducting interviews, helping with analysis, and managing the project. I started a doctoral program not even midway through the project, and I could not have kept it going had it not been for her. Barbara Ramsey made sure that respondents and the project's research assistants got paid.

Tedi Engler deserves special thanks. She started working on this project as an undergraduate student, transcribing interviews, but by 2010 she was conducting interviews, doing analysis, and writing reports. She continued working with me past graduation and was always willing to do anything and everything to help. Likewise with Shawn Pelak, former program manager at the National Poverty Center at the University of Michigan. She is a problem-solver extraordinaire and dealt with many of the administrative issues that go along with a research project and helped keep me sane.

Sheldon Danziger, who was the director of the National Poverty Center at the time, provided much support, both financial and intellectual. Moreover, his support of my research career has been instrumental in getting me to where I am today.

In addition to funding provided by the National Poverty Center, the Center for Local, State, and Urban Policy at the University of Michigan, the Annie E. Casey Foundation, and the U.S. Department of Agriculture all supported the project, allowing me to hire students, provide respondent payments, and have some of my time covered.

Colleagues who were always willing to talk through issues with me include Fred Wherry, Tony Chen, Sandra Danziger, Gerald Suttles, David Reingold, Karen Staller, Rick Rodems, Alix Gould-Werth, Scott Allard, and many others who attended talks I gave on early iterations of this project, including George Galster and his colleagues at Wayne State University. Some of the analyses presented in chapters 5 and 6 were fleshed out more fully in articles that appeared in *Qualitative Social Work* and *Social Service Review,* and I benefited greatly from editors Karen Staller and Susan Lambert and the anonymous reviewers whose comments sharpened those pieces. Alex Murphy and Reuben Miller really helped me work out some of the knots I got myself tied into, and Luke Shaefer has been my main cheerleader during the book-writing process. Kathy Edin provided invaluable guidance and helped me see the bigger picture. I greatly value her generosity in providing me with extensive feedback at several points during the process. Suzanne Nichols at the Russell Sage Foundation believed in this project and shepherded the book from a prospectus to its final version.

To my friends Sarah Burgard, Victor Fanucchi, Laura Lee, and David and Jill Thacher—many, many thanks for always providing me with needed respite and fun. Lucas, Josh, Alaysia, and Aliya— you're too young to read this now, but maybe someday! Katharine Greene read chapter 6 when it was much too long and complicated and also kept assuring me that one day I would learn how to do a backspin in skating. Jason Deveikis put up with me at the rink when my mind was focused on my work and not on my salchow.

Greg Levine provided me with emotional support and pushed me when I needed to be pushed. He also went above and beyond what one could desire from a spouse and read the manuscript multiple times. I'm not sure that I will ever be able to thank him enough.

I have dedicated this book to the memory of Ned Gramlich, former dean of the School of Public Policy at the University of Michigan (now the Gerald R. Ford School) and former governor at the Federal Reserve Board. I benefited greatly over the years from his mentoring and his wisdom. Well before the bursting of the housing bubble, he alerted me to the potential for the bottom to come out from under the housing market in Detroit and encouraged me to look more carefully at what was going on there. Before he passed in 2007, he tried to caution others at the Fed about the perils of subprime mortgages and the lack of regulation of these financial products.

Finally, I must give the greatest and most profuse thanks to all of the women who participated in this study. Their willingness to give their time over so many years and to share some of the most personal details of their lives is a gift that I truly cherish. I very much hope that what follows rings true. My life has been so enriched by meeting and getting to know each and every one of them.

# ⚘ CHAPTER 1 ⚘

## FROM SOCIAL ISOLATION TO
## SOCIAL ABANDONMENT

In 1987, William Julius Wilson's book on urban poverty, *The Truly Disadvantaged*, was released, bringing the terms "concentrated poverty" and "social isolation" into the lexicon of social scientists studying some of the most disadvantaged groups in the United States.[1] Using Chicago as his case study, Wilson argued that within central cities in poor, predominantly black neighborhoods lived certain individuals and families "whose behavior contrasts sharply with that of mainstream America."[2] These individuals were "socially isolated," meaning that they had limited contact with employed individuals, community organizations, and the institutions associated with the working and middle classes. Wilson contended that as job opportunities moved outside of the central city, and as housing discrimination lessened, the African American working and middle classes were able to move out as well. When they left, an important buffer for the poor was gone. No longer did the poor see people going to work each day, and an important source of information about potential jobs and how to navigate the world of work was lost. Institutions such as schools, churches, and community organizations were weakened with the departure of more stable residents.

Economic shifts, beyond the movement of jobs outside of central cities, also reinforced concentrated poverty and social isolation. Manufacturing jobs had provided African Americans with employment opportunities during the first part of the twentieth century, but the latter half of the century had been marked by deindustrial-

1

ization as these jobs moved out of the country (or disappeared altogether through technological innovation). Taking advantage of changes brought about during the civil rights era and by the passage of antidiscrimination laws, some better-educated and middle-class African Americans were able to enter formerly segregated schools and occupations, including employment within the public sector and unionized jobs. As a result, Wilson argued, the condition of poor blacks "deteriorated during the very period in which the most sweeping antidiscrimination legislation and programs have been enacted and implemented. The net effect is a growing economic schism between poor and higher-income blacks."[3] Poor blacks were left behind in neighborhoods that would become characterized by concentrated poverty, joblessness, and other attendant problems, such as welfare "dependency," criminal activity, and neighborhood deterioration.

Now more than twenty-five years have passed since the publication of *The Truly Disadvantaged,* and it remains one of the most highly cited and important works on poverty in the United States. Many of Wilson's descriptions of the conditions and prospects of central city–dwelling African Americans still hold true—the unemployment rates of this group remain high, and mass incarceration, which was only just beginning when Wilson was writing, has affected too many African American men who have been imprisoned and, upon release, marked by a criminal record that makes it nearly impossible to find a job.[4] Present-day Detroit bears striking similarities to Wilson's Chicago of twenty-five years ago, albeit on a much larger scale. An estimated 40 percent of the city's residents live in poverty, and in 2010 the official unemployment rate was 25 percent, although some, including city leaders, believed that, including all of those who had stopped searching for work, it was closer to 50 percent.[5] Decades of white flight and, more recently, black departures left the city overwhelmingly African American, in stark contrast to the mostly white suburbs. By 2010, neighborhoods with poverty rates of 40 percent or higher were no longer scattered here and there throughout Detroit, as they were in 2000, but rather took up most of the city's vast geographical space.[6] Is Detroit, then, a city populated by the truly disadvantaged, its residents left behind by the middle class of both races? The answer is not quite so simple, as I will argue.

Wilson had little to say about those who have left the central city — the workers, churchgoers, and businesspeople who make up the black middle class and whose departure contributed to the social isolation of those left behind. While antidiscrimination legislation has certainly opened up the residential real estate market for African Americans, segregation continues to exist. Middle-class and working-class African Americans may end up in close proximity to poor neighborhoods. Even then, the average black middle-class family typically lives in a neighborhood with lower income than the neighborhood of the average poor white family.[7] And when black families start to integrate formerly white neighborhoods, white flight begins.[8] Black middle-class families are also very likely to have strong ties to poorer relatives, meaning that perhaps the connections between the poor and the middle-class are not severed, as the term "social isolation" might imply.[9] But middle-class status for blacks is tenuous; they are more likely than whites to experience downward mobility, and less likely to experience upward mobility.[10] In a similar vein, Wilson was silent about people who stayed in the central city but had jobs and adhered to other norms that Wilson associated with the middle class, the so-called decent folk that Elijah Anderson describes in *Code of the Street*.[11] According to Anderson, these working-class families valued self-reliance, hard work, and sacrifice for the future.

In this book, I focus on a group I call "strivers." They are Detroit-area residents whom Wilson might have called the "middle class," or Anderson "decent" families. They work, attend postsecondary institutions, and are or aspire to be homeowners. Yet, despite their efforts in striving for middle-class status, they remain poor, near-poor, or precariously clinging to a middle-class status that could easily be lost. Ongoing residential segregation and continued labor market discrimination certainly account for their struggles, but there is another set of factors at work as well. Building upon Wilson's concept of *social isolation*, I argue that these families have been *socially abandoned*. Their social abandonment has come about from economic and policy changes as well as political choices that have altered the structures of opportunity in a way that goes well beyond the social isolation experienced by the urban poor living in high-poverty neighborhoods. It is a result of a new set of social transformations that affect the poor, the near-poor, and the struggling middle class.

## The New Social Transformation and Social Abandonment

By social abandonment I mean that, at a basic level, striving families have been abandoned by institutions that traditionally promoted inclusion and upward mobility. Social abandonment is produced via two mechanisms. First, social abandonment consigns striving families to separate, unequal, and segregated labor, postsecondary, and housing markets that do not offer the same opportunities for advancement and wealth-building that are available to others. Second, protections that were once in place, whether through regulations, social programs, or more informal systems, have been stripped away, leaving families exposed to great financial risk. In the end, not only are striving families unable to move up economically, but they are left in debt from both their investments in the future and their struggles to make ends meet.

The deindustrialization that Wilson documented is now nearly complete. The good manufacturing jobs for less-educated workers in places like Detroit are few and far between. The public-sector jobs that once served as a pathway to the middle class for African Americans are disappearing as well.[12] Instead, job growth has been concentrated in the low-paying service sector. The low-wage labor market grew in the late 1990s and continued to expand into the 2000s. The labor market facing many less-educated workers may offer more job opportunities, but the quality of the jobs may be poor. Studies of low-wage workplaces have documented the challenges of trying to survive economically on these low-paying and irregularly scheduled jobs. Workers who may be classified as full-time find themselves scheduled for very few hours one week, but for many more the next; they may come to work but then be sent home because of a low volume of work.[13] These types of workplace

4

conditions can lead to great instability in earnings, making it difficult to pay bills, as well as challenges in balancing work and family responsibilities and finding child care when schedules are so erratic.[14]

According to Wilson, employment is a mechanism for inclusion in the larger society and stability in one's life. Low pay and erratic scheduling suggest that some workers are not experiencing the full benefits of work that Wilson envisioned. Jobs are increasingly either low-paying or high-paying, with relatively few so-called middle-skill jobs available.[15] But there have been other, less-documented changes in the structure of work that call into question how well employment brings stability into people's lives. I show that strivers often work alone, may never see their employers, and often see coworkers only when they pass them at shift changes. Why does this type of isolation matter? Accompanying the decline of manufacturing has been the erosion of union power, which has left employees with little say about workplace conditions and practices and little protection against workplace abuses. Many of the striving class work for employers that operate outside of the laws and regulations intended to protect workers; as such, they are vulnerable to being fired or feeling compelled to quit before they are dismissed. Moreover, isolation on the job leaves strivers lacking opportunities to build networks that could provide support when they face workplace problems or help when they are looking for a new job. This is the separate and unequal labor market in which strivers work.

Homeownership and a college education are heralded as sure pathways to prosperity in this country. Historically, discriminatory legislation, policies, and practices kept African Americans locked out of the dream of homeownership and confined to segregated neighborhoods.[16] For example, federal housing policies concentrated African Americans in public housing, and racist lending guidelines kept families from securing mortgages. Local zoning ordinances could keep lower-income families out of certain neighborhoods by prohibiting the development of multi-unit housing. And real estate agents steered blacks away from white neighborhoods and did not show them homes there.[17] Although more African

Americans have many more opportunities for homeownership today, the legacy of those policies continues to produce residential segregation. Likewise, outside of the historically black colleges and universities, the doors to higher education were closed to all but a select few African Americans until desegregation efforts started in earnest in the 1960s and the civil rights movement challenged discrimination in university admissions.

Now, not only do striving families continue to face the challenge of residential segregation, but owning their own home is a gamble as opposed to a sure path to upward mobility; families striving for middle-class status may become trapped holding underwater mortgages for a home located in a depopulated neighborhood of foreclosed houses and concentrated poverty. Additionally, deregulation of the financial services sector allowed for the development of high-cost, high-fee mortgages that were targeted to communities of color—a separate and unequal financial product. These mortgages put many families at risk of losing their home altogether. Meanwhile, college enrollment rates have gone up across the board, but changes in the delivery of higher education have led to the expansion of a secondary track of degree acquisition. "Going to school" occurs within a stratified and indeed segregated educational system, one that relegates strivers to online course work, for-profit institutions, and community colleges that provide little in the way of assistance. Obtaining more education in this way can be a long process, resulting in debt from student loans more often than in a degree, and even when a degree is obtained, the payoff is weak. For these families, the promise of homeownership and education as tools for achieving upward mobility has been broken.

Striving families have also been abandoned by the institutions and regulations that are supposed to protect them during difficult times. Specifically, the great difficulties that vulnerable families face in accessing an already stingy safety net leave them exposed to hardship. Retrenchments in the social safety net, most notably welfare reform, have made access to some public assistance benefits much more difficult. Although the welfare recipients interviewed by Kathryn Edin and Laura Lein pre-reform could not make ends meet on a welfare check alone, they at least had a stable monthly benefit upon which to build.[18] Striving families, who often need benefits because their wages are so low, do not receive them in a timely fashion. People who lose jobs may wait weeks, months, or even years to receive the benefits to which they are entitled. An outdated Unemployment Insurance (UI) system favors those who have lost a full-time, year-round job through layoff, even though employment is increasingly irregular and unstable.

When assistance from the safety net is not available, families take on debt (perhaps in addition to the mortgages and student loans they already carry). However, the financial products (including mortgages) they are offered frequently have bad terms, such as high interest rates and penalties. Deregulation of the financial sector has opened access to credit for people with low income, but the dark side of easy credit is the predatory nature of those products. Families can find themselves trapped in a cycle of debt, never able to pay down balances, let alone make a dent in the debt they might have accrued in the past. These striving families have become modern-day sharecroppers, always owing someone and never able to fully "settle up." Problems making payments may also lead to a low credit score. In addition to the continued financial repercussions of a low score (for example, being unable to get additional credit or credit with good terms), credit scores can be used by employers in making hiring decisions and landlords when they are screening applicants; strivers "marked" by very low credit scores are thus hurt in other markets. Holding debt also puts families at risk of having their wages or tax refunds garnished by creditors, a practice that disrupts the already fragile financial situation of families in debt.

Finally, carrying debt negatively affects the ability of striving families to accumulate and build wealth. To build wealth, one does not need to be debt-free; however, it is almost impossible for families striving to reach the middle class to get out from under debt, especially when the debt they have taken on for purposes of investment has proved worthless. For other families, taking out loans for college or a mortgage on a home might be significant drivers in building wealth; the cost of student loans might be more than repaid through higher future earnings. For many striving families, however, the debts that might otherwise translate into investments instead become mechanisms of wealth-stripping. In short, these striving families are left to become abandoned families.

Social abandonment can also help explain the maintenance and growth of income and wealth inequality between blacks and whites. In 2007, for example, blacks' median income was $41,400, whereas for whites it was $58,200. Differences are even more stark when we examine net worth (the difference between assets and debts): median assets among blacks amounted to $31,800, while for whites the figure was $192,800—six times the median net worth of blacks.[19] Further, a college-educated African American has only one-third as much wealth as a white high school dropout.[20] Social abandonment may also help explain low rates of intergenerational mobility. Two-thirds of black families living in the poorest neighborhoods will continue to do so a generation later. This generational experience is much less common among whites, and far fewer whites ever live in the poorest neighborhoods, making this intergenerational transmission of neighborhood poverty a phenomenon that disproportionately affects blacks.[21]

The struggles faced by striving families in trying to achieve upward mobility demonstrate how difficult it is and how difficult building wealth can be. Their jobs give them few opportunities to move up, whether because of the lack of career ladders or because of workplace isolation; their homes are worth less than they owe on them; and their college education, if they are even able to complete a degree, leaves them in debt and usually with a job that does not pay much better. Poor children tend to fare better in places that have more integrated neighborhoods, but many poor families find it too expensive to live in such a neighborhood.[22] And striving families who do move to such neighborhoods may find themselves isolated from the rest of the community.

In discussing social abandonment, I use terms such as "separate and unequal," "segregated," and "sharecropping" very deliberately because, as I argue, social abandonment represents the latest set of policy choices and institutional changes that serve to perpetuate racial inequality. Poor and lower-income whites have been affected by social abandonment, but fundamentally social abandonment is tied to past and ongoing discrimination as well as racial residential segregation and the predatory lending practices that are deployed much more frequently against people of color.

# The Study

I did not start out intending to study social abandonment. The conclusions I draw come from analyzing interview data and placing those findings in the context of larger social trends and the findings of other studies. I interviewed forty-five women living in the Detroit metropolitan area. With a couple of exceptions, each woman was interviewed yearly between 2006 and 2011, for a total of six interviews. The sample includes women from a range of socioeconomic positions (but including more poor and near-poor families), from families both with and without minor-aged children (but more with minor-aged children), and from a mix of races and ethnicities. The resulting sample is predominantly African American (thirty-eight women), with four non-Hispanic white women, one Latina, and two Arab American immigrants. (See the methodological appendix for more detail about the study design, sample, and interview questions.)

Originally, I was interested in understanding how economically vulnerable families were faring during the first significant economic downturn since a number of major social policy changes had been implemented, most notably welfare reform and the expansion of the Earned Income Tax Credit (EITC), policies that mandated and rewarded work, respectively. Once in the field, however, it quickly became clear to me that welfare reform and the EITC were very small parts of a larger story. I also soon realized that my purposeful focus on women was not necessarily detrimental: women, particularly women of color, were more likely to be targets for subprime housing loans, and among African Americans, enrollment in postsecondary education was higher for women than for men.[23]

With the exception of a few women who were struggling with severe health problems, one trait shared by these women quickly became apparent: they were all trying hard to improve their situation. They were holding down jobs, going to school, and buying and keeping up homes. They did not have outsized ambitions or plans; rather, they wanted better jobs (to be a nurse instead of a home health aide, for instance), to live in a nicer neighborhood, to maybe take a vacation with their kids. They were striving for something better. Yet, six years after the study began, the majority of these women still had incomes around or below the federal poverty line, and even those with higher incomes were struggling to maintain their economic position. This stasis led me to ask: What is it about the jobs that these striving individuals hold, their higher educational pursuits, and the neighborhoods in which they live that might explain their difficulties moving up? What happens to striving families that they are not able to realize their dreams, despite their attempts to follow the same paths that for decades have produced upward mobility for others?

Through the experiences of these women in Detroit, we can see how those striving for upward mobility are abandoned at various turns by the systems and institutions that should have assisted them in their quest for better lives. Among these striving women was Geneva, who lost her job when she was injured at work. Her employer faced no penalties but instead contested her claim for public benefits, making her go months without any cash coming into her household. Geneva sought to better her situation by returning to school, but when she finished she was unable to find a job in the field for which she was trained. She was saddled with large student loans she took out to finance her education at a for-profit institution. Geneva had once been married and had considered herself middle-class, but job loss, health problems, and divorce left her with income barely above the federal poverty line and a home that was in foreclosure. Another woman at the head of an abandoned family was Yvette, a steadily employed telecommunications worker and a single mother. She had significant student loan debt from an online school through which she had earned a degree that, as she said, only allowed her to get a job one step above fast-food work. She held a mortgage on her home on Detroit's east side that was much greater than the house's value. And Yvette had thousands of dollars of credit card debt from trying to make ends meet. No matter how much she paid, the balance never seemed to go down.

Finally, social abandonment hits the poorest families particularly hard. These women may have once been strivers, but serious health problems kept them out of the labor market, out of school, and sometimes unable to hang on to their homes. Their nonexistent credit scores kept them from securing any type of financial products. Relegated to the very fringes, they were given disability payments but otherwise left on their own to manage their various problems.

It is worth noting that data collection for this project covers the period of the Great Recession and the subsequent slow recovery. Plausibly, what I am observing could simply be the effect of the recession rather than what I am calling social abandonment. However, the recession served more as a backdrop than as an actor in these women's stories. Most of them, when asked how the recession was affecting them, could point to a few friends and family members who had been laid off, and there was a general sense that it was difficult to find jobs, but only a couple of women saw themselves as being affected by the recession. In fact, employment rates among the women peaked at about 75 percent in 2008 and 2009, at the height of the Great Recession. Certainly the subprime mortgage crisis and bursting of the housing bubble played a role in draining these families of any wealth they had hoped to accrue through homeownership; in other parts of the country, however, housing prices have been climbing back to pre-recession values, while in Detroit, as in other predominantly African American communities, the recovery has not happened.

Is social abandonment merely a story about families in Detroit? Again, I argue no. The data on homeownership, college enrollment and student loan debt, predatory lending, and other trends lend credence to the argument that this is a national phenomenon that is helping to reproduce and maintain racial inequalities. The experiences of the Detroit-area women in this study illustrate how social abandonment occurs across the country.

The final issue to consider is marriage. The majority, although not all, of the women in this study were single mothers, and seventeen had never been married. More than 30 percent of single-mother households are poor, compared to about 6 percent of married-parent families.[24] Achieving middle-class status can be much easier with two incomes compared to one. The families in Karyn Lacy's study of the black upper-middle class were all married couples.[25] Wilson devotes considerable attention to rising rates of births outside of marriage and female-headed households in the central city; however, his analysis focuses on changes in larger social values, such as the increasing acceptance of divorce and single-parenting, as well as labor market changes that gave women increasing economic independence from men. With other social commentators focused on the availability of welfare payments as the explanation for declines in marriage among the poor, Wilson argues that male joblessness is the primary obstacle to marriage. Quite simply, there are not enough "marriageable men" (his term) within central cities for women to consider marriage.[26] More recent studies find that poor men and women indeed value marriage as an institution, but believe that they need to be financially secure before they take this step. This requirement is not in place for childbearing, researchers Kathryn Edin and Maria Kefalas argue, because parenthood is one of the few positive identities available to poor people, given their meager labor market prospects.[27] A large literature has taken on the challenge of understanding increases in childbearing outside of marriage and in single-parenting. Nevertheless, by the mid-2000s single motherhood could hardly be called an aberrant behavior. Just under one-quarter of all children and half of African American children lived with a single mother, while fewer than half of all children lived in the so-called traditional family with two married, heterosexual parents in their first marriage.[28]

Would the women in this study have been better off financially if they had been married? Perhaps. Those with the highest household incomes — Lisa, Gwen, and Leah — were all married, but they faced the struggles of underwater mortgages and high levels of debt. Marriage did not boost the economic prospects of Sandra and Cynthia, whose husbands were frequently out of work. Marriage, it seems, is not a protective factor against social abandonment.

# An Outline of the Book

The next chapter orients the reader to the location of the study — Detroit, the poster child for social abandonment. Once one of the largest cities in the country and a center of manufacturing, the city is now depopulated, filled with vacant properties, and lacking in money to properly fund city services. Some might argue that Detroit is a city with unique challenges and that the issues faced by its residents cannot be generalized beyond the city limits (or at least Michigan). Although Detroit is the first major U.S. city to file for bankruptcy, many other cities around the country are "financially distressed," including not only other former industrial cities, like Syracuse, New York, and Reading, Pennsylvania, but also places perceived to be wealthier, like Miami and the greater Los Angeles metropolitan area.

The next three chapters focus on the spheres in which social abandonment occurs. Chapter 3 discusses social abandonment in the workplace, where it thwarts the promise of social integration that work is supposed to provide. Low-paying service-sector jobs have been growing the fastest. They do not pay well, they offer few if any benefits, and they are highly unstable. In these jobs, much of an employee's work is performed in isolation from coworkers, or apart from any meaningful contact with supervisors. The repercussion of lack of connections to others in the workplace, coupled with low pay and other workplace conditions, is to maintain and exacerbate social isolation.

Chapter 4 discusses the role of social abandonment in shutting out individuals and families from the promise of upward mobility that higher education and homeownership once offered. College enrollment rates have risen over time, yet those in abandoned families who enroll in college may get a degree from an online program or a for-profit school that leaves them deep in debt and with no chance at a better job. Or they may go to an understaffed and underresourced community college, working for years toward a degree they may never obtain.

Social abandonment also plays out in our public safety net system. Chapter 5 documents these women's experiences with trying to secure benefits when they lost jobs and to maintain those benefits once approved. Those who are abandoned by the safety net often must fight for those benefits for months or even years.

Social abandonment results in debt, the subject of chapter 6. Families are mired in debt, with little hope of escaping. They go into debt when the safety net fails them, they go into debt when their jobs fail them, and they go into debt trying to better their situations. They are caught in a cycle of perpetually owing money. Social abandonment is like sharecropping in that it keeps people from getting ahead and keeps them forever in debt.

The book concludes with recommendations for addressing social abandonment and undoing the harms it has caused. In the current political climate, some of these suggestions may seem like pie in the sky, but the consequences of social abandonment for those who experience it are too dire to ignore.

Finally, while the story about social abandonment told here is one of structural impediments to upward mobility, as seen through a decidedly racial lens, I do not at all want to suggest that individual agency plays no role. The women profiled here are not passive victims. They are smart and savvy and have weathered circumstances that would have immobilized others. But like all of us, they have sometimes made choices that some people may find questionable and that even they themselves sometimes later regretted. We must remember, however, that they made their decisions within a system that stacks formidable odds against their upward mobility.

# ✺ CHAPTER 2 ✺

## *ABANDONED DETROIT*

Driving up to the house where Annette lived was always a bit surreal. Once off the highway, I would drive down a stretch of road in a neighborhood that had clearly seen better days. She lived in an older area of the city, not all that far away from where the city's infamous riot of 1967 had broken out. The houses still standing were large, two-story wood or brick homes, but many lots were vacant; an entire side of one block had no structures on it whatsoever. The sidewalks were overgrown with weeds and looked more like dirt paths than paved walkways. Several blocks farther along this road, a boarded-up brick building was still standing; it looked like it had once been something official—a school or perhaps a post office. Other buildings that had presumably once housed businesses were now crumbling, their window panes broken. This desolation was made even more unreal by the sudden appearance, looming high over the vacant buildings, of a billboard advertising the arrival of a famous chef at one of the casinos downtown.

From a bit of a distance, the condition of Annette's block did not appear to be as bad, with houses lining both sides of the street. But as it turned out, the first two were just shells—they had been burned out. The house across the street from Annette's was barely even a shell: both the inside and outside had been torched, and part of the roof had caved in. But right next to that house was a freshly painted, occupied home with a beautifully landscaped yard.

Detroit is perhaps one of the most compelling symbols of abandonment in this country, and thus a fitting site for a discussion of social abandonment in particular. Once one of the largest cities in the United States, with a peak population of about 1.8 million residents in 1950, the city is now home to fewer than 700,000 people. With rapid population loss came abandonment of homes, factories, and all other types of structures. In 2010, one-third of all lots in Detroit, it was estimated, were vacant or abandoned.[1] A burgeoning number of websites feature the so-called ruins of Detroit. Followers of this "ruin porn," as well as many others living outside of Detroit, have come to associate the city with the abandoned Central Rail Station, an old Packard manufacturing plant, or the once-grand Michigan Theatre, now used to park cars.

With abandonment has come an increase in both the number of people living in areas of concentrated poverty and the geographic reach of those areas as those with more resources leave the city for the suburbs. When William Julius Wilson was writing about Chicago in the 1980s, he documented an increase in the number of neighborhoods in which 30 percent or more of households had incomes below the federal poverty line: eight of the city's seventy-seven communities met this criterion in 1970, and twelve did in 1980; indeed, some neighborhoods that were poor in 1970 became even poorer. These neighborhoods were primarily located in one part of the city, and they were home to many African Americans. Contrast Wilson's Chicago of 1980 with current-day Detroit, where more than 180 of the city's census tracts are high-poverty, triple the number in 2000 and a much higher number than in 1980.[2] Although the units of analysis are not comparable (neighborhoods are larger units than tracts), the visual difference between the two cities is striking. In Chicago, areas of concentrated poverty have spread over time, but mainly outward from historically high-poverty areas; most of the north and northwest sides of the city remain untouched by rising neighborhood poverty.[3] In Detroit, by contrast, just a handful of census tracts have poverty rates lower than 20 percent, and more neighborhoods have become poorer over time.[4]

Detroiters themselves have been blamed for their city's demise; taken to task for many misdeeds, they have been criticized for electing corrupt officials and feeling "entitled" to good-paying jobs like those previously offered by the auto industry. Even more than twenty years later, it is not uncommon to hear some white Michigan residents say that Coleman Young, the city's first African American mayor (serving from 1974 to 1994), "ruined" Detroit— coded language expressing the racially motivated animosity, thinly veiled, that emanates from people who seem to believe that Detroit was taken away from them.[5] Such blame and anger not only obscure the phenomenon of social abandonment but also erase the consequences of decades of depopulation and deindustrialization in Detroit, as well as the impact of federal and state policies that exacerbated the effects of these changes.

# A Brief History of the Abandonment of Detroit

White flight from Detroit began in the 1950s, when federal funds were used to build freeways that allowed easy access to suburban areas. Previously, blacks were relegated to a small number of neighborhoods in the central city. While white movement out of the city gave African Americans the opportunity to move into neighborhoods that were formerly off-limits, restrictive covenants and racial violence kept them inside the city. Orville Hubbard, the thirteen-term mayor (from the 1940s through the 1970s) of Dearborn, the city immediately to Detroit's west, vowed to keep that city "lily white," fought hard against the construction of public housing in Dearborn, and went on record as being in favor of segregation. The pace of white flight accelerated after large-scale rioting broke out in the city in 1967. Further, much of the city was designed around automakers' needs, including the development of numerous nearby communities that were annexed to provide housing for the burgeoning workforce. But when whites and their money and the auto companies and their plants began to relocate from the city to the suburbs, the city's tax base was decimated and many properties, including many large factories, were abandoned.[6]

During the Great Recession of 2007 to 2009, Detroit teetered on the precipice of financial insolvency. The federal government rescued two auto companies that were going under, but there was no bailout for the city. Detroit was also a prime target of predatory lenders, and the resulting foreclosure crisis only exacerbated the city's financial crisis, with revenue continuing to decline because of lost property tax payments when homes were foreclosed upon and the value of occupied housing declined. Although corruption and risky financial maneuvering during former mayor Kwame Kilpatrick's time in office (2002 to 2008) have also been blamed for contributing to the city's poor fiscal health, the abandonment of a promise made between Kilpatrick and then-governor John Engler to keep stable the funds received through revenue-sharing hurt the city much more than Kilpatrick's racketeering and extortion schemes.[7] Detroit's financial distress culminated in a bankruptcy filing in 2013, making it to date the largest city to do so. Current governor Rick Snyder installed an "emergency manager" to oversee the city's finances and its path out of bankruptcy.

But there was no rescue for the families living in an abandoned city, nor for those in the suburbs surrounding Detroit. Scrapping, squatting, and arson were problems that most Detroit residents had encountered at some point. Living in the suburbs did not necessarily improve one's situation. Schools there were better for children, but rents were higher, forcing some families to live in apartment complexes isolated from the rest of the community. Many poor and low-wage workers struggled to find stable housing, and some never did. Strivers who had become homeowners watched their neighborhoods slide into disarray as homes were vacated; their own property values plummeted, leaving them with the choice of staying in a declining area or walking away from what should have been a source of wealth. As city officials, entrepreneurs, and newly arrived young creative types began making plans for the city's comeback, long-term residents who had stayed in Detroit while others left were excluded from this "revitalization" of Detroit.

## Detroit and Its Neighborhoods

Detroit was not an abandoned city to thirty-five of the women in this study; it was their home for some or all of the time between 2006 and 2011, and for many it was the only place they had ever lived. Detroit does not have the strong neighborhood identities that one finds in Chicago or some other large cities. Except for people living in Mexicantown and the more recent, more affluent, and generally white residents flocking to the fashionable areas of Midtown and other areas close to downtown, most residents identify their location as either the "west side" or the "east side" of Woodward Avenue, a main thoroughfare that runs north to south through roughly the middle of the city. The two sides contain different types of neighborhoods with different histories and problems. When the factories were up and running, more were located on the east side, which had more of an industrial feel in certain areas. (The factories may have contributed to the high levels of lead found in the blood of children living on the east side; industrial toxins produced long ago can stay in the soil for decades.[8]) According to data compiled by Data Driven Detroit, a nonprofit "data hub" that provides detailed information on various aspects of Detroit and the metro area, compared to the west side, census block areas on the east side have proportionally more housing in very poor condition, more vacant lots, a higher proportion of adults without a high school or equivalent degree, and lower per capita income.[9]

Slightly more than half of the Detroit residents I interviewed lived on the east side. Several had spent at least some time in the east side's Osborn neighborhood (or in the area immediately to its west), a neighborhood characterized in 2011 by the *Detroit News* as "Detroit's Deadliest Neighborhood" because of the large number of homicides and shootings.[10] Osborn has also been the site of a number of public and philanthropic efforts aimed at solidifying the area. Yet the streets on which these women lived did not seem to have changed at all. Erica lived on the fringes of Osborn for a couple of years. Her street seemed peaceful enough during all my visits there, but she referred to the neighborhood as "the hood" and believed that most people living on the street had their utilities connected illegally—usually by finding someone to scale a utility pole and rig some sort of connection—and were dealing drugs or engaging in other hustles. Lisa, one of the better-off women in the study, moved to Osborn with her husband, who remembered it from childhood as "one of the nicer areas of Detroit." Even before they moved in, their house was broken into and their air conditioning system was stolen. Lisa also witnessed an armed robbery directly in front of their house.

Other east siders lived in relatively close proximity to Outer Drive, a boulevard that encircles a large part of the city. Outer Drive is winding and can be quite confusing to drive, but along much of it the homes are beautiful brick two-stories, some quite luxurious. Yards are mostly well maintained (lawn service workers can often be seen there in the middle of the day, tending to the landscaping). However, not too far off of Outer Drive are blocks that, while hanging on, are experiencing the effects of increased vacancies—untended yards, boarded-up homes, and lots that have become dumping grounds. Miss Price referred to the neighborhood she moved into in 2009—an area of Detroit that seems to lack a moniker—as "the ghetto," although at first glance, one might not think this. Her block, like nearly all the neighborhoods I visited, was lined with single-family homes.

High-rise apartments, which for better or worse are synonymous with public housing and "the ghetto," are few and far between in Detroit. In part, this is because of Detroit's wide geographic spread and the preponderance of one-story, single-family homes. As is often noted, in terms of land size, San Francisco, Boston, and the isle of Manhattan together would all fit into the 139 square miles inside the city limits of Detroit, with a little bit of room left over. Because of its large size, the pressure to construct high-rise, high-density housing has been minimal. Aside from the older, centrally located areas of the city, neighborhoods consist primarily of small Cape Cod houses, either brick or wood frame, built in the 1920s or 1930s or after World War II, in the late 1940s and early 1950s. Despite ample land, Detroit has faced housing shortages at a number of points in its history, including during the Great Depression, World War II, and the immediate postwar years. These shortages affected both blacks and whites, but the situation was much worse for African Americans, who for decades were kept out of many neighborhoods and relegated primarily to the highly overcrowded areas of Paradise Valley and Black Bottom, neighborhoods that were demolished in the early 1960s as part of "slum clearance" projects and paved over by Interstate 75.[11]

But housing projects do exist in Detroit. The Brewster Homes, one of the nation's first large-scale public housing complexes, sits close to the downtown area. In the early 1950s the projects were expanded, with the addition of four "high-rises" (only fourteen stories tall) called the Douglass Towers; the overall project became known as Brewster-Douglass and was home to Diana Ross, Smokey Robinson, and Lily Tomlin in their youth. The high-rises later emptied out, and eventually some buildings were demolished, while others have been renovated into senior housing.

For most of the time I knew her, Tykia, a young mother with one son, lived in an apartment on the east side in what remained of the Charles Terrace public housing complex, built in the same era as Brewster. According to the Detroit Public Housing Commission, Charles Terrace originally consisted of thirty-nine buildings, but only seven or eight buildings still stood—in a large, empty, and dust-covered field—when Tykia lived there. The buildings of Charles Terrace resembled barracks more than apartments. The complex was torn down beginning in 2012 and replaced by the Emerald Springs development, financed in part by federal Hope VI funds, which are designated for the express purpose of demolishing old public housing complexes and replacing them with new, sometimes mixed-income developments. The Emerald Springs development consists of brick townhomes, and tenants will have access to a fitness room and a clubhouse, amenities that Tykia never enjoyed. She had been promised occupancy in one of the units but moved out in 2011, two years before her building was demolished.

The west side neighborhoods I visited looked fairly similar. Most of the residential streets run south to north, with major commercial arteries cutting through west to east. Many of the homes were built in the 1930s and 1940s for autoworkers, and during the postwar period, given the shortage of housing in the city, more houses were put up quickly; at the time one developer estimated that construction of a single home would take twelve person-days of labor—or two if the prospective owner was in a hurry and was able to pay for more workers. Given the rapid construction, the homes were and continue to be nothing fancy—single-story wood frame homes with an attic, usually about 900 square feet.[12] The Grandmont-Rosedale

21

area on the west side is one of the more stable neighborhoods in the area. Residents tend to be better educated and to have higher incomes compared to residents of other areas of Detroit. More than 80 percent of homes are owner-occupied, and in contrast to the quickly constructed Cape Cods of other neighborhoods, most are stately brick two-stories or ranches. But right next to Grandmont-Rosedale is the neighborhood of Brightmoor, which has been in significant decline, leading some people to refer to it as "Blight More."

Southwest Detroit is home to one of the city's few "ethnic" neighborhoods, Mexicantown. During labor shortages in World War II, Mexicans were recruited to come north and work in Detroit's wartime production, and many settled in this neighborhood.[13] The area is more diverse than most of Detroit, with Latinos, rather than African Americans, constituting the majority of residents. Although parts of Southwest Detroit have been revitalized, particularly Mexicantown, whose restaurants are popular among suburbanites, the area is also the base for the Latin Counts, a gang that has been the target of a joint FBI–Detroit Police effort to reduce violent crime in the city.[14]

Marie owned a home in Southwest Detroit. The first time I turned off the main road and into her neighborhood, a very large dog ran out in front of my car, barking ferociously and not backing down when I honked. (It finally ran off when I started inching the car forward.) Marie assumed that the local drug dealers had set the dog out. A few years earlier, drug dealers had moved directly across the street from her. Marie reported that she was determined to get them out of the neighborhood, saying, "I chased them away. I just got in fights with them, I said, 'You gonna call me a snitch? I'm gonna take a picture of you while you're selling it and write the license plate. I'll really be a snitch!'" Marie is long gone from her house, but drug dealers remain on the street.

A few areas of Detroit have remained stable enclaves of higher-income residents. These include Palmer Woods, Boston-Edison, and Indian Village. None of the women in this study ever lived in these areas. A number of areas have become popular destinations for new arrivals to the city, including downtown and midtown (near Wayne State University), where rental occupancy rates top 95 percent.[15] Another popular area is Corktown, which is one of the oldest parts of the city and has become a hipster hangout. Judy was the only woman in the study who had ventured into one of these revitalized areas. In 2011 she moved into an apartment in downtown Detroit. Although a native Detroiter, Judy talked about her new neighborhood as if she had moved to a completely different city: "It's just a different environment, period, down here. To put— to use my mother's word, it's more 'upscale' down here." She was having difficulty finding her way around, noting that many of the streets were one-way and not set on a grid. One day she decided to walk over to Greektown, a small entertainment district downtown with a casino and some restaurants, close to the baseball park and football stadium. Even though it was a short walk, it was an adventure for Judy, since she didn't know where she was going and the street names were unfamiliar. She said, "When they say, 'Go to Congress [Street], I'm like, 'Where is Congress?'" For visitors to Detroit, Greektown, the ballparks, and the cultural venues like the Detroit Institute of Art are usual stops, but for residents like Judy, they are a whole different world.

## Living in an Abandoned City

The sheer magnitude of abandonment within some Detroit neighborhoods can be shocking for first-time visitors (and can continue to be no matter how many times one has been to the city). A survey of residential parcels conducted by a consortium of nonprofits in 2009 found that 26 percent were vacant—that is, no house or other dwelling structure was present. Ninety-five percent of homes were categorized as habitable (that is, in good condition or needing only minor repairs). In the report released by the consortium, one of the nonprofit directors says, "This important survey busts the national media myth that all of Detroit has fallen into complete disarray."[16] However, the consortium's "drive-by" approach in gathering its data may have led it to understate some of the housing and neighborhood challenges faced by residents—or at least by the women I interviewed. Teams of three surveyors, many of them University of Michigan students, drove down every residential street in the city, making note of the number of vacant properties and the quality of still-standing houses. The immense effort undertaken to document the status of residential properties in the city should not be discounted, but as the report's authors note, the survey teams never left their cars as they made their best visual guesses as to the tenancy and adequacy of the structures. Outside appearances, however, can be deceiving. Sometimes a property is just very old and run-down rather than uninhabited. According to census data, nearly six in ten homes in Detroit were built before 1950.[17] Although older housing is not necessarily in worse condition than newer structures, a house that has had more owners, who may not have been able to afford repairs, over a longer period of time, can become more deteriorated. The house in which Annette lived, owned by her boyfriend, was built in the 1920s and needed a great deal of work. The first time I visited I wondered if I had the right address, because from the outside the house appeared to be abandoned. It looked run-down and tired — the roof was sagging inward, and the front porch steps were crumbling. Inside, parts of the dining room ceiling had come down, exposing wooden beams.

When Dave Bing, a former NBA player and the owner of an extremely successful steel company, became Detroit's mayor in 2009, he pledged to tear down more than ten thousand abandoned homes, and he received federal funds to help accomplish his goal. (One of the houses subjected to the wrecking ball was a childhood home of 2012 presidential candidate Mitt Romney.[18]) Vacant lots could be a mixed bag for those who remained in the neighborhood. Tamara's street already consisted of more empty lots than homes when I first started coming to her house in 2006. On her block, several of the homes still standing were burned-out shells, including one that looked like it had once been a grand brick home. The presence of these homes at the entrance to her block gave the impression of entering a war zone. At the other end of the street, where she lived, was a grouping of about seven or eight occupied homes. The yards were all well-kept and tidy. At that time the sidewalks stretched down both sides of the street, even in front of the many abandoned properties and the vacant lots. Tamara had moved into the house after her grandparents, still the owners, became too frail to live on their own. She had known the home and the neighborhood for all of her life and had fond memories of the area from her childhood. At one point she said wistfully, "This whole neighborhood used to be—it was the place to be, you know, honestly. We used to give lawn parties over in this yard [referring to the lot next door, which her grandparents owned]. Right here, that was really nice. The whole neighborhood would come. We used to have like block parties—you know it was just really, it was really nice." But now she would not let her children go outside unsupervised. "It's a lot of drug dealings," she said. "It's a lot of people like, almost every night you can hear, any given night you can hear gunshots going off. And it's not even so much as during the night, it can be during the day."

A few years later the block seemed emptier, and when I remarked upon this, Tamara said, "Yeah, they burned down one house, um, they sold the four-family flat across the street, and the back neighbors destroyed the house on the corner, so it's, it seem like it's three, four houses left on this block now." Some of the vacant lots had become extremely overgrown with long grass and weedlike trees called "Tree of Heaven" (which, despite their idyllic-sounding name, were invasive and ugly). Five-foot-four Tamara noted that the grass on one lot had grown taller than her. Sidewalks in front of empty lots had crumbled or were overgrown with weeds.

In addition to being an eyesore, vacant lots can attract people who are looking to illegally dispose of trash, and not regular household trash. Despite all of its problems, the city seemed to manage to pick up household trash every week, but not larger items such as tires, old furniture, pipes, and other remnants from demolished buildings. When I entered Tamara's neighborhood that year, I had been greeted by the sight of three men emptying out what looked to be industrial refuse into a vacant yard. As one of my colleagues, Margaret Dewar, an urban planning professor, said in an interview, "Detroit is a dumping ground for a lot of stuff. There is no one to watch. There is no capacity to enforce laws about dumping. There is a perception you can dump and no one will report it."[19]

The area in which Miss Price lived until 2010 was so abandoned that it resembled the countryside more than a neighborhood well within the city limits. When I turned onto her street, the homes appeared tidy, with mowed lawns. But the view changed very quickly. One side of the street had tall trees growing to nearly the edge of the sidewalk (which was crumbled and barely discernible — more like a path than a sidewalk). The few houses that stood on that side were mostly obscured from view. The farther down the block I drove the more I started to feel as if I were in a rural area; most of the houses were small and wood frame, and the road itself was narrow, with weeds popping up from cracks in the pavement. The three vacant and overgrown lots to the east of Miss Price's house, which sat back from the road, contributed to the country feel.

By no means was every neighborhood as desolate as Tamara's or Miss Price's. Although Sandra's west side street had vacant properties, they were far outnumbered by occupied homes. Since Sandra worked during the week, I typically interviewed her on a Saturday or Sunday. During the weekend, adults were outside, mowing lawns and washing cars, and children rode their bikes up and down the street. A sign of welcome marked the entrance to Geri's east side neighborhood (although the lower portion of the sign warned any potential troublemakers that the neighborhood watch was active). A small corner grocery store did a very brisk walk-in business, and on nice days families would sit outside on their front porches, speaking to each other across the street or wandering over to chat. Barbecue grills sat on numerous lawns. And unlike any other neighborhoods I visited for this project, the block was integrated. However, Geri's neighborhood was showing signs of visible decline the last couple of years I was there. The corner store had closed, and homes that I remembered as being occupied were now vacant and boarded up in an attempt to keep out intruders. A focus on demolition rather than investment, restoration, and occupancy was leading the neighborhoods in which these women lived to become even more abandoned.

The high rates of vacancy exacerbate another problem that many Detroiters deal with, either directly or indirectly: scrapping. Scrapping is the practice of looking for metals such as steel or copper that can be sold on the secondary market at scrap, junk, or salvage yards. Scrapping is not necessarily illegal. Items that are left out on the curb to be picked up as trash are often considered free for the taking, and homeowners and businesses may wish to have someone else haul away old appliances, whose component parts contain metals. At times when she needed money and when she had a car, Marie would "go scrapping," even though she knew it was illegal (although one can obtain a "junk" license from the city of Detroit and legally haul scrap to a scrap yard). However, with so many structures abandoned, the price of some metals rising, and the dearth of jobs, organized groups of thieves or individuals looking to earn extra money now engage in scrapping. Scrappers have been known to strip entire buildings of wiring, plumbing, and appliances, not only leaving many owners unable to rehab or resell their property, but often leaving the buildings in unsafe condition from extensive structural damage.[20] It is an industry that thrives on people's losses—the loss of their home, their rental properties, and their businesses. Scrap metal theft, however, is not a problem only in Detroit. Nationwide, it is one of the fastest-growing crimes.[21]

The stripping of appliances and metal does not just happen to vacant homes. Some of the siding was stolen off of the side of Tanya's west side house, during the middle of the day while she was at work. Lisa's house, despite being just minutes away from the very affluent and upscale Grosse Pointe, was in a very high-crime neighborhood. Before she and her family had even moved in, their house was broken into. "They broke in this window here," Lisa said. "Came in, and took part of the air conditioner, central air conditioner from the basement. Whatever part that is. And then they took the unit from outside. And then after we got the alarms, someone had broken in the window. They probably didn't think we were living here yet. Because it did look vacant because we had plastic bags [with our possessions]. We actually hadn't moved in yet." Once they settled in, her husband's car was stolen. Cars have street value in and of themselves, but they are also a target for scrappers, since parts are valuable for the metal they contain.

Despite some statistics that might indicate otherwise, most of the women I interviewed did not believe that crime was a large problem in their neighborhoods, although it became clear that they considered "problem crime" to be something very serious, like shootings and murders. By contrast, they viewed theft, assaults, and robbery as commonplace occurrences.

Those who were victimized by these crimes could expect little to no help from the police. Detroit routinely lands at or near the top of lists of "America's most violent cities," yet the police force has been shrinking. With the city under severe budget constraints, vacant positions have not been filled, and low pay has led some officers to leave the city's force.[22] The average police response time is fifty-eight minutes, compared to eleven minutes nationwide.[23] And the city is so strapped for funds that private donors have pitched in and bought one hundred new police cars for the department. The department has also been criticized for abandoning its residents — there is ample police presence in the downtown area to protect visitors, but the force has little visibility in the rest of the city. During all the time I spent in Detroit for this project, I never saw a police cruiser in any of the neighborhoods until one of my last visits in 2011.

Someone attempted to break into Geneva's house when she and her children were at home. The culprit unscrewed all of the floodlights she had installed for safety, but luckily her son scared off the intruder. The police did respond to Geneva's call, but the officer's reaction unsettled her. "He asked me if I had a weapon," she said, "and I told him I had [baseball] bats. I mean, we have kitchen knives and things like that, but he said, 'Have you ever considered getting a weapon?' And I said, 'To be honest with you, I wouldn't use it on anybody.' I couldn't shoot anybody. I just, even if, even if they come into your house. I can't, it's just not, I mean I don't know what I would do if, if somebody came after me or my kids. I don't know, you never know what you do, that is not something that I am interested in. I am terrified of guns." However, "do it yourself" policing has become common in parts of Detroit. The wealthy northwest Detroit enclave of Palmer Woods hired its own private security firm to patrol the neighborhood, and other neighborhoods have organized citizen patrols, another indication of the extent to which Detroiters have been abandoned by their city.[24]

Geneva attributed some of the neighborhood's problems to the presence of squatters. Along with scrapping, the large number of abandoned or foreclosed-upon properties encourages squatting —

occupying a home without a valid lease or purchase agreement. Although it is impossible to quantify the number of squatters in Detroit, given the under-the-radar nature of this activity, news and anecdotal reports indicate that squatting became a big issue sometime around 2011.[25] A popular narrative, and one to which Geneva subscribed, is that squatters are drug dealers.

Unfortunately, homeowners who want to rid themselves of squatters may face an uphill battle. Until 2014, Michigan law required that landlords go through a formal eviction process, which required court action and could be a long and drawn-out process in a state that has historically had strong protections for tenants. Because squatting was viewed as a civil matter, city police would not remove those living illegally in a residence (although many in the community consider the actions of squatters akin to breaking and entering). For instance, Cynthia found squatters living in the downstairs unit of the two-story flat she purchased in 2008. While she went through the formal process of evicting them, she and her family were confined to the much smaller upstairs unit. In 2014, the state passed legislation to make squatting a criminal offense.[26]

Sometimes squatters are just people looking for housing or taking an opportunity to live somewhere rent-free. In 2012, Maureen Taylor, the longtime leader of Michigan's Welfare Rights Organization, started collecting addresses of foreclosed properties in the city and moving single-mother families into houses that were in good shape. By Taylor's reckoning, the banks that owned the homes were unlikely to find out about their new occupants for at least five to six months, given the backlogs in processing foreclosures.[27] Although the moves were criticized in the media as encouraging theft, a few women in this study noted that certain types of squatters, such as the families Taylor was assisting, might be beneficial to a neighborhood. Carol, herself a single mother, said, "Like, I was watching the news, it must have been last night, I think it said something about the squatters. The squatters had moved into a house and the neighbors were complaining—'But I don't want no squatters coming in there selling drugs.' . . . I think people who squat in houses, if they're legit people you know, not drug dealers, and if they could improve the house, after a year or so you know, shit, they should have a house. It's better than vacant and an eyesore." Even though Cynthia had to remove squatters from her own home, she drew a distinction between men who squatted and women who did. "A lot of guys, they do move over here, move in these houses to sell drugs and stuff out of these houses. But you have younger women that move over here with kids that don't have nowhere to go. They move in, they squat, they take care of these homes."

Although none of the women I interviewed acknowledged that they had moved into a house with the intention of squatting (and I have no reason to believe otherwise), at least two were unintentional squatters. Dorothy, as well as Cynthia, found out that the homes they had moved into and were intending to purchase did not belong to the person purporting to be the owner. Dorothy was desperate to move from an apartment building that had no working elevators (and a landlord who had no intention of fixing them). Health problems made it extremely difficult for her to walk up and down the stairs. Through a friend, she was introduced to a man who told her that for $1,500 down and monthly payments of $400, she could move into a house he owned, with the plan that Dorothy would eventually purchase it via a land contract. In this type of arrangement, a buyer purchases a piece of real estate by paying the owner in installments. The buyer gains possession of the property right away but typically the owner retains the title to the property until such time as the purchaser's installment payments are equal to the negotiated selling price. No mortgage is involved.[28]

Although the house lacked a hot-water heater, Dorothy moved in with two of her adult children, a grandchild, and her boyfriend. The house needed some repairs as well, but nothing got fixed, because Dorothy found out that the man who represented himself as the landlord was in fact not the owner of the house. The house was a "HUD house": the U.S. Department of Housing and Urban Development (HUD) had acquired the property owing to foreclosure on an owner who had purchased the property with a Federal Housing Administration (FHA) loan. One day housing officials came by the house and told Dorothy that she would need to leave, since she was occupying the property illegally and the house was not fit for occupancy.

Prior to purchasing the home with squatters in the downstairs unit, Cynthia had found out that she was living illegally in the home she was renting when she and a neighbor went to city hall to look into some property tax issues. Cynthia had been hoping to purchase the home via land contract from the man to whom she had been paying rent, but a check of the property tax records showed that the city was the owner. Cynthia was able to find a new home (albeit the one with squatters) and move out on her own time table, but Dorothy and her family were thrown into chaos—they had just a week to find a new place to live. They ended up staying in a foreclosed home previously owned by a family friend. The house lacked a working furnace, so in the four months they lived there, from late fall into early winter, they used space heaters and the oven for heat—which put them at risk for a house fire—and lived in just a couple of rooms.

Along with vacant houses, scrapping, and squatting, fires have been a problem in Detroit for many decades. Every winter people die in fires caused by faulty space heaters, which are used by households that may either lack utilities or want to save on heating costs by relying on a cheaper alternative to gas heat. In addition, arson has become a hallmark of city living. "Devil's Night," the night before Halloween, had long been marked in Detroit by acts of vandalism and other petty crimes, but in the 1970s and 1980s arson was added to the mix. The city has made great strides in reducing the number of Devil's Night fires, but arson in the city continues. Many residents believe that insurance fraud is at the root of the approximately five thousand arsons the city experiences each year. Lisa believed that the fire that destroyed her home in 2007 was set by the owner of the vacant house next door, who wanted to collect an insurance payment.[29] Karla said that she was unable to obtain affordable homeowner's insurance when she moved to Detroit in 2010 because of the prevalence of arson for insurance scams.

Experience with fires, whether due to arson or accidents, was eerily common among the women in this study, underscoring how prevalent an issue this is for city residents. Aleta had lost a home when her son accidentally left something cooking on the stove; Judy had a fire in her apartment on Christmas Day — she was trying to bring extra heat into the space by keeping the oven door open, but a roll of paper towels fell in and hit the oven's heating element. Lisa's home burned after flames from the burning house next door reached her property. Marie's home burned to the ground under suspicious circumstances. The house next door to Miss Price was set on fire with Molotov cocktails (kerosene-soaked rags are stuffed in bottles and then set on fire). Tamara had to deal with a continual onslaught of fires in abandoned houses in her neighborhood until the city finally tore them all down. And Tamara's smoke detectors often did not seem to be working. For at least three years in a row, a smoke detector made repeated "beeps" throughout our interview, indicating that the battery needed to be replaced. Tamara's house was not the only place where I heard the chirp of a smoke detector that needed batteries; it was often background noise during an interview. Four houses on Charlene's short block burned in 2009, all of which she thought were caused by arson to claim insurance. It was one thing for Charlene to look out her window and see boarded-up homes, but the fires left her with a view of the charred remains of homes and only intensified her desire to leave Detroit.

# The Suburbs

Whites were not the only demographic group to leave the city of Detroit; over time African Americans have followed the exodus, although patterns of segregation still remain. African Americans living in the suburbs tend to reside in "inner ring" or "first" suburbs. These are older suburbs that experienced growth in the 1940s and 1950s as whites began to move out of the city. Some of these places are more industrial in nature, but most functioned as bedroom communities for people affiliated with the auto industries. Over time many of these suburbs started experiencing problems similar to Detroit's, such as high property vacancy rates and a declining tax base, though on a smaller scale. These inner-ring suburbs no longer draw more affluent families, who instead have moved farther outside the city or to suburbs that are close to Detroit but also adjacent to Lake St. Clair.

Sheila, who is African American, and Sharon, who is white, lived in Western Wayne County in two different cities that were contiguous to each other and difficult to distinguish in terms of the types of houses in the neighborhoods (modest), the types of businesses (small mom-and-pop stores interspersed with abandoned storefronts), and their general condition (worn down). Sheila lived in the city that was experiencing a rapid growth in the number of African American residents, however, while Sharon's city remained overwhelmingly white. Although someone passing through would find it difficult to tell where one city ends and the other begins, the patterns of residential segregation are nonetheless stark.

Debbie, Teresa, and Brianna lived "downriver," a descriptor used for communities located to the south of Detroit along the Detroit River. Many of the downriver communities grew once the auto companies began locating plants on the fringes of Detroit or in these suburbs themselves. As white flight from Detroit accelerated, these inner-ring suburbs became the landing spot for many blue-collar workers looking to leave the city. Despite an increase in the number of blacks leaving Detroit over the past two decades, many of the downriver communities remain predominantly white. Layla and Amala lived in Dearborn, due west of Detroit. Dearborn, known as the home of Henry Ford, is the city once governed by Orville Hubbard, the mayor who publicly stated that he wanted to keep it "lily white." Dearborn now has a large population of Arab Americans, including many from Lebanon, like Layla and Amala. But some suburbs are more racially mixed or even predominantly African American. Inkster housed blacks who worked at Ford's Rouge plant in Dearborn but were unable to live in Dearborn because of segregationist housing policies. The city of Southfield did not have the reputation for racial hostility that Dearborn did (although now many whites are leaving) and is now majority black. River Rouge, the downriver community where Brianna, an African American, lived, is racially and ethnically mixed and heavily industrialized (and as a result, is often not very pleasant-smelling).[30]

Not surprisingly, given Detroit's history of segregation and white flight, the suburbs were where I found all but one of the white, non-Hispanic or non-immigrant participants in the study; only Beth, married to an African American man, lived in Detroit. These women—Debbie, Sharon, and Teresa—grew up in suburban communities and had little connection to Detroit. African American suburban dwellers did have roots in Detroit, however—or, in the case of Pamela, in Pontiac, an industrial city to the north of Detroit. Leah lived in Detroit for twenty-five years before moving to the suburbs; Brianna grew up in Detroit, and the rest of her family still lived there. Danielle grew up in the Herman Gardens public housing complex in Detroit; when those buildings were demolished, she moved to a public housing complex just on the other side of Eight Mile Road, the infamous boundary line between Detroit and its northern suburbs. Mary was a longtime Detroiter who had moved when she was fed up with the city.

Leah lived in Eastpointe, which borders Detroit's northeast side and is in Macomb County. Eastpointe was originally called East Detroit, but in the early 1990s residents elected to change its name. The city's website says that the change was made because the city "suffered a lack of identity as the city was often confused with its larger neighbor, Detroit."[31] The conventional wisdom, however, is that Eastpointe did not want the stigma associated with Detroit so instead adopted the "pointe," which aligns the city with its much wealthier suburbs to the south—Grosse Pointe, Grosse Pointe Parks, Grosse Pointe Farms, Grosse Pointe Shores, and Grosse Pointe Woods (collectively referred to as "the Pointes"). Danielle, Pamela, and Mary lived in suburbs to the north of the city, in Oakland County, one of the wealthiest counties in the state (as well as the nation), but the communities in which they resided were considerably less well-off compared to the cities farther north, where million-dollar-plus residences are not uncommon.

Unlike the stately homes one sees in Grosse Pointe, the housing in many of the inner-ring suburbs surrounding Detroit resembles some of the neighborhoods in Detroit. Debbie's neighborhood in a near Western Wayne County suburb had the same small Cape Cod houses as Detroit, although yards were larger in this suburb. The only real difference between the street Teresa lived on for many years in a downriver town and Beth's street in Detroit was the absence of boarded-up homes on the former, although that did not mean that there were no abandoned houses in the suburbs. Real estate listings for the inner-ring suburbs show large numbers of foreclosed properties up for sale.[32] On other measures, however, the suburbs come out ahead. The public schools are generally better, crime is lower, and job opportunities are greater.

For these reasons, some public policy efforts have sought to bring poor African Americans out of central cities, where opportunities may be limited, and into the suburbs. The Moving to Opportunity (MTO) experiment, for instance, provided poor families residing in public housing with the opportunity to relocate to better neighborhoods. MTO operated as a randomized evaluation: residents who volunteered for the program were randomly assigned to a control group (the status quo) or to one of two treatment groups. Those in one treatment group received a Section 8 voucher (now a "housing choice" voucher), which they could use to move out of public housing and into any rental unit where the voucher was accepted; those in the second treatment group received the voucher with the stipulation that they had to use it to move to an area with a poverty rate of less than 10 percent. (This group also received assistance in identifying such neighborhoods). MTO was not necessarily designed to move families to the suburbs, but the hope was that by moving to higher-income neighborhoods (some of which would likely be in the suburbs), these families would find their lives improving along a number of dimensions, including their children's school performance and their own employment. Interim evaluation evidence found few positive impacts of MTO, however, probably for a number of reasons, including changes in the circumstances of the control group (who were being relocated as public housing complexes were torn down), the relatively low number of moves that actually occurred (just under 50 percent of families in the treatment groups moved), and the deterioration of low-poverty neighborhoods over time.[33] More recent work has shown improvements, however, in college attendance and earnings for young adults who were younger than thirteen when they moved.[34]

Detroit was not part of MTO, and between 2006 and 2011, only five women in the study moved with their families out of Detroit to lower-poverty neighborhoods in suburban Detroit. For much of the latter part of the twentieth century, a move to the suburbs was a signal of upward mobility and status attainment. It meant that the family could afford to leave the city and purchase a larger home, perhaps with a nice yard and garages for the cars. It is difficult to know, however, whether moving improved the lot of these striving families. In some respects, these moves seemed not to have changed the families' situations at all, possibly in part because their move was short-lived, because the suburbs themselves were declining, or because the families found themselves in isolating circumstances after they moved.

Yvette did not stay in the suburbs for very long. After declaring bankruptcy and walking away from her home on Detroit's east side, Yvette, a tall and striking African American woman, moved far out of the city, to a mostly white suburb in northern Macomb County. The apartment complex into which she moved was located on the fringes of the suburb. Yvette had a number of motives for moving out of the city. First, she hoped that she could eventually leave Michigan, but to do so she would need to go to court to change her custody agreement with her younger children's father. Even before she left Detroit, she was thinking about a suburban move in terms of how it might accelerate her plans to relocate out of state. The Wayne County court system is notoriously back-logged, but, as Yvette said, "Well, I know the other county's court system, I think, is a little more together. I will move to a different county first, and then if I still decide to move out of state, I'll petition that county for an approval for me to move out of state." But after she moved, other issues, such as her health and her son's newly diagnosed learning challenges, consumed her time and she never went to court.

Yvette spent only two years in the suburb before moving back to the city, although technically not to within the city limits — she moved to Hamtramck. Hamtramck and Highland Park are two municipalities that are embedded within Detroit. Although Detroit started expanding its boundaries in the 1800s, from roughly 1900 to 1920, Detroit was busily annexing neighboring communities and growing larger geographically, but Hamtramck and Highland Park resisted and remained independent.[35] Highland Park is a very financially stressed community, albeit on a smaller scale than Detroit. At one point, the city disconnected most of the streetlights (and the utility company repossessed some of the light fixtures) and asked citizens to keep on their porch lights as a way to illuminate residential streets.[36] Hamtramck is in better fiscal health, but the city, once known as a Polish ethnic enclave, has had its share of difficulties and, like Detroit, has a history of racial strife. In the 1960s, Hamtramck officials razed a predominantly African American neighborhood in order to build a civic center. Former residents sued, and the city was ordered to build homes for those who were displaced. But the lawsuit dragged on and on. Hamtramck's African American population declined dramatically, and some residents were just getting rehoused in 2012.[37]

Yvette's family had not been displaced, and in fact she returned to her childhood home. After going on extended and only partially paid sick leave from work, she decided that she needed to figure out how to reduce her expenses. Her mother had recently retired and moved south, so Yvette decided to move into the family home, where she would not have to pay rent.

How her younger children would do in school was the one concern Yvette had about moving back. The first time I interviewed her in her suburban apartment, the kids were still in school, and she excitedly talked about the many activities available for them that were nonexistent in Detroit. Pulling out a flyer from her purse, she said, "Here it is — soccer team, swimming team. All this for the little kids. All this little stuff, you know, that they — they have out here. . . . They, you know, do all these nice little things out here for the school system, and the parents are really involved." Yvette's son had also started receiving specialized services in school after he was diagnosed as being on the autism spectrum. During his time in a Detroit public school, no teachers had ever raised this possibility. Yvette said, "I was just kind of shocked that, at that age, to have been in school for so long, that it had never been brought to my attention before." The suburban school immediately put a plan into place to have him work with specialists.

Janelle was also impressed with suburban schools. She moved to a nearby suburb after spending many weekends with a friend who lived there. Rents were higher than in Detroit, and all Janelle could afford was an apartment. She and her two daughters moved into the same complex where her friend lived. A year later, she was back in Detroit, living in a house on the west side. When asked why, she said, "When I stayed in the apartment it was like, too small for the kids. So the kids have a little bit more freedom to run around [now]. It was too loud in the apartment, so we got complaints all the time." Although the apartment manager never threatened her with eviction, Janelle decided she should move back into the city, where her girls would have more room.[38] She wanted to keep her daughters in the same school, however, because she believed it was much better than the schools in Detroit. The last time we talked she and her girls were all spending a lot of time away from home. Janelle would drop the girls off at school and either go back to her mother's house, which was closer than Janelle's own house, or to work, which was also in the same suburb. After picking up the girls, they would all return to her mother's house, where they would end up staying all week. She said, "It's like pretty much difficult to get back and forth and to get home. . . . I am so glad school is out, because it's like so terrible trying to get them back and forth." Janelle had no plans, however, to change this arrangement.

Along with stronger schools, another appeal of the suburbs was the possibility of finding a home in a nice, quiet neighborhood. For these women, relocating to the suburbs usually meant moving, as Janelle did, into an apartment complex that was more affordable than a house but also isolated from the rest of the community. The suburban apartment complexes that Janelle and Tykia moved to were both located on very busy, multiple-lane roads. There was nowhere close by for children to play, which was probably why neighbors complained about Janelle's children being noisy. The complex in which Yvette lived did have a playground and was in a fairly secluded area, but Yvette found the rest of the residents to be noisy. "I thought it would be a lot more peaceful out here," she said, ". . . and it probably is in other areas. It's probably just this apartment building, so I can't wait until we can, you know, get out of this apartment building." She hoped to rent a home but could not afford any in the suburbs.

Cheryl lived in two different complexes after moving out of Detroit. The first was in the same suburb where Sharon lived. While Sharon lived on a quiet, tree-lined street, Cheryl's initial suburban experience was living in a rather old and run-down complex of tightly packed buildings separated by small parking lots. After that, she moved farther outside of Detroit, to a town built up around a large auto plant (since closed). The complex she lived in was huge (I got lost trying to find her apartment) and much newer, with many amenities (including a playground and a swimming pool). The rent was substantially cheaper and the school system even better than the first suburban school her children attended, but the apartment complex was fairly isolated from anything else. It was off a busy road with no sidewalks, so Cheryl had to drive everywhere.

Families in this study who were striving for upward mobility were abandoned by the promise of the suburbs. While their children may have attended better schools in the suburbs, these families who moved were relegated to apartment complexes isolated from other areas of the community. A move to a suburb can increase opportunities, but there are costs as well, and one may be isolation. Further, without a car, getting around in the suburbs is nearly impossible.[39] All of these women had cars, but one accident or unaffordable repair would have left them stranded. When I asked Cheryl if her car was running well, she knocked on a nearby (wooden) shelf to signify that it was and that she hoped it would continue to do so. Because of Detroit's abysmal public transportation system, Detroit residents in this study called on nearby friends and family to help out with rides when their cars broke down. This was not possible for those who had moved to the suburbs. Building new relationships was also difficult. Tykia was excited when another young mother moved into the same suburban apartment complex; she hoped that they would be friends, but her son would take a two-hour bus ride on the weekends to visit friends in Detroit, and when he was home he stayed inside playing video games. Cheryl would have been happy to never set foot in the city again—

Detroit was "like the Night of the Living Dead to me," she said — even though all of her family still lived there. None of her immediate family had cars, so she had not seen them in months. Cheryl was signed up with a temp agency, but her work assignments had been few and far between. When I asked her what she had been doing with herself since moving, she said, "There's a park down on that road. So I take [the kids'] bikes up there. They have like a, a trail, a forest that you can go through. . . . There's a dance class that they wanted to take. And then the library has a lot of activities, so we've been going to library. They're in the little book club. You know, they pick out a book and then read it for I think like a month and then they go back and if the book has a movie, they go back and see the movie and they discuss it." When I asked if she ever did anything for herself, she replied with a laugh, "Now that's my problem! I don't go out. I don't do much or much grown-up time." For these women, a suburban move did not help them to become more socially integrated.

# Moving and Loss

During one's adult life, moving, whether within the same city or to another geographic area, is to be expected. A life course theory of residential mobility posits that young adults move out of their parents' homes, then move several times before starting a family; as they enter their thirties they might move one or two times as their families grow larger, and once they are older, with grown children, they move again to a smaller place.[40] Poor and near-poor families tend to move more, perhaps because of the higher rates of renting among these groups as well as opportunities to move into better housing.[41] But not all changes in residence are positive. Frequent moves may be a sign of "housing instability," that is, not having secure housing. Housing instability is conceptualized differently in different studies, but experiencing homelessness, being evicted, and moving frequently are often markers.[42] Hypermobility, a form of housing instability, is characterized by very frequent moving, perhaps a couple of times during the course of a year.[43] Experiences of housing instability have been shown to be negatively associated with various health outcomes for adults and with poor educational outcomes for children.[44] Including those who moved from Detroit to the suburbs, twenty-five people in the study moved at some point between 2006 and 2011, and fifteen of those moved more than once. Nichelle and Dorothy moved most frequently—a total of ten times for each of them. Some moves fit the life course model, but others were indicative of instability. And that instability resulted in the loss of more than just housing.

Nichelle was one of the most unstably housed. She moved from Michigan to a Southern state when she decided to leave her abusive husband. She and her three sons boarded a bus and landed in a shelter for those escaping domestic violence. The shelter helped her find a house to rent, partially subsidized the rent, and provided her with other services. Eventually Nichelle found a job at a local university. It seemed like her life was on an upward trajectory, but the next year she was back in the Detroit area, living in a hotel. The shelter in the South had a time limit on its services, and Nichelle had reached it. When Nichelle lost her job, she was unable to afford the rent (which the shelter was no longer subsidizing). She found another place to live only to have the home flooded (and many of her possessions ruined) when a water main burst. And two of her children were diagnosed with serious health problems. She said, "I actually had not planned on coming back, but just so much was happening." She thought she had found a place to live in Detroit, but the current tenant of the house would not vacate, and eviction proceedings would take months. (She did not find this out until after she lost several hundred dollars by renting a moving van and keeping it for several days because the landlord kept telling her that the tenant was on the way out.) Her mother offered to take in Nichelle and her three sons, but four other people were already staying in the house, and Nichelle and the kids would have to sleep on couches in the basement. So she ended up in the hotel. The monthly rent there was just under $800, but she and her sons were confined to a very small space; the room had two double beds, a few dressers, a TV, and a very small kitchenette with a small refrigerator and a stovetop for cooking. With no job at the time, and having spent all of her money moving back to Detroit and then having her tax refund garnished for a student loan, Nichelle had no way to save up for a security deposit on a rental. After staying in the hotel for a year, Nichelle bounced around a few more times, eventually landing once again in a homeless shelter. The possessions she had not lost when her house flooded remained packed in boxes in a storage locker.

When Annette and Karla went through divorce and job loss, they tried to hang on to some of their possessions by putting them in storage. Annette lost her home through foreclosure, and Karla was homeless off and on for a couple of years after a divorce and job loss. When Annette could no longer afford the monthly storage rental fees and stopped paying, the contents of her storage unit were presumably auctioned off. Karla was going through a bankruptcy and thought that the contents of her storage unit were protected from liquidation, but they were not. When I asked her what she lost, she said, "Three bedroom suites—my son's bedroom suite, mine, my daughter's. I had a living room set, dining room set, computers, toys, pictures. Every picture of my kids from the time they were born. Pictures of my grandkids that I'll never be able to get back. My pictures was the main thing."

Detroit artist Tyree Guyton is well known for the Heidelberg Project, an open-air art exhibit that revolves around abandoned houses in a near–east side neighborhood. Guyton uses items from vacant houses (and the houses themselves) to create his pieces. For example, the "Doll House" is an abandoned home that he covered with children's stuffed animals; other items he has used include unpaired shoes, vacuum cleaners, and chairs. Viewers of the Heidelberg Project may think of his art as employing "discarded" objects or even "garbage," but in all likelihood at least some of his artwork is constructed out of the belongings that families must abandon when they move.

Moving can also slowly whittle down what few possessions families own. Dorothy moved at least ten times during the period I knew her, although the last few years she moved so much that I might have missed a move or two. When we met her in 2006, she lived in a rental home on Detroit's east side, but she would be there for only a year before finding out that the property was being foreclosed upon and she would have to leave. After that she moved to an apartment just a few blocks away from Tamara's house. The building's elevator did not work, and after Dorothy had knee surgery she decided she could not live there anymore. From there she moved into the "HUD" house in 2008—an arrangement that did not last long, since she was unknowingly squatting. In need of housing quickly, and with no money for a security deposit, she then moved into a home that had been owned by a friend but was in foreclosure at the time. She stayed there for a couple of months during the fall and early winter until the bank repossessed the house. The house had electricity but no working furnace, so she and her family kept warm by using the oven for heat.

The next house Dorothy found seemed like it would provide her with some stability. The house was bigger than others she had lived in, it had a nice yard, and the landlords, a married couple, were "the best landlords in the world!" Knowing that Dorothy was in poor health, they called her every week to see how she was doing. When her brother passed, they let Dorothy use her rent money to help pay for his funeral, giving her a free month in the house. But that arrangement also did not work out. A group of men broke into the house when Dorothy was home. They kicked down the door, but somehow the police arrived before the intruders took anything or hurt anyone. Feeling unsafe there, Dorothy quickly found another place to live, but that did not work out either. The landlord had not paid the utility bill for the house, so Dorothy could not get the lights turned on. When a different friend offered Dorothy the opportunity to live in a house the friend owned, Dorothy took it.

For all of these moves, various members of Dorothy's family came with her, including two grandchildren, both under the age of five. Sometimes her adult children would live with her, other times not. Dorothy was usually the only one with a steady income—her $700 SSI (Supplemental Security Income) check. What often did not come with her were her possessions. Being unstably housed, or even moving just once, often entails abandoning one's possessions. When she moved out of the first house, Dorothy had no one who could carry her appliances out of the basement, so she had to leave behind her washing machine and her deep freezer, a huge loss for her. Women who owned a separate freezer could stock up on certain foods when they went on sale. If there were more mouths to feed some months, or if the welfare office cut off their food stamps, this stock could get them through. Dorothy talked about her old deep freezer for several years. For a different move, Dorothy hired a friend's son who had a truck to help them; he never delivered the last load, stealing some of Dorothy's possessions. A few people were able to rent vans when they moved, but most had to make do with their own cars or a friend's truck, since they had no money to pay for a rental. They moved what they could and left behind what was too big to haul.

When people are evicted from their home—that is, forcibly removed because they have not paid the rent or have violated some other term of the lease—the landlord (or a sheriff, depending on the eviction laws) may remove their possessions from the house. It is not all that uncommon when driving around Detroit's neighborhoods (or poor neighborhoods in other places) to see furniture and other remnants of families' lives tossed to the curb. But couches, dressers, and children's toys sitting in piles on a lawn can also be a sign that someone moved for other reasons and simply left behind much of what they owned.

The last time I saw Dorothy was in 2011 as she was getting ready to leave an apartment she was renting in a crime-riddled part of the Mexicantown area of Detroit, some distance away from the tourist-frequented restaurants. As I waited in the building's entryway for Dorothy to let me in, I was propositioned by a woman who may or may not have lived in the building; Dorothy yelled at her to get lost when she came to the door. Dorothy's apartment was tiny, consisting of a living room with a stove and refrigerator on one wall and a bedroom with a mattress leaning up against the wall. There was one upholstered chair and two wooden chairs. Dorothy moved me over to one of the wooden chairs after I sat in the cloth-covered chair; she believed the chair was infested with bugs. Roaches of all sizes were scurrying everywhere, and Dorothy was clearly disgusted and embarrassed by the infestation. She was hoping to move to another friend's house the next day, and if that did not work out, she would go to a shelter. Besides the few pieces of furniture, the rest of her belongings fit into a few garbage bags.

Aside from a few of the better-off women, most women in the study did not have much in the way of furniture and other possessions. A living room might have one couch, a kitchen just a table and two chairs. Most people had televisions, but in general living spaces were sparsely furnished. One year I interviewed Erica in one of the upstairs bedrooms of her house. A couple of mattresses lay directly on the floor; she had no money to buy frames. She also lacked any dressers with drawers, so all of her clothes were either in piles on the floor or in plastic garbage bags. Low income prevented these women from accumulating furniture and other household items, but their moves whittled down their material goods even further.

## "Saving" Detroit

Because of the proliferation of "abandoned" neighborhoods, "right sizing" the city became a popular policy term, one that reflected then-mayor Dave Bing's desire to shrink the footprint of the city to better accommodate the smaller population. What "right sizing" might actually mean was never clear: Would certain neighborhoods be bulldozed under and allowed to return to nature? Would parcels of land be used for urban farming, an enterprise that took off with great gusto during the economic downturn? Would some neighborhoods be deprived of city services, such as garbage collection, so that the city could more efficiently target the deployment of resources?

At first, the message coming from the mayor's office seemed to raise all these possibilities. Most of the women who had heard about this plan thought it was ridiculous. Annette was probably the most adamant in voicing her opposition. Her voice rising, she said:

> So what you're going to do, you're just going to uproot somebody out of the home that they done had all of their life? You're just going to take something that belongs to that person and tell them that they've got to get out? That's crazy! That's crazy.

45

How are you just going to—I don't understand. That's wrong, that's wrong! That will be like them come telling you, "I want your house, so get the hell out." That's not, you don't do people like that. I mean, I can understand when there ain't but one house in the whole neighborhood, but if you're going to do that, give them what they should be getting, don't just give them four or five thousand dollars and tell them to move out and that's wrong. And that's what they're going to do. They ain't going to give the people what they should be getting.

Bing left office at the end of 2013. Many abandoned properties were demolished under his administration, but the implementation of any plans to "right size" the city were put aside by Detroit's significant financial troubles and its eventual filing for bankruptcy. Bing was succeeded by Mike Duggan, the first white mayor of Detroit since the early 1970s, and since Detroit became a majority–African American city. "Right sizing" has not been part of the Duggan administration's vocabulary, but revitalization efforts in the city since 2010, when looked at in conjunction with the election of a white mayor, indicate that Detroiters like the women in this study are being abandoned by the "new" Detroit. A new three-mile-long rail line is being built along Woodward Avenue. The line will only serve downtown, midtown, and the "New Center" areas. (The New Center is a commercial area north of midtown.) People in the neighborhoods are left to be serviced by Detroit's abysmal bus system, long known for its delays. The core downtown/midtown area is thriving, with new restaurants and quirky boutiques opening on a seemingly regular basis. Go to one of these venues and chances are you will see only white people.

Dan Gilbert, CEO of Quicken Loans, has received a great deal of attention in the press for his contributions to the renaissance of Detroit. Gilbert relocated his company's headquarters to Detroit, bought up numerous buildings downtown, and has been welcomed with open arms by the mayor and others who are happy to let the private sector lead the way in rebuilding the city. There is now a Whole Foods grocery store in the midtown area. Meanwhile, much of the rest of the city lacks quick access to a full-service grocery store. There are numerous examples of native Detroiters engaging in various efforts to stabilize and revitalize their community, but their endeavors have been overshadowed in the media by Gilbert and other young and mostly white entrepreneurs who are praised for their "bravery" in putting down roots in Detroit.

Meanwhile, longtime residents who live outside of the central area of the city seem forgotten. Lorraine noted this disjuncture the last time we spoke. She said, "There is no focus on the neighborhoods. . . . If you don't build the neighborhoods, you have no city. I don't care what you put downtown to attract people to come and see, you know, the Red Wings [hockey team] and all of that. That's a come and go. The residents of the city are a permanent fixture, so you need to address our issues as a priority." Unfortunately, in the zeal to remake Detroit, ordinary citizens like Lorraine, while not "right sized" out of her neighborhood, may be abandoned.[45]

# Conclusion

For the women in this study, living in Detroit could be difficult, but moving away posed challenges as well. The neighborhoods where they lived in the city were marked by blight and vacancy, and arson and other crimes were very real threats, but police could not be counted upon to respond in a timely fashion. Scrappers stripped away the last materials of value in unoccupied homes, making an industry out of other people's losses. The palpable physical abandonment in much of the city is emblematic of the dismissal of the people living in these neighborhoods. It sends the message that what they have and where they live are not worth protecting and nurturing.

All of these factors left residents like Lorraine feeling as if there was "no focus on the neighborhoods." Indeed, the strategy pursued by the city focused on demolishing unoccupied buildings in the outlying neighborhoods while investing mainly in the downtown areas. Although the numbers remain small, whites are beginning to return to the downtown and nearby areas. A new pattern of racial residential segregation is starting to emerge, with two separate and distinct cities within Detroit's geographic boundaries.

47

Detroit is not necessarily unique in this sense. A number of large U.S. cities with significant African American populations have witnessed recent influxes of whites, including Washington, D.C., Atlanta, and Raleigh, North Carolina.[46] Further, poor neighborhoods in other cities, such as Chicago and Baltimore, are facing the same kinds of challenges that decades of neglect bring about—blight, abandoned structures, and segregation. For the women in the study, moving to the suburbs brought a different type of segregation—isolation in far-flung apartment complexes, where they were cut off from the rest of the community. Moving, whether out of the city or within the city, also often entailed leaving behind or losing their possessions. A couch or kitchen table might have been replaceable, but family pictures and heirlooms were not.

# ↝ CHAPTER 3 ↜

## *ABANDONED BY INSTITUTIONS OF INCLUSION AND STABILITY: THE FAILED PROMISE OF EMPLOYMENT*

Rhonda worked overnight as a home health care aide. Since the clients were sleeping, she interacted with them only when she fed them breakfast. Rhonda never seemed very excited about her job, but it was one she could easily get without having a high school degree. Although it had never happened to her, at multiple points during her interview she voiced concern about the clients becoming violent, noting that other aides who worked during the day had been assaulted by patients. Rhonda had been given some minimal training in how to handle such a situation, and if worse came to worst, she could call 911. But she would be alone until then. Rhonda did not have this worry for very long, however, since she quit this particular job when she feared that she was going to be fired—even though she believed that she had been wrongly accused of a misdoing. She got subsequent home health care jobs, but all of them were the same—working by herself on the midnight shift and earning less than $8 an hour.

In the late 1980s and early 1990s, researchers and policymakers voiced concern about low levels of work among poor individuals. Wilson drew attention to joblessness as a critical problem facing black men and affecting central-city neighborhoods. Today black male unemployment remains a looming problem, and high levels of criminal convictions and continued discrimination keep many black men on the fringes of the formal labor market or out of it altogether. Wilson advocated for an employment policy, but mass incarceration has instead become the policy focused on black men. At the same time, policymakers from both the left and the right have sought ways to move single mothers—both black and white—off of welfare rolls and into employment, and the employment rates of single mothers have grown tremendously. Among unmarried women with a high school degree only, employment rates increased from about 50 percent in the early 1990s to 76 percent in 2000, matching the employment rate for single women without children and surpassing the employment rate for married mothers.[1] Employment rates for all high school–educated women have dropped since then, but single mothers' employment rate remains on par with that of single women without children. This shift has variously been attributed to a tough welfare regime that enforces work requirements, an expansion of tax credits to low-wage workers, a booming economy, or some combination of these factors. "Welfare-dependent" is not an appropriate descriptor for the vast majority of single mothers.

But did employment provide the mechanism for social integration that Wilson envisioned? In the United States, work is one of the most central activities for adults. It not only brings in income but also organizes our time and helps us build networks of people we can call on when looking for a new job. In that sense, increases in employment among single mothers should improve their well-being. In Wilson's framework, families who left the central city were able to do so because they were always working. Once housing discrimination was made illegal, it was their earnings that allowed them to move away, perhaps on a path toward further prosperity. Yet changes in the labor market, which were well under way and recognized by Wilson when he was writing, call into question whether the types of jobs that low-income single mothers obtain serve to integrate them fully into society.

Indeed, the jobs of the middle class are no longer secure today. Across the board, declines in job tenure, increases in the use of temporary or contingent labor, the growth of the global labor pool, and the replacement of jobs through technology have all served to increase the precariousness of work for workers and downgrade the quality of jobs.[2] Job growth in the past decade has been concentrated in the low-paying service sector and in low-level health care jobs with limited to no advancement opportunities.[3] Income inequality has grown, driven partially by the bifurcation of the labor market into jobs that are considered "low-skill" and thus are low paid, on the one hand, and jobs that require more education and specialized knowledge and are highly paid, on the other.[4] The proportion of workers who are members of unions or other collective bargaining units has declined dramatically, from about 20 percent of all workers in the mid-1980s to around 12 percent in the late 2000s, while the number of temporary employees increased from about 1 million employees in 1990 to 2.7 million in 2000.[5] Public-sector jobs, once so crucial in building the African American middle class, are shrinking in number.[6] The desire of companies to reduce costs and maximize profits has led to an increased demand for "flexible" labor, which enables employers to institute "just in time" scheduling whereby workers may need to be available on short notice to come in to work or may be sent home when business is slow.[7] Employers also expect "flexible" workers to work off hours. These are all well-established trends in the labor market and are characteristics of the jobs held by the majority of women in this study. Many of the jobs were isolating rather than integrating, put these women at the mercy of their employer on many different levels, and did not provide them with economic stability, let alone a strong footing within the middle class.

Table 3.1 provides a summary of the sectors in which these women worked, the median pay of those sectors, and whether the women had ever been a member of a union or worked in a temporary position. Jobs in the health care field, usually as home health aides, were the most commonly held. Fast-food and other restaurant jobs were the least well paid: the median wage was only $8 an hour. With the exception of the women in professional, salaried positions, most of the jobs held by the women in this study paid low wages of between $10 and $12 an hour. Only 11 percent had ever worked in a temporary job (one acquired through a staffing agency or by design not leading to a permanent position), and the same number had held a unionized job.

The segments of the labor market in which most of these women

51

Table 3.1　Job Characteristics and Median Pay of Respondents, 2006–2011

|  | Percentage of Respondents[a] | Median Pay |
|---|---|---|
| Sector |  |  |
| Fast food or other restaurant | 11 | $8.00/hour |
| Manufacturing | 11 | $12.00/hour |
| Health care | 24 | $10.00/hour |
| Retail | 16 | $11.50/hour |
| Other professional | 16 | $47,000/year |
| Other service | 11 | $11.50/hour |
| Never employed | 20 | — |
| Has held a temporary position[b] | 11 | — |
| Has been a union member | 11 | $45,000/year |

*Source*: Author's calculations.

[a]Does not add to 100 percent because some women worked multiple jobs in different sectors.

[b]Because temporary positions were short in duration, we were unable to get full data on wages earned.

labored had other characteristics that, coupled with the low wages, instability, and unpredictable schedules, made workers socially abandoned. In talking to them about their jobs, including what they did in a typical day and how they lost and found jobs, many said that not only were their jobs low-paying and lacking in opportunities for advancement, but the working conditions were isolating — they felt cut off from coworkers and supervisors. As a result, they were unable to count on fellow employees for support, and they also missed out on networking opportunities and chances to build connections that might help them later. In total, sixteen of the forty-five women worked in a job that could be considered isolating, a condition that often left them feeling vulnerable when problems arose at work. Rather than being able to seek help from fellow workers or find strength in numbers, they sometimes quit their jobs preemptively to avoid being fired. Other women were subjected to violations of employment law and other regulations. In short, the promise of employment as a mechanism for social inclusion had been broken for these working women; social abandonment in the workplace had made them invisible and expendable, and they were afforded few, if any, protections from abusive workplace practices.

Women working in higher-paying jobs tended to have better working conditions, although not always. For these women, however, working by itself did not provide enough income for the economic security they envisioned. They and their families hoped to achieve that stability and perhaps become upwardly mobile through their entrepreneurial efforts. But these attempts were fraught with difficulties. By contrast, the poorest women had very limited contact, if any, with the formal labor market. In a country where so many workers cannot achieve economic stability, those cut off from employment are left on the sidelines; though sometimes provided with meager public assistance benefits, these women were left alone and truly abandoned.

## What Does Isolation at Work Look Like?

Shanice was just nineteen years old when we started interviewing her. At that time, she was looking for a job, but she had already had many different positions, some in light manufacturing and others in retail. None of the jobs had lasted very long, partly because she obtained many of them through a temporary placement agency, so they were not designed to be permanent. Shanice had dropped out of high school in the twelfth grade, not liking the alternative school she had been sent to when she got pregnant, and she believed that the lack of a degree was holding her back from getting a better job. The next year she was excited to report that she had completed training to become a certified nursing assistant (CNA) and had just passed the state certification exam. CNAs typically perform routine tasks such as bathing and feeding patients as well as lifting them, but the jobs are low-paying and typically have high turnover.[8] Shanice said that she had always wanted to get more education, but, as she said, "I didn't finish high school, so that kind of like discouraged me from wanting to pursue that. You know a lot of people, it's not that they don't want to do things, it's just they be scared of failing at something that they're trying to attempt to do, so that

holds a lot of people back from doing the things they want to do."
Shanice had the opportunity to enroll in a program where her tuition would be paid by the state, so she decided to do it. She had not
yet found a job, but her certification was brand-new and she felt
very confident.

The following year Shanice had a job, but not as a CNA. She
worked for an agency that sent her out to people's homes to, as she
described it, "bathe them, dress them, clean up for them, help them
with their prescriptions." Although Shanice had certainly received
CNA training in all of these areas, she was essentially functioning
as a home health care aide. According to federal data, most CNAs
work in hospitals, nursing homes, and other facilities where they
are under the direct supervision of a nurse. CNAs also typically
make more money than home health aides, largely because home
health aides do not receive as much formal training.[9]

Shanice did not have a nurse as a supervisor; in fact, she had little
supervision at all. When I asked her how much supervision she
received, she said, "I'm basically on my own." As for coworkers,
she said that "I pretty much don't even see my coworkers." She
often faxed in her timesheets and rarely went to the agency's office.
How many hours Shanice worked was completely dependent on
the number and type of cases the agency had. In one day, she might
be assigned to visit two people in their homes, one of whom would
need a two-hour visit and the other a three-hour visit. She would
also be paid for the time it took her to travel between the two assignments (but not reimbursed for mileage, so she had to pay for
gas as she drove all over the metro Detroit area). Thus, if it took one
hour to travel between her patients' homes, she would be paid for
a six-hour day. However, sometimes she was unable to work more
than six hours if the agency had no other cases or if the other available cases involved patient requirements and travel time that would
put her over eight hours a day. The agency did not want to pay
overtime, and Shanice needed to be home for her children. How
many times a week she saw each client also varied. "I might get a
case that I only go two times a week," she explained. "I might have
a case that I go five times a week. I might have a case I go just on the
weekends. So it varies." If a client moved into a facility, went to the

hospital, or, in the worst case, died, Shanice lost those hours until the agency had another case to assign her. Given all of these variables, Shanice often worked only ten to fifteen hours a week instead of forty. At a wage of $8 an hour, she wasn't making much at all. By 2011, work had slowed down so much that Shanice was not getting any hours at all, and she finally quit.

One of the hallmarks of low-wage jobs is lack of autonomy and arbitrary supervision, but Shanice had no one watching over her to correct any mistakes she might make, provide support, or commend her on a job well done.[10] A client could certainly complain about how Shanice carried out her duties, or a family member of that client could do so on the client's behalf, but in the absence of such complaints, Shanice was left to her own devices, effectively abandoned by her employer. The agency she worked for checked up on her by phone to make sure she saw all of the clients she was scheduled to visit, and she faxed or sometimes mailed in a worksheet on which she checked off the various tasks she had performed for the client. Otherwise, Shanice was all but invisible to her immediate supervisor.

The kind of workplace isolation that Shanice experienced was also common among the other low-wage workers in the study. They were more likely to work overnight shifts, when staffing levels are skeletal, and to work in settings, such as home health care, where the norm, as in Shanice's experience, was to rarely see other employees and to pay few visits to the work site of their employer. Eleven of the women were home health aides for at least some amount of time between 2006 and 2011, and all of them experienced this type of isolation.

Slightly higher-paying jobs could be isolating as well, particularly those that involved working from home. Nichelle at times worked at home as a "virtual office assistant." Typically, virtual assistants are independent contractors who take on short-term projects or provide administrative support off-site to clients who may not want to hire a full-time in-house administrative assistant. In 2006, Nichelle described her work: "You set up your website, and, you might do, you know, you do your brochures and business cards. I had joined a lot of different groups that were on Yahoo that dealt with—they even had a group, Michigan Virtual Assistants. They also had, like, a website where they have virtual assistants that's in the Michigan area. So like, small businesses, entrepreneurs—people like that that can actually go and if they need a one-time project or they just need somebody. They may not need someone full-time." Nichelle was contracted to perform a number of different jobs, including setting up appointments for a businessperson and doing some short-term accounting work and website design. For a mother of three, a job like this certainly had many benefits. Being able to work when it was most convenient, Nichelle could take her children to and from school and run other errands. But the job kept her at home, with her unemployed and abusive husband, and it cut her off from any community she might have been able to build if she had been employed in an actual office.

Several years later, after she had left her husband, Nichelle was unemployed and trying to get herself back into virtual office assistant work. All the websites providing information on becoming a virtual assistant stress the importance of being self-motivated and able to stay on task, but in 2009 Nichelle was having a lot of difficulties, both financial and personal. She said, "It's just the last year and a half, I kind of have not been focused. I think I'd be a lot further with a lot of things, but because everything that's happened, you know, there's been times when I've been really depressed. Or just like, 'What am I doing? Why am I even . . .?' You know? And I get up and push myself and be really into it. Then there's something else happens." At that point, Nichelle had been moving from place to place before finally settling in at a long-term residence hotel. The instability in her life, the stress she was experiencing, and not un-importantly, the lack of a reliable Internet connection made doing virtual assistant work extremely difficult.

Erica lived in a run-down house on Detroit's east side, with very little furniture. Lacking a vacuum cleaner, it was difficult for her to keep the carpeted floors clean, despite her efforts in taking a broom to them. In 2011, Erica moved to the South, hoping for better opportunities. Erica had training and skills related to computer maintenance, but the only job she could find was working from home and taking calls from people having difficulty with their computers. There was enough work to keep her working forty hours a week, more if she wanted. I never saw Erica's new place, but she described it on the phone as "a real shit hole," full of roaches half the size of a Mounds candy bar (her point of reference). A few years later, I learned that she had found a different job, one she was eager to take because she would no longer have to work from home.

Rhonda described her work setting when she was employed by a custodial company cleaning office buildings: "Mostly I worked in a building by myself. But it was like, two different departments, but the building was connected together, so it was one coworker that worked on the other side of the building, and I worked on one side. So I barely seen him unless I went over there to get supplies or something like that. Other than that, I worked by myself." When asked what she liked best about the job, she said it was the peace and quiet of working alone, after all of the building's employees had left. (Rhonda's four children, ranging in age from six to eighteen, were quite active and lively.) But the peace and quiet could have a downside: "Sometimes it used to get a little scary, when it get late. When I was working more hours, I used to be there late, like, eleven o'clock, and sometimes people come back in the building when I think I'm there by myself, and I see somebody walk past, and I didn't like that."

Aside from concerns about safety (though that is obviously an important issue), why should we care if workers labor alone? Many workers across the occupational spectrum do just that. Telecommuting has become much more popular in the past ten years. The number of workers who telecommute is estimated to have increased 79 percent between 2005 and 2012, accounting for 3.2 million workers.[11] In writing this book, I spent many hours working at home by myself. However, neither my job nor the jobs of many who telecommute are intrinsically isolated ones. I have meetings to attend and classes to teach, and I spend time on a busy and bustling campus. Employees who work remotely may find themselves more isolated than if they were in an office; perhaps avoiding such isolation is a reason for the rising popularity of "coworking" spaces that individuals can rent and share with others who are similarly working independently.[12] There is a key difference, however, between the potential isolation faced by a telecommuter (or someone who does not always work in an office) and the isolation experienced by the women in this study in their work settings.

Telecommuters are likely to be set up with the technology and other tools they need to keep in communication with others. Email, Skype, and other forms of online communication have made telecommuting much more feasible because the employee is not completely off on her own. For many home health care workers like Shanice, however, working alone really means working alone. She might have interactions with her clients, but many of them were quite incapacitated. Because Rhonda worked nights when she started working as a home health aide, "the clients are asleep, and I don't wake them up until like six in the morning." With her shift ending at 7:00 AM, Rhonda would have only an hour to interact with clients. The working conditions of home health aides vary — as mentioned, some work in group home settings or adult day programs — but working inside clients' homes, as Shanice and Rhonda did, is the norm.[13] Home health aide work is a fast-growing occupation in the United States: the average growth rate for U.S. occupations is about 7 percent, but the number of home health aide jobs is projected to increase 38 percent in the next twenty years.[14] Thus, we might expect a growing number of low-wage workers to experience isolating work.

Another reason to be concerned about isolating work is that these workers do not accrue the benefits of working with others. Having coworkers can help acclimate new employees to workplace norms and create and reinforce solidarity among them.[15] In addition, working alongside one another creates bonds between workers, which may be particularly important when working conditions are bad.[16] Coworkers can provide emotional support in those circumstances, since they have a shared understanding of what they are all experiencing. For example, Erica, who dealt alone with customers all day, had no coworkers with whom she could vent about a particularly irate individual or share different strategies for resolving problems. Although sometimes workers may be able to mobilize and push for changes in their workplace, isolated workers more often have no real peers who understand what they are going through. Labor organizers, knowing that "dense networks" of interconnection between coworkers are needed to move from individual to collective action, are concerned that isolating work prohibits the formation of such ties.[17]

Having the social skills to enable such interaction, moreover, may be a key for future success in the labor market. The automation of job tasks has significantly reduced the number of jobs and eliminated some altogether. In the Detroit area, people are very aware of this trend, having watched friends and family members lose good-paying factory jobs as their work is shipped to plants in Mexico or taken over by robots. But even on the low end of the wage distribution, jobs are being eliminated via technology. Shoppers can check themselves out at stores with self-serve kiosks and pay a machine in a parking garage instead of an attendant. The jobs that are much more difficult to automate are ones in which human interaction is important to the completion of tasks.[18] Collaboration with coworkers provides important experience in social interaction; indeed, the "ability to work in a team" is often listed as a requirement for many jobs.

Organizational sites such as the workplace are extremely important in shaping interactions. In his study of child care centers, Mario Luis Small has found that the way these centers are structured can encourage or impede the building of ties between parents.[19] Centers that mobilize parent volunteers for field trips, for example, help start friendships, which are important to mothers whose social networks are otherwise limited. These mothers also have lower rates of depression. Parents also build networks at pick-up and drop-off times when they share information. This does not happen, however, in centers where pick-up and drop-off do not occur at specific times or where space is too tight to allow for mingling between parents. These sorts of everyday exchanges, while seemingly mundane, form the building blocks of strong social networks. Women who work in isolation have no opportunity to form these connections through their jobs.

Even when their jobs presented opportunities for interaction and collaboration, some women in the study were reluctant to take them. Yvette and several other women noted that their workplaces were dominated by other women and this, they believed, led to an undue amount of "drama." For Yvette, getting "caught up" in such drama could have real economic repercussions. She worked in a combination sales and customer service position and spent most of her day on the phone. Part of her pay came from commissions she made on sales. "If you get caught up or drawn into that stuff," she said of the workplace drama, "then you'll see how your performance can easily be affected." Workers who engaged in this drama and in idle conversations, she believed, did not earn as much money on commissions. Judy, a nurse's aide, also believed that it was best for her to avoid much contact with her coworkers — also all women. She said, "Women tend to keep a whole buncha stuff started. You tell one person something, they'll blow it up, and then next thing you know . . . it's that confrontation thing." Like Yvette, Judy greeted her coworkers and talked with them when she needed help with a patient, but otherwise kept to herself. As she said, "I don't [talk to my coworkers]. They're women, and I don't. I just find that to be bad policy."[20]

Not engaging with coworkers was also a protective strategy used by those whose employers had very little sympathy toward their workforce. Yvette's comment about her performance being negatively affected if she talked to her peers was not just about making money. It was also a way to deal with the relentless pressure to meet corporate standards. In 2007, Yvette explained in great detail how she was evaluated on each shift. Even though she was dealing with customers over the phone and did not have control over what they said or did, she was held accountable. For example, she explained "final call resolution": "That means that if a customer [I talked to] calls back within thirty days, then I'm marked down on my final call resolution, because whatever happened on that call initially, I did not resolve their concern completely and that customer had to call back." Then there was the "save rate percentage," which "has to be 52 percent or higher. So for the amount of customers that call in and say that they want to disconnect their services, if a hundred people call in and I disconnect ninety of the accounts, then my save percent is only 10 percent. So, out of all those customers who are calling in, I should be able to save the business for the company. At least 52 percent of the calls that come in within that thirty-day period." Of course, this was a job Yvette held during the economic downturn, and as she noted, many customers were leaving the state to seek jobs elsewhere, and many others just did not have the money to afford the company's services. Nevertheless, since Yvette was penalized for these terminations of services, she believed that keeping to herself was necessary to avoid such penalties. Adding to her isolation was the fact that her employer structured its workplace operations to keep "idle time" to a minimum, thus denying employees opportunities for potentially positive social interactions, information sharing, and solidarity building.

## The Preemptive Quit

Lacking connections with coworkers, and particularly with supervisors, contributed to what I call the "preemptive quit": quitting a job because of worry about being fired. Due to isolating work conditions, these women were unable to build relationships with others and develop trust, so when a problem arose they quit as a way to protect their reputation. Preemptive quitting occurred in all types of jobs but was more common in low-wage jobs. Of the thirty-seven women who held at least one job between 2006 and 2011, seven preemptively quit a job.

After working as a custodian, Rhonda moved into a home health care job. When I asked her if she was happier in this job than in the janitorial position, she said, "I guess I can say I'm happy, compared to the last job." But when I probed for reasons why, she listed the ways in which her home health care job was worse, including the amount of lifting she had to do and company policies she did not like, such as the last-minute scheduling of shifts. Unlike Shanice, Rhonda did see her supervisor on a regular basis, since the supervisor worked the shift prior to Rhonda. But they would mostly just see each other in passing, and if the supervisor wanted Rhonda to do something different from the normal routine, she would leave a note. One day she left a note telling Rhonda to feed the clients some fruit with their breakfast. Rhonda could not find any fruit in the refrigerator, so she gave them their regular breakfast. The next day her supervisor confronted Rhonda and told her that the fruit was in a can in the cupboard; Rhonda had not thought to look there. As a consequence, Rhonda said, "I got wrote up for not giving the clients some fruit with their breakfast. And the manager said that I withheld food from them, like as if I was starving them, because I didn't give them fruit with their breakfast. So if she sent that in, it would have been on my record and I wouldn't have been able to do this kind of work anymore." Rhonda decided that it would be better to quit than to have an infraction in her file, so that was what she did.

As Nichelle was setting up her own business (discussed in more detail later in the chapter) she continued to work for a fund-raising organization. It was a full-time job, and aside from a few minor issues with her boss, she really enjoyed it. But she also wanted to pursue her passion. She was just about to open her store when her boss found out about it. Her boss confronted Nichelle, wanting to know if Nichelle was going to quit. Nichelle had no plans to leave the job in the near future; she needed the steady paycheck the job provided until she was sure her business could support her and her children. Later in the week, according to Nichelle, her employer started questioning her about whether she used the office's equipment and supplies for her own business, which she did not. Then she started talking to Nichelle about conflicts of commitment, worrying about how Nichelle was going to be able to do her job as well as run her own business. Nichelle recounted part of the conversation:

> [My boss said,] "I'm going to have to explain to the board how you can do two things at the same time." I mean it was just a lot of this, and I just was really, I really was hurt. And I was really angry because I had just got a performance evaluation, probably about three weeks prior. And I had gotten 3.8 out of 4. And I was doing two jobs for one thing, you know, dealing with the events coordination and trying to deal with the financial side. And I just was really hurt. I mean all the time I've put into this job. . . . So when I left out of there, I just felt, I felt really, really, just like, wow, you know? When I went on my lunch break I took a long drive, and I just really thought and I was like, you know, you're going to have to resign because there's going be any little thing you do, whether you take a day off, whatever,

she's going to find something and she's going to make it hard.
Where, you know, I would end up getting fired.

Nichelle's reaction to her boss's concerns and Rhonda's worry about her future employment prospects illustrate a phenomenon that Judith Levine describes in her book *Ain't No Trust*. In the low-wage labor market, Levine argues, workers believe, often very correctly, that they have no rights. If a conflict arises, they do not trust that their employer will do the right thing, and so they quit.[21] Nichelle worried that her boss's concerns would escalate into something worse, so she quit. The preemptive quits that Rhonda, Nichelle, and others made were also a reaction to feeling threatened. Although Rhonda did not say so explicitly, I understood her as saying that her supervisor was threatening to make a report of elder neglect to the state, which might very well have ended her career as a caregiver. Nichelle was not threatened in the same way as Rhonda, but in her retelling of the story, her boss repeatedly and over the course of several interactions raised her concern that Nichelle might be using the organization's resources to further her business efforts. Her boss also brought up long-ago incidents in which Nichelle had technically violated the organization's policies. For example, Nichelle had on a couple of occasions brought her boys into work with her, a practice that was common among the staff, she said, when kids had the day off from school. What Nichelle actually thought her boss would do with this information was not clear, but she believed that a threat was there and so she quit.

Such preemptive quits could very well be justified. Jen and Tasha had both been fired under dubious circumstances. A young mother of one, Jen had also taken custody of her niece, who was about the same age as her daughter. She worked in an administrative position for one of the large health care systems in Detroit. The job paid well, and wage increases put her earnings above the poverty line by 2011. Then the health system was bought out by another company, and Jen found herself fired for an infraction that was not even her fault: when her employee ID card failed to register after Jen "swiped in" one day, she officially was not at work though in fact she was. Tasha was fired after a year of turmoil on her job. Work rules would change arbitrarily, and morale was very low. She began to use her accrued vacation time because the stress of the job was wearing her down, but then she was fired for lack of attendance. Both women were shocked that they had been fired after years of having no performance problems on their jobs. Preemptive quits at least allowed women to leave on their own terms.

# Unlawful Practices

Employers also reportedly violated worker's rights, and with no repercussions. Geneva tried to go back to her job after she was mostly healed from the back injury she incurred after falling in the company's parking lot. But she needed some accommodations: to have her desk moved closer to the restroom so that she would not have to walk very far, to gain access to a handicapped parking space in the lot, and to have a special chair with lumbar support. Her desk did not get moved, but she did get the chair—for a short time. She related the story of what happened: "They took my chair, because other people started complaining, 'She has a special chair, and her chair does this and that.' And so they took my chair. And told me I had to have, I would have to sit in a regular chair because they were getting too many complaints about this chair." Shortly after her special chair was taken away, Geneva was fired for attendance issues: she often had to miss work when her pain got bad. Admittedly, this retelling of the firing includes only Geneva's point of view, but the incident with the chair nevertheless seems to be a clear violation of the Americans with Disabilities Act (ADA). Geneva had a doctor's prescription for a special chair. Under the ADA, if Geneva could perform the essential functions of her job with reasonable accommodations, she should have been provided with those accommodations. The chair was one, and allowing her some flexibility in her schedule might have been another reasonable accommodation. Geneva litigated the disputed worker's compensation claim, but she did not know that she might have been able to also sue for ADA noncompliance.

Erica was a victim of a "bait and switch" job offer that unfortunately was not necessarily illegal. Erica had a college degree and was very skilled at programming and repairing computers. Given the high demand for tech-related skills, one would think that she would have had no trouble finding work. Initially, she did not, getting an interview with a large firm. Only after she was hired did she learn that the job she was hired into was not the job for which she thought she was applying and that in fact she was employed by a subsidiary of the company. She received much less comprehensive benefits than the benefits offered by the parent company to its employees. The company's tuition reimbursement package had been particularly attractive to her, since she wanted to acquire additional computer certifications, but as an employee of the subsidiary, Erica would not have that benefit. She would also be making less than $12 an hour, whereas those employed by the parent company were making $17.

Erica thought the entire setup was rooted in racism. She believed that in order to fulfill its contract with the city of Detroit, the parent company had to agree to hire a certain number of Detroit residents. She may have been correct in this speculation, since this is common practice when the city issues large contracts, but less arguable was the discriminatory treatment she saw day to day on the job. Erica reported that when she approached a supervisor about getting more on-the-job training, "she said, 'No. I can't train you because you're not network plus certified.' But all these other people is dancing around here, learning all these new things that are not networks plus certified, which is mainly white people. I'm going to sound prejudiced, I mean, I'm not like that. I went to a white college and all that kind of stuff, but this stuff do happen. And like right now, I really feel like I'm experiencing it." It was important to Erica to clarify that she was not someone who "went looking" for racism (perhaps because she was talking to me, a white person); she had gone to a small liberal arts college in a rural part of Michigan, and she often worked side by side with people who were not African American. Her suspicions were raised even further when the work started slowing down. There were rumors that the subsidiary employees were going to be laid off, which would have qualified them for unemployment benefits. But suddenly supervisors were writing up the employees, including Erica, for very minor infractions, like submitting a time sheet a little bit late. Fearing that she would be fired rather than laid off, a distinction that matters for unemployment benefits, Erica preemptively quit and left the job. (Unfortunately for her, quitting also does not help one claim benefits.)

Erica might have had some recourse if she had taken her chances and stayed with the employer. If she had been fired, perhaps she could have alleged racial discrimination in the firing process. She might have been able to show disparate treatment in opportunities for advancement or in compensation and benefits.[22] She could have filed a complaint with the Equal Employment Opportunity Commission (EEOC), the federal agency charged with enforcing the nation's antidiscrimination laws. The EEOC investigates such claims, and if it determines that a case should move forward, it files a lawsuit against the employer. However, the EEOC pursues lawsuits for only a small number of the complaints that are filed; in fiscal year 2010, for instance, about 90,000 claims were filed, but only 271 resulted in EEOC lawsuits.[23] If the EEOC had declined to take the case to court, Erica could have filed a lawsuit herself, although that would have required legal representation, which Erica certainly could not afford. Racial discrimination was not an issue brought up by most of the other women, possibly because they were not comfortable doing so with a white woman (although the topic did not come up when African American students conducted interviews). However, most of them worked in racially segregated environments in which all staff and supervisors were of the same race and most of their customers or clients were racially homogenous as well.

Other workplace illegalities to which the women were exposed were violations of various regulatory practices. Tamara reported that the assisted living facility in which she worked was supposed to admit only people who were mobile, but that changed when the company was bought out. She explained: "If [the patients] got to the point to where they couldn't walk or couldn't stand, we would transfer them to a nursing home. Once they changed management, we started getting residents that couldn't walk and that was in wheelchairs. We had to do more lifting, and, you know, things like that." The facility lacked any special equipment to help with moving patients, and Tamara suspected all the additional lifting caused her back injury. Rhonda was asked to give out medication by one of the home health care agencies she worked for, but first she needed to go to a training to get certified. The agency did not want to pay for that and kept pressuring Rhonda to take on the responsibility anyway. Rhonda again preemptively quit a job, concerned that either she would be fired or she would give out medication and then be held responsible if something went wrong.

These women, like the majority of the U.S. workforce, were "at will" employees. Those employed at will are not covered by a contract, collective bargaining agreement, statute, or any legal agreement that specifies the terms of their employment. In theory, employment at will is supposed to benefit both employees and employers equally. At will employees are free to take whatever jobs they want and to leave when they want, and employers are free to hire whoever they want and to fire employees whenever they want. This model is supposed to promote economic efficiency. Firms can downsize when necessary, and workers can take their labor to where it is needed. However, employment at will does not give employers the right to break state or federal laws such as the ADA or employment discrimination statutes. The courts have also provided for exceptions to employment at will; absent these provisions, however, an employer is allowed to fire an employee without giving a reason.[24] Employees who believe that they have been fired unjustly may take action against an employer by pursuing their case through legal channels, but particularly in the low-wage labor market, workers are unlikely to go this route since they lack the money and time to engage in a court case. They may also lack knowledge about their rights. Having previously endured abusive behavior in the workplace, they may not know that recourse is available. And because they are often isolated, they cannot share information with coworkers.

## Searching for Work

Not only were aspects of their actual jobs isolating, but many of the women in the study found the job search process to be isolating as well. Key to Wilson's concept of social isolation is that the poor are excluded "from the job network system that permeates other neighborhoods and that is so important in learning about or being recommended for jobs."[25] In other words, they lack the social networks that could connect them to jobs. The literature on job searching stresses the importance of networking and making connections with others in finding jobs. In his classic work on finding employment, Mark Granovetter argues that an activity like searching for a job requires being able to tap into the networks of one's acquaintances rather than turn to one's own family and friends. Why? Because the former group is less likely to know each other and have similar social networks, while the latter are often embedded within some of the same networks.[26] To illustrate, if I want to find a new job, I would be better off asking people I do not consider close to me whether they know about any opportunities. If I ask three acquaintances, each might go back to his or her network and consult people in that group about job openings. I would thus have expanded my network to include people I may not even know. By contrast, my close friends and I are all largely in the same network. Asking three of my friends for job leads would not yield more information beyond what those three could provide, since all their consultations with network members would be with each other. This scenario illustrates what Granovetter calls the "strength of weak ties," that is, the greater ability to obtain needed information from people whom we know less well. Given the environments in which many women in the study worked—alone and rarely interacting with others—sharing information and building "weak ties" at work was never a possibility.

The Internet and social media have drastically changed the way we network, but only a few of these women used Facebook or other social media, and even those who did tended to use it to stay in touch with friends and family, not as a tool for finding jobs and making professional connections. (The exception was Nichelle, who had a very strong professional social media presence.) However, they did use the Internet to try to find jobs. Increasingly, employers had moved to online applications, and women mostly submitted job applications and résumés electronically.[27] They also uploaded their résumés to online services such as Monster.com, which allows employers to locate potential applicants and job-seekers to apply online for jobs. The state of Michigan runs a "Talent Bank," which performs the same service for Michigan residents and employers.

Job searching online, however, could be at least as lonely and demoralizing as many of the jobs these women were able to find. Submitting applications online could feel like sending material off into a void. They might apply for dozens of jobs online and never hear anything from an employer. For Tamara, this method of job search felt like just "waiting, waiting, waiting." She had to wait for an employer to contact her since most online job applications do not supply contact information, and sites like Monster.com are designed for employers to initiate contact. Erica, a college graduate, longed to have a network of people with more than a high school degree with whom she could discuss jobs. But according to her, being poor put her in a circle in which most people did not have the type of education she had. She said, "I don't really have nobody to talk to, give me some like, good jobs leads [for the] type of thing I might want to do. Because you know, everybody I talk to . . . it's not very many people with high school diplomas. And you know, or they just, all they jobs is hard labor type of work. You know, I don't necessarily have to do no hard labor type thing, you know? And it's not the same."

While most of the women's networks of friends and family did not consist of "laborers," their peers did tend to work in the same types of isolating, low-wage jobs. Their parents and older relatives might have better jobs, working in factories or in civil service positions, but those jobs had all but dried up. The strength of these "strong ties" was not very strong at all.

# Entrepreneurship

Some of the women in this study viewed starting their own business as a way to have control over at least a portion of the income they might have coming in. And working for one's self also eased the fear of being fired. During times of high unemployment, entrepreneurship may be the only solution for bringing in income.

African American women in particular can deal with thwarted opportunities in the wage labor market, where they face dual disadvantages based on their race and gender, by opening a business.[28] Of course, starting a business is extremely difficult. About half of small businesses fail—that is, they no longer exist five years later.[29] There are start-up costs, operating costs, and the cost of forgoing other activities while running the business. Further, minority small business owners are more likely to have their business loan applications rejected, in part because these businesses are frequently located in minority neighborhoods, which lenders consider risky.[30] Without money from loans, minority-owned businesses may then have to expend more of their own capital. Finally, most of the businesses that women in this study started required cultivating some sort of clientele, which may have been made more difficult by their experience working jobs in which they interacted with few people. And obtaining payment for services was sometimes difficult.

Lisa and her husband had dreams of being self-employed entrepreneurs, but acting on those dreams had put them on the very edge of financial solvency. Lisa's husband usually made a fairly good salary as a skilled tradesperson, although he sometimes was unemployed and often had to work in locations far from home. (The last time I saw Lisa her husband was working on the West Coast.) But they had always wanted a business of their own. As Lisa said, with her own business, "I don't have to work hard to make someone else's company successful." Lisa had stopped working at an office job, frustrated by the politics in the workplace, so having their own business would be a way to bring in a second income over which they might have more control. Their first attempt at a small business did not work out because, according to Lisa, they could not find reliable employees. Next they tried to open up a home day care. They spent about $12,000 of their own money finishing their basement, purchasing toys and equipment, and installing the safety features required by the state licensing agency, such as adding a second exit. They had been running the day care for only a few months, and Lisa was caring for several children, when disaster struck. The neighbor's house caught fire, and Lisa's house caught fire as well. Lisa and her family not only lost their

Detroit home but lost their business as well. Although the basement where the day care was located was not burned, it was completely flooded by the water used to extinguish the blaze.

Luckily, Lisa and her husband had homeowner's insurance. The insurance company paid for them to stay in an apartment while they figured out what to do next. Instead of rebuilding their home, however, the couple decided to use the insurance money to pay off their mortgage. They then combined the leftover cash with some of their own money to invest in learning about the real estate business. A late night infomercial by a house-flipping "guru" inspired the couple to spend about $40,000 to enroll in his seminars and learn his marketing techniques, purchase various marketing tools (such as postcards), and buy other proprietary materials, such as lists of potential buyers kept by the company and access to software containing property listings. After about a year of not having any luck finding a property to purchase, let alone flip, and with the insurance payments for their rental apartment about to stop, they decided to purchase a home that they would live in while fixing it up with the intention of selling it and moving on to something better.

We might think that Lisa and her husband were making unwise decisions in their efforts to be entrepreneurs. While the fire that damaged their house and day care business could not have been expected, why did they spend so much money, we might ask, to learn about the real estate business, particularly when the housing bubble had recently burst? The answer is that, for Lisa, paying an expert seemed reasonable. She had no one in her family to whom she could go for financial and business advice. The one piece of financial advice that her mother gave her was that it was important to save, and Lisa followed her advice, putting aside money from her paycheck, and later her husband's, each payday. The money they saved was what they used for their business endeavors (although spending that money left them with no reserves). Moreover, there were many radio commercials at that time for businesses, such as the one used by Lisa, with the message that the abundance of homes in the Detroit area that were up for sale provided a real opportunity for people to make money. And indeed, as Detroit started becoming a trendy locale, investors, including foreign ones, started buying up real estate.[31] The housing market in Detroit was getting better—but not in all areas of the city. Also, Lisa and her husband would be newcomers going up against real estate professionals with much more experience.

These types of schemes offer hope to people who are trying desperately to maintain and even elevate their economic status. Furthermore, these "experts" often present themselves as people who worked hard to rise up from humble beginnings and are now trying to "give back" by sharing the secrets of their success. They provide a message of hope, encapsulating the Horatio Alger story that has long been a part of the American social fabric. For strivers like Lisa and her husband, who were trying to restart their lives after the fire and who always wanted to be their own bosses, the seminars seemed like an easy way to get the tools and skills that would take them "from rags to riches." What is often ignored, however, is the role played by luck (including the luck of being born into a family with some resources) in these success stories.

Starting a business while living on the edge of financial stability is also difficult for the simple reason that extra cash is not available. Sandra and her husband also tried to start a business—in their case a transportation service for seniors and people with mobility issues. They already owned a van, and as Sandra said, "transportation is a good [business]. That's a good one because everybody rely on it and they do need the transportation." However, they had yet to transport a client. They had obtained a tax identification number, but their van had not yet passed inspection. On their first try, the regulatory agency found issues that needed to be corrected, but Sandra lacked the funds to make the repairs. Unlike Lisa, Sandra and her husband had not invested any money in the business (just their own time and effort), and lack of money stalled their plans.

Figuring out the prices to charge in order to stay in business is another challenge. Karla was in the midst of setting up her own business when I last saw her. She had moved to Detroit in 2010, when she bought a house for about $10,000. The house needed many renovations, and she was still in the middle of that when I saw her the next year. Despite that, soon after moving in she started providing child care to the children of various family members, most of whose child care payments were at least partially subsidized by the state's human services agency. Karla had yet to see any of those state payments, but even once she got paid, she would not be making much money. She charged $20 a day per child. By comparison, in Ann Arbor (where Karla lived for a couple of years), child care in a center might cost $50 to $60 a day. Family day care homes like the one Karla was operating tended to cost less, but not by much. Karla was caring for five children, but not each day; one might come three days a week, another two, and another just half-days. She said that she had made as much as $300 in a week, but also as little as $30.

Nichelle's efforts at entrepreneurship had left her in the red. She had her own business long before we met her, making beauty products. For several years she sold them in a handful of local stores. She stopped for a couple of years, but after she moved to the South, she decided that her life was stable enough to launch her own brick-and-mortar business. Her dream was to eventually start a franchise. She rented a storefront in a small mall that had a couple of other tenants, not realizing that it was in an area of town without much traffic going past. Soon after she opened, one of the other shops closed. Nichelle's store stayed open for six weeks until she ran out of money to keep the operation going. By that time, she estimated, she had spent at least $10,000 she had saved up over the past year. She said, "I invested quite a bit in shelves and you know, trying to decorate and . . . supplies, furniture."

Even those women who succeeded in selling their services encountered challenges in getting customers to pay. Mary took a course in decorating and flower design and started to offer her services in party planning. She made balloon bouquets, centerpieces, and other decorations for events such as weddings. She said that the experience was a lot of fun, but that it had shown her "that people do not want to support you. People, you know, different family member, different friends. When I come to them and tell them my price . . . nuh uh. So I end up doing it . . . I'll say, 'Whatever you give me is fine.' I have had a friend of mine that I had over thirty years give me forty dollars to decorate a party." The money people gave her did not even cover the cost of supplies.

# Employment for
# Those on the Margins

For a few of these women, their days of being strivers were either long past or had never come to anything. These were some of the poorest women in the study, and they were very much on the fringes of the labor market; some had been ejected from it altogether. Marie had once worked at a packaging plant, but she started missing work and was fired. She said that she had liked the job but it gave her carpel tunnel syndrome. In 2011 she was applying for disability benefits. Dorothy said that she had last worked in 2005, at a day care center, but had been laid off. It was difficult to picture her ever working again in light of how poor her health was: she was using a walker when I saw her in 2011, and she had recently had a series of mini-strokes. She was in her midfifties but looked much older. Dorothy received a monthly disability check, but usually three or four other unemployed family members looked to her for some support, since she was the only one with a stable (albeit small) source of income. Miss Price was also in poor health. She was as thin as a stick owing to a thyroid disorder. She also had some neurological problems. The last job she had held was in 2002, working as a machine operator in a small manufacturing firm. She was on temporary layoff and when her employer called her back, she never returned the phone call. She said, "You know, maybe I should have called them back, you know, a while back, to try and get my position back. But you know I, it's just one of those things." Eventually she started receiving disability benefits.

Raeanne worked more than the rest of the lowest-income women, but when she was caught leaving her custodial job with a bag of stolen goods that her niece had handed her, nobody asked her to explain what had happened; she was arrested and sent to jail. Danisha worked very sporadically, citing her son's asthma as the reason she could not hold a job. (She often needed to take him to the ER when he had an attack.) The only income that she and her three children had coming in was from her son's disability benefits ($674) and about $600 in food stamps. And Danielle's employment, braiding hair or occasionally selling meals, was off the books, with very sporadic income. She too was seeking disability benefits.

Like those documented by Wilson in Chicago, these women were relegated to the sidelines of social and economic life. Disability benefits allowed them to (barely) get by, but no one checked on their health or their need for assistance. Not only were they abandoned by the promise of employment as a path to social inclusion and stability, but when their health, criminal record, or other challenges limited their ability to even look for a job, they were provided with a small (often difficult-to-obtain) disability check and largely left to their own devices. For example, no one checked on Dorothy after she had knee surgery. She tried to sign up for a visiting nurse, but never heard anything. When she developed an infection, she could not get doctors to pay attention and later needed multiple surgeries to repair the damage. Raeanne's already high blood pressure went up higher after her arrest and subsequent conviction. She was sent off by the welfare office to look for a job but ended up in a hospital, where she died, much too young, after having a stroke. In a world that stresses work as the main activity for the poor, being kept out of the labor market by their poor health had left these women truly abandoned — and left Raeanne's five children without a mother.

# Conclusion

For those women in the study who could work, bad pay, fluctuating hours, and lack of benefits — commonly recognized problems with the low-wage labor market — were not the only challenges they faced. The conditions of their jobs left them isolated and lacking a community at work. Isolation caused them to miss opportunities for developing a network of people who might help them find better jobs. And the isolating nature of their work left these women on their own to deal with problems, without support from others. Some of them, experiencing work as a place where they felt threatened, quit when they feared they would be fired. Workplace rules and laws were violated. The decline in union participation and power has left workers with few protections, but for these women, the added layer of workplace isolation made it that much more difficult to feel supported. Even women in the study whose earnings ostensibly put them into the middle class experienced some of these problems.

The promise of employment as a mechanism for social inclusion and stability has been turned on its head, and many people who are striving to get ahead or trying to maintain some stability in their lives have been abandoned.

# ❧ Chapter 4 ❧

## Abandoned by Institutions of Mobility: The Failed Promise of Postsecondary Education and Homeownership

Despite having her first and second children at a young age, Yvette completed her bachelor's degree in business management. But that degree was a long time in coming. "It took me about twelve years," she said, "one class at a time. . . . But I just stuck with it, because when I had my oldest child, everybody said my life was over, ruined, you know. But I still had that get-up-and-go about me." For a striver like Yvette, that "get-up-and-go" translated into working a full-time job, raising her sons (she had her second child shortly after the first), and, of course, taking one class at a time. Originally she enrolled in a community college in the state where she was living at the time. Upon moving back to Michigan, she started taking some classes at Wayne State University. Eventually, she obtained her degree from the University of Phoenix, a largely online, for-profit degree-granting institution. The cost of attending community college and Wayne State was low enough that Yvette could afford to pay tuition out of her own pocket, but when she moved to the University of Phoenix, she needed to take out loans to pay tuition—$30,000 in total. Ten years after finishing, she proclaimed the degree "worthless": "I'm paying $30,000 on this student loan for something that is giving me a job one step above McDonald's." In that stressful and isolating job, she was earning $45,000 a year.

Yvette was also a homeowner when I first met her. She had put

77

time and money into remodeling her modest brick home on the east side of Detroit. The house had new windows and flooring, and she had spent some money fixing up the basement. She had refinanced her mortgage a number of times, always hoping to get a loan with better terms. In 2008 she still owed about $105,000 on her mortgage, but by that time the house was worth only about $60,000, according to an appraisal Yvette had done when she decided to put the house on the market. She said:

> I had it up for sale for almost a year and a half, and nobody wanted to buy it. And I don't blame them. If I was preapproved for a mortgage for $120,000, I wouldn't buy a house in a neighborhood that, you know, there's no recreation center within walking distance, the school systems are crappy, the—you know, politics of the city is crappy, the taxes are high. You're not getting anything for your tax money. Your insurance is high, your utilities are high. You know, if I had got approved for a mortgage of $100,000 or $120,000, I would move to an area that has a great school system, and I would get the cheapest house.

Yvette ended up letting her home go into foreclosure and losing all that she had invested in the property. The stress of the foreclosure as well as other financial problems took its toll on Yvette: she always had beautiful, intricate braids, but that year her hair started falling out in clumps.

Yvette had experienced the ultimate abandonment by the promise of the American Dream. The degree, which she had spent years working on, did not result in a position within her chosen field of business administration; rather, she answered phones all day and tried to convince cash-strapped customers, who were trying to disconnect their phones and cable, to purchase more services from a telecommunications firm. Her home was rapidly depreciating in value rather than becoming an asset for her future. And she had financed her shot at the American Dream through loans, which she needed to pay back.

Furthering one's education beyond high school has been one of the pathways to prosperity for several generations of Americans.

The so-called wage premium of having additional education is substantial. Bachelor's degree holders earn on average $430 a week more than those with a high school degree. Over a forty-year career, the typical college graduate earns $650,000 more than someone holding only a high school diploma.[1] However, the experiences of the women like Yvette who were enrolled in postsecondary programs were markedly different from those of a student attending a four-year institution full-time, living on campus, and taking classes in an actual classroom with other students and an instructor who are there in person. These women were relegated to a segment of the educational market that is separate from and not equal to the traditional system of higher education: attending for-profit institutions and community colleges, they took most or all of their classes online, a lonely and isolated enterprise. Further, some of them lacked examples in their networks of people who had gone to school, so they often did not understand the implications of enrolling part-time or of choosing or changing majors. Yet they were largely left on their own to navigate the process of choosing classes and monitoring their progress.

Most importantly, completing a degree provided these women with little upward mobility. The returns to education are gradual, but more education is supposed to result in improved earnings over the course of one's time in the labor market. Six years—the time over which we followed these women—may not have been long enough to see whether the investment had paid off for these families. However, early indications about the success of their additional education were not promising.

The other mechanism for upward mobility in the United States has been buying a home. Historically, home equity has been the largest source of wealth for families—that is, until the housing crisis of 2007. Many of the homeowning women in this study had purchased their house during the run-up to the housing crisis, when homeownership was being promoted in low-income communities as a way to build wealth and predatory lending and the promotion of high-risk mortgages were at their peak.[2] Mortgages were also being promoted as a way to access quick cash. A few women in the study had taken out mortgages on a home that they owned outright or that was close to being paid off. When housing values across the country collapsed, the situation in Detroit and the surrounding suburbs was particularly dismal. Housing prices in Detroit peaked in early 2006 and bottomed out in 2011, by which time housing values had dropped almost 50 percent. The market has since recovered somewhat, but the value of the average home purchased in Detroit in 2006 was still down by 23 percent in 2014.[3] All of the mortgage holders in this study owed more on their homes than they were worth, and many of the houses needed additional work requiring more outlays of cash. The families in this study had been abandoned by the traditional institutions of upward mobility.

# Going to School

Only four women in this study lacked a high school degree or a GED: Shanice, Danielle, Dorothy, and Marie had all dropped out of high school and never completed a GED. The other forty-one women were in a position to obtain postsecondary education, including graduate degrees for those who already had gone to college. During the study period, more than half of these women were enrolled in a degree or certificate program at some point, but only eight finished their course of study and obtained the degree or certificate. And for those eight women, better jobs and improved earnings had not materialized.

There are a number of reasons why we might expect degree completion rates to be lower among people who have more financial challenges. The families of wealthier students can use home equity, savings, and other assets to finance attendance at college. Students who do not have family resources may have to take time away from their studies to work while attending school. Furthermore, some students leave before finishing a degree because the need to earn money overwhelms the desire for more education. Additionally, the cost of higher education has grown tremendously over the past two decades: tuition at a public four-year institution rose from $3,350 in 1991 to $8,660 in 2012 (in 2012 dollars).[4] Tuition at community colleges has also gone up, although more slowly and generally from a much lower base. In addition to tuition costs, students with children face challenges in balancing the demands of school-work and parenting, perhaps having to do their own homework even as they are helping with their children's. And finally, researchers have pointed to the role of a lack of academic preparation for college in low degree completion rates.

Twelve of those enrolled in educational programs were hoping to obtain an associate's degree, four were in shorter-term certificate programs to train for a specific occupation, two were trying to get a bachelor's degree, another two were in graduate programs, and one woman had just started taking some classes as a way to ease herself back into school. They attended a variety of institutions: nine were enrolled at the local community college, seven at for-profit institutions, and four at private not-for-profit universities or colleges that had multiple campuses around the state. I do not know the type of school Judy attended; she dropped out fairly soon after enrolling. Two women did all of their course work online, and many others took online classes along with classes on campus.

Community colleges are sometimes referred to as "democratizing institutions" because of their open enrollment policies and low cost of attendance. They have also been criticized for offering subpar educations, catering too much to the demands of business in the classes and class content they offer, and perpetuating inequalities by granting degrees that are not valued in the labor market compared to those from four-year institutions.[5] That said, community college enrollment grew over the 2000s, leveling off at just over eight million students in 2011.[6]

Community colleges are primarily funded through state budget allocations, tuition and fees, and federal dollars. In some states local tax dollars support community colleges, but the proportion of total funding that comes from this source has dropped dramatically over time.[7] Compared to public universities, and factoring out money received for research purposes, community colleges receive far less funding per pupil even though the average community college student has many more academic and other needs than the average public university student.[8] Community colleges are also much less likely to receive large donations from wealthy alumni or other benefactors and so are particularly vulnerable to cuts in state appropriations or, as occurred during the most recent growth in enrollments, flat funding.

Degree completion rates at community colleges are quite low. Only 20 percent of students enrolling in two-year community college degree programs have completed them three years later; that figure rises to just 35 percent five years later, with substantial proportions having dropped out along the way.[9] Since African Americans and Latinos are overrepresented among community college attendees, every legitimate criticism of community colleges also points to the reproduction of racial inequalities.[10] Many community college students are "nontraditional" students who do not enter college straight after graduating from high school; the average age of a community college student is twenty-eight.[11] While older students may possess the maturity to know what they want to do, they may also be parents who have other demands on their time and are trying to balance school with family life.

Tamara's attempt at getting more education illustrates these challenges. She had always regretted that she did not attend college right after graduating from high school. One year she told me the story of what happened.

> I got accepted into Grambling [State] when I graduated and didn't go because my mom told me that she didn't think that I was ready to go. So I didn't go. And I'm regretting that now. I feel like if I would have went, I would have had the opportunity to do, you know, to do something. And I was like, okay, I'll just go next year. And then next year went to the next year after that, and then the next year after that, and then the next year after that. And then heck, I was pregnant so you know? It just never happened. So now, I'm going to rectify that situation. That's why I'm in school now.

Tamara was enrolled in a program at the county's community college to become a licensed practical nurse (LPN). When I met her in 2006, she said that she had another year and a half left in the program. But in 2011 she had still not finished it. One reason was that she took only two classes per semester and none in the summer. She said that she could only handle two classes since she was working and a single parent, but she did not realize what this pace meant for how quickly she would finish. Getting frustrated with her slow progress, in 2008 she tried taking three classes per term. In 2011 she thought she had only two classes—or maybe three (she was not sure)—to go before she got an associate's degree "in either general studies or liberal arts" (she did not know which). She would need to complete more course work for the LPN degree.

In addition to being a single parent and needing to work in order to support her family, Tamara also was trying to navigate her way through the program largely on her own. All community colleges have academic advisers, but they are usually overworked and overwhelmed by the sheer number of students they have to serve. They may have caseloads upwards of one thousand students and thus never see many of them; about half of community college students are unaware that they have an adviser.[12] Geri could have also benefited from an adviser. Like Tamara, Geri was unsure about when she would graduate and with which of two possible degrees (although from what I could tell by looking at the college's materials, there was not much difference between the two). Geri was struggling with the slow pace of her course work. She had gotten bogged down with the developmental education courses she needed to take but had finally completed them. Then she had to satisfy the general education requirements for all students obtaining an associate's degree. After she finished those, she learned that she might have been better off taking them in the summer: "What I should have done was take these three major classes—Biology, Sociology, and Psychology—in the summertime 'cause they move faster." She then explained that she could have taken more criminal justice courses (her major) during the regular academic year, when there were more choices.

The majority of community college students are like Geri in that they are put into developmental education courses because they are judged as academically underprepared for college course work. Entering students are typically given assessment tests to determine their skill levels in reading, math, and writing. Students can use their financial aid to pay for these courses, but they do not receive college credit. Some students may have to take only a course or two at the developmental level, but others may end up spending five semesters in what are essentially remediation courses before moving on to their degree program. Older adults and low-income students are more likely to be placed in developmental education. Remediation is costly to both the community college and the student. An estimated $2.3 billion goes to support remedial education in community colleges and other postsecondary degree-granting institutions, yet students who are put in developmental education courses are more likely to drop out, and fewer than one-quarter complete their program within eight years.[13]

When I asked Geri about advising at her school, she tried to show me the online advising system provided by the community college. First, she had difficulty logging in. Then she could not find the links to take her to the information she wanted to find. Geri was not computer-illiterate, but she had been out of school for more than twenty years and the system was confusing, even to me. After she gave up, she started talking about whether or not she should change the focus of her studies. She said, "You know something, I'm thinking about changing my major, because it's hard when you're in college, you learn these things and you think, oh man. I really want to be a criminal justice probation officer for juveniles, right? But I also want to do biology, or something in science. I like science. So right now, to be honest with you, I'm kind of torn between, I like all three of these subjects." Her enthusiasm for being in school and for learning was great to see, particularly since for the previous two years she had been so stressed about her debt. But what were the implications of switching majors? Would she be in school longer? Would the federal program paying for her schooling continue to pay? What kind of jobs could she get with an associate's degree in biology? These were all questions Geri had not considered.

Karla also changed her mind about what type of program she wanted to pursue. In 2011, after she moved to Detroit, she was taking classes at the county community college, also in the criminal justice program. When I first met her, she was enrolled at a different community college, working toward a certificate in early childhood education. Then she was taking business classes. Next, she started classes for a degree in human resource management. She

84

did not complete any of these programs. Changing majors is quite common among young students at four-year institutions. We rarely expect those students to have made up their mind about the field they want to pursue when they first enter college, so it's not surprising that Geri was toying with the idea of changing gears and Karla already had. Some guidance about how to make those decisions could have really helped these two students who knew very little about navigating the world of higher education, but when Karla tried to make an appointment with a counselor, she was told, "They don't work during the summer."

Lack of academic guidance often combined with their slow progress (as a result of part-time schooling) and the need to take prerequisites made enrollment in school exceedingly hard for these women and increased their chances of being put on academic probation. In addition, their economic difficulties often spilled over into school. In 2010, after Nichelle's business failed, she attempted to return to school, hoping to finish with an associate's degree in business. Initially, school was a positive experience. She was doing well in her classes, and she and her sons would study together at night. But then her car broke down. Nichelle had been attending a private, nonprofit college with campuses all over the state, but none were close to where she lived. Previously, she had taken her children to their respective schools and then headed to her classes on campus. Once the car broke down, she and her sons needed to leave the house at 5:00 AM in order to take all of the various buses to get to their schools. And then Nichelle needed to get on yet another bus and make the long trek to her classes. She hoped to use her income tax refund to get the car repaired, but because she had not worked all that much in the previous year, her refund was fairly small.

Sometimes when Nichelle did not have enough money to pay everyone's bus fare she did not go to class. Sometimes all of them stayed home—often enough that the district's truant officer sent a warning letter, noting that if her sons missed any more days of school they could be held back. Unable to manage, Nichelle ended up withdrawing from several of her classes. She had already received a sizable amount of financial aid as well as a loan, but between tuition and bills, that money was gone. Since she did not complete the number of credit hours commensurate with her financial aid package, the school put her on probation. When we met that summer, she did not know what being on probation meant, whether she would be able to enroll again in the fall, or whether she would have to pay back some of the financial aid.

When Jen was put on academic probation, she was very upset. She had asked if she could send her final paper to her instructor via email, which she said she did. Only when she got a failing grade for the class did she find out that the instructor claimed not to have received the paper. Jen was put on academic probation and told that she could not re-enroll for another year. She was irate: "I was just, I was really just disgusted, and I just, I decided, let me just get out for a while. I just got really upset about that because I just felt like they, just that teacher, ooh if I see her it's on!! Because I don't appreciate her even doing that to me!" A year later, the for-profit institution she had been attending was bought out by another company, and many of the credits she had accumulated did not count toward a degree. Her understanding was that she would need to take classes for another year rather than just one more semester. Discouraged, she decided to "sit out" for a while longer before trying to go back to school. Later, she enrolled in online courses through a major national online university, failed her courses, and then was sent a bill for the classes because financial aid covered her course work only if she passed.

Institutions can set their own standards for continued receipt of federal financial aid, including the requirement that a certain grade point average be maintained, the criteria for making satisfactory progress to completion of a degree, and the consequences for failing to meet those standards.[14] It is likely that Nichelle and Jen did not meet a requirement for making satisfactory progress, but neither reported being asked about their situation and what had caused them to miss classes or otherwise fail in their course work. The women in the study were striving to better their situations, but with little help and guidance. They often slipped through the cracks, casualties of the separate and unequal school system in which they were embedded.

Even within this separate and unequal system, not all degrees may be seen as equivalent in the labor market; employers may value degrees from certain institutions more than others. For example, degrees from for-profit schools may be viewed as of lower quality than those from traditional public or private nonprofit schools. Enrollment in these institutions has grown tremendously: between 1990 and 2013, the number of students enrolled in for-profit schools increased by 565 percent, although enrollment levels are still well below those of public institutions.[15] For-profits are thought to be more "nimble" than traditional educational institutions, because their management can add new types of degrees and courses quickly.[16] They have come under scrutiny, however, for their high cost and the high unemployment levels among graduates, all while collecting millions of dollars in federal student aid monies each year.[17] Additionally, for-profit schools have been accused of engaging in predatory recruitment tactics, targeting economically disadvantaged students with promises of significant (and sometimes unrealistic) earnings upon graduation.[18] African Americans are overrepresented among students attending these types of institutions, making up 27 percent of enrollees in 2008.[19]

How these women made the choice to attend a for-profit school rather than a community college was not always clear. In some cases, the decision was based on the type of training offered and how long it would take. Training in medical billing and coding, for example, was offered by numerous for-profit schools in the Detroit area, so if courses at the community college were filled, students interested in this field had many other options. Location and convenience also were factors. For Charlene, the for-profit school where she was enrolled was much closer than the nearest campus of the community college. For others, the choice of where to enroll was driven by the ability to take classes online. Online education, in theory, is supposed to increase access to educational opportunities for students who cannot attend campus-based classes because of distance or schedules or who prefer the flexibility offered by online course work. The number of online courses has proliferated over the past fifteen years, but evidence about its effectiveness as a learning method is mixed.[20] The major challenges to course completion cited by online students are lack of consistent access to computers, lack of support, lack of structure, and feelings of isolation.[21] Cynthia spoke to the importance of motivation in completing online work:

> Only thing is, I guess you have to be a person to say, "Okay, well, I'ma sit down and do it." You have to make yourself sit down and do what you need to do. Because it's not nothing where they make you or you have to go in and sit down and in front of instructors. You go, you do your work, and that's it. I can get up at three, four o'clock in the morning and do my work, or in the evening, whenever I feel like I need to get on the computer to do it. The only other thing about that is, it's a fast track. Everything is faster than the normal.

Cynthia failed a couple of classes because she had difficulty understanding the material, and the outcome might not have been different if she had taken the class in a classroom. Since Cynthia said that she sometimes did her course work in the middle of the night, her study habits might have also contributed to her difficulties. Students at traditional brick-and-mortar institutions may often stay up late and pull "all-nighters," but very few of those students, unlike Cynthia, have full-time jobs. Cynthia also took care of her three children and sometimes her husband's four sons, so her time was tight. A challenge for her when I last spoke to her was figuring out how to continue on with her bachelor's degree. She expressed a desire to be on a campus to take classes, but she didn't know if that would be possible. She had completed her associate's degree through an online university that also had a few physical locations. However, the closest one was more than several states away. The upside of staying with the same institution was that her associate's course work would count toward her BA. If she attended a different college or university, she did not know whether all of her credits would transfer; if they did not, she might have to start over almost completely.

Lorraine liked her experience with an online degree program. In addition to the flexibility, she said, the courses were set up in a way to encourage interaction. People were assigned to respond to each other's papers by email, and the instructor was also available by phone or email. But how are online degrees viewed by employers? A recent study found that job applicants with a degree from an online institution were less likely to get calls for a job interview.[22] As noted at the beginning of the chapter, Yvette had firsthand experience with this: "I really didn't want to go to an online program because, like, that degree [I have from an online institution] is worthless. It's so worthless. So that's like, I'm paying $30,000 on this student loan for something that is giving me a job one step above McDonald's."

Among the few who finished, the additional schooling did not help them make more money. As a teacher, Lorraine said, she needed a master's degree in order to advance. She completed a master's degree through an online school, but the degree provided no upward mobility. She went from being a teacher in a charter school to an instructional coach at a private tutoring company, and her pay decreased from about $39,000 a year to $32,000. Tanya was promised by the proprietary school she attended that she would quickly find a job after completing training in the supposedly "high-growth" and well-paying occupation of medical billing and coding. When Tanya finished, all the jobs she found were for positions paying less than she was making at her current job as a teacher's aide. The school she attended had a placement office, but the job they found for her "was like eight or nine dollars an hour," Tanya said. "So I'm like, already struggling. I really can't take a cut like that." Tanya's training had been paid for by a special state initiative that provided tuition assistance to certain unemployed and underemployed workers, but she had still invested a full year of her time in training for a job she was unlikely to take.

Despite their own experiences, most of these women still adamantly believed that higher education was necessary to do well economically in the twenty-first century and were pushing their children to attend college, even though financially this was difficult. Lorraine's daughter was attending a prestigious historically black university and had secured an internship in a noted medical center, but after Lorraine's husband lost his job, they worried about how they would continue to pay the tuition. When Geneva's family started having real financial difficulties, her son left one of the state's public four-year universities and planned to enroll in the local community college. However, because he owed money to the university, Geneva said, "he can't get his transcripts. So now he's got to go to a little — I don't know what you call those little medical schools. He's home and he's going to school, but he can't get his transcripts. Everything that he's done for the last three and a half years has just been held up." By "little medical school" Geneva meant a for-profit institution specializing in health-related programs that did not require the transcripts that the community college wanted. This was just the kind of place where Geneva would later earn a certificate for a job she was unable to get. Thus, a second generation of students, relegated to a different tier of schools and degrees, separate and unequal, faced the same abandonment as their parents.

# Financing Education

The majority of students (or their parents) borrow money to pay for postsecondary education. After mortgages, student loan debt is the largest source of consumer debt for U.S. households. Compared to those who graduated in the early 1990s, the median bachelor degree holder graduating in 2011–2012 had more than double the amount of debt ($26,885 compared to $12,434, in 2013 dollars), and more graduates had taken out loans. In 2011, 69 percent of those graduating with a bachelor's degree had taken out some loans, whereas in 1990 fewer than half (49 percent) of graduates financed at least some of their education through student loans.[23] Borrowing among graduates of associate's degree and professional certificate programs has also increased, despite the shorter duration of these programs and their lower cost, especially for degrees obtained at a community college. However, for-profit institutions, which offer two-year and four-year degrees as well as short-term certificates, have tripled their enrollment since 2000. These institutions disproportionately serve low-income students and students of color, and they have come under fire because their students, compared to community college students, have relatively low degree completion rates, higher unemployment, and higher rates of loan default.[24] Almost *90 percent* of those who do obtain an associate's degree or a certificate from a for-profit school leave with debt, compared to about 40 percent of those obtaining the same credentials from a community college. In 2011, borrowers who obtained a credential from a for-profit school left with nearly $25,000 in debt, compared to about $13,000 for those who finished at a community college.[25] Finally, student loan debt is an issue affecting not just young, recent college graduates. One-third of those with loan balances in 2011 were in their thirties, and just under one-third were forty or older. Some of this debt may be from degrees completed longer ago, but many older adults are returning to school and borrowing money in order to do so.[26]

The federal government plays a very large role in financing higher education, particularly for low- and middle-income students. Pell grants, the largest source of federal aid that is not loan-based, are awarded based on financial need, although eligibility criteria have changed over time; the maximum grant amount in 2011 was $5,550. About 60 percent of Pell recipients are classified as "nontraditional" students, that is, they are over twenty-four, live independently from their parents, and are married or have children.[27] Other forms of aid include work-study, which awards students an amount of aid that is paid out as the student works. Until 2011, Brianna had been financing her schooling with Pell grants and a work-study position with her college's student services office. For low-income women like Brianna who attended a community college in their county of residence, a Pell grant typically covered the cost of tuition and, depending on a student's financial situation, books and other supplies, with some left over to pay for other expenses, such as housing and food.[28]

Loans are the other component of financial aid. With the exception of the federal Perkins loan program, in which the lender is the student's school, the Department of Education is the lender, and borrowers do not have to be deemed creditworthy in order to receive a loan. Direct subsidized loans are available to students with financial need, and the Department of Education pays the interest on the loan while the borrower is in school and for the first six months after degree completion. Direct unsubsidized loans are not need-based, and the interest that accumulates must be paid by the borrower during periods of enrollment as well as after completion of the degree. Parents as well as graduate and professional school students may borrow through the PLUS program for expenses not covered through other forms of financial aid. Perkins loans are for students with great financial need. The amount of aid — both grants and loans — is determined by the school based on the student's completion of the Free Application for Federal Student Aid (FAFSA). Each type of aid has yearly caps on the amount that can be received, and Pell grants have a lifetime limit.

Janelle had both subsidized and unsubsidized loans. She knew that "one has interest, the other doesn't," but she didn't keep track of the balance on either, or the interest rate on the unsubsidized loan. She would worry about that once she finished. "As long as I stay in school," she said, "I don't have to pay." She was correct, but while the interest on one loan was being subsidized while she was enrolled, she would eventually be responsible for paying back the interest that accumulated on the other.

Students can also borrow from private institutions, assuming they are deemed worth the risk. Typically, the terms of these loans are less favorable than those for federal loans. Whereas interest rates for federal loans are fixed, private loan interest rates may be not only higher but variable. And just as was the case in the mortgage industry, in the lead-up to the Great Recession private lenders extended student loans to those with poorer credit. Additionally, lenders began marketing loans directly to students instead of working through schools' financial aid offices. These loans are more prevalent among students in for-profit institutions. Among students enrolled in two-year schools, more than two in five at for-profit schools took out a private loan in 2008, compared to just 5 percent at community colleges.[29]

Geneva had just finished a program in medical billing and coding when I talked to her in 2011. She attended a private, for-profit institution whose tuition and fees were well beyond what she could receive in federal grants; the total cost was $16,000 for a program that took less than one year to complete. She ended up taking out two loans, one federally subsidized and the other a private loan, that together totaled $10,000. She obtained the latter through her school, which had specifically developed this loan for its students; this for-profit institution was later investigated for engaging in predatory lending practices.

The high level of debt with which students are saddled today has been well covered in the media. The soaring costs of college tuition are often pointed to as an underlying cause, although net college costs (the actual price paid once grants and scholarships have been factored in) declined somewhat during the last half of the 2000s, after steadily climbing over the prior decade.[30] Further, debt from student loans is expected to pay off in the form of significantly increased wages over the life course.[31] According to the U.S. Bureau of Labor Statistics, median weekly earnings for someone with a high school degree was $678 in 2015, whereas this figure was $798 for a holder of an associate's degree and $1,137 for someone with a bachelor's. But the ability to reap the rewards from higher education may not come until some point well after finishing a degree, whereas payments toward student loan debt, with some exceptions, must start being made after a student graduates—or departs from school for other reasons.

Women in the study took out loans to improve their skills and marketability, in the hopes of obtaining better jobs and better lives for themselves. Most of them (and their spouses) who held loans had also received some federal financial aid to pay for their schooling, but for a variety of reasons the aid alone had not been enough. Sometimes grants and scholarships did not cover the full cost of the program. Even if the student was enrolled in a lower-cost institution, such as a community college, and the aid she received through programs like the Pell grant paid for all school-related expenses, a loan could supplement that aid and help pay for her living expenses. Brianna stopped working when she was in an associate's degree program. Initially, her Pell grant and federal work-study money went far enough to cover her tuition, the cost of books, and her living expenses. But by her last semester she felt stretched very thin financially. She took out a federally subsidized student loan so that she would have some money if unexpected expenses arose.

Brianna described the financial aid seminar she attended when she was applying for her loan: "And they were saying in the seminar that, you know, if you don't pay this loan back, they coming after you by any means necessary to get it. And so the only way will probably be, you don't have to pay it if you die." In some respects, Brianna was correct. Federal student loans are nearly always excluded from bankruptcy proceedings and can be forgiven or canceled only under rare circumstances. A loan holder can stop paying and go into default, but the consequences of doing so can be quite harsh: the entire loan can be called due, the holder becomes no longer eligible for federal aid in the future, wages and tax refunds can be withheld to go toward payment, and the holder's credit rating is negatively affected for years.[32] For people in difficult financial circumstances, options do exist for delaying payment. Those who are currently enrolled in school at least part-time are exempt from making payments on their federal loans, and federal loan holders can request "deferment" of their payments if, among other circumstances, they are unemployed or facing economic hardship.[33] Deferment in these situations may last for up to three years, and holders of Perkins loans, direct subsidized loans, and subsidized federal Stafford loans may also be able to avoid the accrual of interest during these times.[34]

Between the two of them, Leah and her husband owed more than $100,000 in student loans for graduate professional school. Although their combined income put them over six figures, Leah hoped that she would have some of her student loan forgiven. Some teachers, certain members of the military, public service employees, and those in some other professions can apply to have portions of their loans forgiven. Public service employees are eligible if they make 120 on-time, full payments toward the loan. Only federal direct loans are eligible for forgiveness.[35] As a social worker employed by the state of Michigan, Leah thought she met the criteria, although she said that a coworker once told her that only certain types of state social workers qualified. Leah intended to explore this option but had not done so by 2011.

Loans made by private entities are not covered by the government's deferment and forbearance programs. Geneva had received a six-month deferment on payments toward her federal loan, but she needed to begin making payments on the private loan immediately upon receiving it. While in school, she made $20 payments toward the $1,000 loan. The payment increased to $34 a month once she finished school. Although $34 is not a large sum of money, Geneva was working in a low-paying job, she had lost all of her public benefits (food stamps and disability), and in fact she was earning less from working than she had been receiving on public assistance. Furthermore, this smaller loan carried a very high interest rate, around 15 percent, more than twice the rate charged on federal loans. If Geneva continued making payments, she could have the loan paid off in about three years, but by then she would have paid more than $350 in interest and fees.[36]

Geneva attended a school that was overseen by Corinthian Colleges, at the time one of the largest for-profit college companies in the country but also one that was under investigation by the U.S. Department of Education and the Consumer Financial Protection Bureau for predatory lending practices and deceptive reporting of graduation rates. In mid-2015, Corinthian Colleges filed for bankruptcy and closed down some schools; others were purchased by another company. The Department of Education announced debt relief for students who were enrolled in the programs that were terminated and for students who believed themselves to be victims of fraud.[37] Geneva never talked about feeling pressured into taking out student loans. However, when she started the medical billing program, she was told that when she finished she might be able to get a job making $19 an hour. Instead, Geneva ended up working as a van driver for a social service agency and was, as she put it "still poor."

Those who did not qualify for deferment status were making payments on their loans, although most were not making much headway. Tykia and Judy were able to pay off their loans, but their loan amounts had been relatively small ($3,000 and $4,500, respectively); other women owed anywhere from $10,000 to more than $100,000. Many were not making payments on their loans. Most had qualified for deferment—some because they were enrolled in school, but others because their income was so low, perhaps an indication that their additional schooling had provided no real benefit.

Not only did the separate and unequal schooling that many of the women in the study received during their postsecondary careers make it difficult for them to complete degrees and obtain better-paying jobs, but any earnings- and wealth-building potential of those degrees was offset, at least for the foreseeable future, by their large debt from student loans.

# Homeownership

Homeownership has long been considered one of the fundamental markers of achieving the "American Dream." But owning a home is not just a marker of realizing that dream: it is also one of the most important assets a family can have. For these striving families, however, homeownership was often more of a nightmare than a dream, a drain on their wealth rather than a building block of it.

Just under half of the women were homeowners at some point between 2006 and 2011. A few owned their home outright because they had paid a relatively small amount of cash (usually less than $2,000) for it at a county auction of tax-foreclosed properties or a sale made by the U.S. Department of Housing and Urban Development (HUD) for a property foreclosed after a default on a Federal Housing Administration (FHA) loan. In Mona's case, she and her husband had lived in their house for so many years that they had paid off their mortgage. (They later purchased a "HUD home.") The rest of the women had mortgages and were underwater — they owed more money than their homes were currently worth. But even outright ownership did not protect these homeowners from an outlay of costs. Property taxes in Detroit are the highest in the nation, despite how little the properties were worth.[38] Most of the homes owned by the women in the study were in some state of disrepair or in need of updates on important and expensive features like furnaces and roofs, so these families were pouring more money into homes that were already declining in value.

The homes these women owned were typically modest — one-story Cape Cods built in the 1940s and 1950s, some of which looked as if they had not been updated much since then. Sandra purchased such a home on the west side of Detroit, directly next door to her sister. She recalled being very skeptical about the house when she first saw it: "This house was raggedy! When I say raggedy, there was nothing done to it." Her husband convinced her that the house had "potential," so they began a rent-to-own arrangement with the landlord. Before they even owned the home they had painted, plastered, and done other repairs. "We put in everything," Sandra said. "Everything you see, yes, we've done it. Because it was holes in the walls, there was no floors down, all there was was wood, dirt. It was awful, it was awful."

Karla also had to put in a great deal of effort to get her home into livable shape. When she purchased it, the kitchen had no appliances and no cupboards. She received quite a bit of assistance from her siblings in financing the renovations, including the labor supplied by her brother, but because she was calling in favors, the work was done very slowly. A year after she moved in, the kitchen still wasn't completely finished; granite countertops were waiting to be installed, and the refrigerator sat in the middle of the room. Despite all of the money being poured into the house (which Karla bought for $10,000), "I don't even have homeowner's insurance right now," she said, "because when I bought the house, after I signed I went to go get insurance, and they was like, 'Well, you could be trying to buy a house and, and trying to burn it down so you can get the insurance.' I was like, 'Lady look!' You know, but that's what the story is for the city of Detroit." Karla reasoned that she would try again once she was done with the renovations, which would show the insurers that she was serious about living in the home and not just trying to get an insurance payment. In the meantime, however, if any damage occurred or she was robbed, she would not be covered.

When Karla said, "That's what the story is for the city of Detroit," in explaining why she could not get insurance, she added, "See, Detroit is redlined." What Karla was referring to was the practice outlawed in 1968 whereby lenders had color-coded maps and drawn red lines around minority neighborhoods in order to deny loans (or in Karla's case, homeowner's insurance) to those who resided there, regardless of their income. Redlining reinforced segregation by keeping African Americans out of white neighborhoods, although it did create the mixed-class black neighborhoods that Wilson described as being a protective factor for poor residents. African Americans attempting to move into white areas were kept out via a number of other mechanisms: real estate agents would not show African Americans properties in white areas (or would not provide services to African Americans at all): restrictive covenants were used to disallow the sale of a property to a person of color; and those who broke through these barriers and moved into white areas were often met with outright violence and intimidation.[39] Although the Fair Housing Act of 1968 outlawed redlining and any other forms of discrimination in lending practices, redlining clearly continues, albeit in less overt ways, and some real estate agents continue to steer people of color toward or away from certain neighborhoods.[40] When Gina and her partner were looking to buy their first home, they had difficulty getting their agent to show them properties that were not run-down and in bad neighborhoods. She said, "It was to the point where I was getting upset with the real estate people. I was telling them—they just trying to sell us anything because we're black. . . . And this lady would always take us to these bad neighborhoods. And then I just came out saying, 'Look, I'm tired of going to these neighborhoods. Just 'cause we black don't mean we want to live in the ghetto.' So I guess she caught on to that, and the next houses she started showing were nice houses." Gina and her partner ended up purchasing a home in a mixed-race neighborhood, but the house itself still needed repairs.

Most of the houses the women and their families bought were ones that more affluent buyers might call "starter homes"—that is, smaller, cheaper houses marking a family's entrée into the world of homeownership. For many decades, the U.S. housing market has relied on the multiple purchases made by homeowning households over the life course: starting with the "starter home," buying a larger house as children are born, and then perhaps downsizing in retirement. For the families in this study, however, the houses they bought were likely to be all that they would ever be able to afford, and if they tried to sell, they were unlikely to get their money back and more likely to take a heavy loss.

Moreover, for those living in a large home (as opposed to a 900-square-foot Cape Cod) or in a well-maintained house (as opposed to a "fixer-upper"), the likelihood that ownership would yield a return on their investment did not increase. Cynthia had by far the largest house of any of the homeowners, and Carol had one of the nicest (in that it was in very good condition when she moved in). Cynthia had purchased a two-story brick home that had been converted into two units, one upstairs and one downstairs. (See chapter 2 for what she found when she moved in.) The entire street was lined with these types of houses, many with attached one- or two-story brick porches. The neighborhood bordered Boston Edison, a historic area of Detroit that was once home to Henry Ford and other luminaries of the auto industry. Although the houses in Cynthia's neighborhood, most of them built between 1915 and 1925, were not as grand as those in Boston Edison, they were still imposing structures. Cynthia's home had the original hardwood floors, which they had refinished, and large windows that gave the home lots of light. Cynthia and her husband paid $18,000 for the house, borrowing money from a family friend to help make the purchase. Despite the presence of large, well-built homes and its proximity to one of the finer neighborhoods in the city, Cynthia's neighborhood was experiencing significant decline, with many homes in tax foreclosure status. (Cynthia eventually faced the same fate.) The fact that nearly four in ten properties were owned by the city of Detroit, the Wayne County treasurer, or other public entities had significantly decreased the value of the neighborhood's homes: houses in Cynthia's neighborhood that had been auctioned off had gone for as little as $1,000.[41]

Carol moved to the Bagley neighborhood in 2009. This area is close to the campus of the University of Detroit as well as Palmer Woods, perhaps the most upscale neighborhood in Detroit, and a relatively thriving retail corridor. Carol's brick house had gleaming hardwood floors, thick plaster walls (which Carol painted in bright colors), and a newer kitchen. The steeply graded roof and the turret over the entryway gave the house the look of a miniature castle. Although Carol purchased the home after the housing market crashed, and even though the home was in a stable neighborhood, the property's value was continuing to decline. Homeownership, for some, had become a nightmare rather than a realization of the American Dream.

## Financing the American Dream

As mentioned earlier, for many decades African Americans were denied access to the American Dream of homeownership through redlining, as well as through other practices that made obtaining financing extremely difficult. While the rationale for redlining was that these borrowers were "too risky," the practice was meant to discourage blacks from moving into white neighborhoods, thus enforcing racial segregation. Rates of black homeownership began to increase with the passage of antidiscrimination legislation; between the late 1970s and late 1990s, homeownership among African Americans stood at 42 to 44 percent, but by 2004 that rate had increased to nearly 50 percent (which was still well below white ownership rates of about 75 percent).[42] This increase came about after changes in the mortgage industry made loans more widely accessible to lower-income families and those with lower credit ratings.[43] However, now borrowers who were deemed high-risk typically received loans with worse terms—these so-called subprime loans carried higher interest rates and penalties. In pursuit of more borrowers, some lenders engaged in predatory practices, such as charging excessive fees and including penalties for prepayment (paying off the loan early). Unscrupulous lenders systematically targeted predominantly minority neighborhoods for subprime and predatory lending. Compared to whites with similar characteristics, African Americans were more likely to receive subprime loans and to be subjected to predatory lending practices.[44]

Geneva was a victim of predatory lending. She purchased a home in 2008, although she did not realize right away that she was doing so. After separating from her husband, Geneva and her kids stayed with several different family members, but after not being able to find her own place, they ended up returning to the house where her husband was living. She said:

100

> I was living down in the house my husband was in, and I didn't
> want to. There were too many people living there, and we were
> staying in the basement. I told him I wanted to get my own
> house, so what I did was, I was going to rent, knowing that my
> credit was ruined. . . . I answered an ad in the paper, and it was
> rent to own. So I wasn't sure what the program was, and they
> told us. I went down [to the office] and they told me about the
> program. I was like, "Okay. Whatever. That would be fine."
> They would take one hundred dollars off the rent and put that
> towards the purchase of the house. I was like, "Okay that's
> fine, you know, that's good." And then when it all came down
> to it, they said, "You can actually buy this house based on your
> credit." And I'm going, "My credit score is 575, are you kid-
> ding me?" And she said, "No, you qualify."

Geneva remained incredulous that she could possibly qualify for a
mortgage, but the woman from the "rent to own" company kept
showing her houses. Geneva ended up thinking she was not going
to be able to buy a house, however, since everything the woman
from the "rent to own" company showed her was too small—everything, that is, except for one house that already had a potential
buyer.

Then the house became available. Geneva and the rent-to-own
agent, along with a person she referred to as "a little man," went
back one more time, although Geneva thought it was just to take a
look. Geneva recounted what happened next:

> The lady said, "You can get the house if you want to," and she
> had me sign this, I don't know what it was, it was just a book of
> things, but, it was my closing. She didn't tell me that, you
> know. . . . She didn't tell me that we actually closed on the
> house. . . . We sat on the floor in, in the kitchen, and she said,
> "Sign this, and sign this," and I'm going, "Okay, what the heck
> am I doing here, you know?" Then at the end, the little man
> left, and he shook my hand, and he said, "Congratulations!"
> And I didn't know what he was talking about. Then she said,
> "Well, I think we're all done here." And then she gave me a
> coffee mug. She said, "Well, you should be hearing something

shortly. You should have the keys to your house in a little while
... just look in the coffee mug." I was like, "What the heck is
wrong with this lady?" She left, and I looked in the coffee mug,
and it said: Congratulations, Geneva, here are your keys!

At first Geneva was thrilled, thinking all of her housing problems
had been solved. Only later did she realize that she had been a victim of predatory lending. She admitted that she should have looked
more carefully at what she was signing, but as she said, "I thought
I was just signing another million papers, because I had been doing
that the whole time, just signing all these different papers, you
know, to check the credit, to get permission to do this, do that and
the other." When she had a friend look over the terms of the sale,
she saw just how bad a deal she had received. Her monthly mortgage payment was about $760, which would be tight for Geneva,
but doable. However, the monthly payment did not include her
city property taxes, as she had thought it did; she had not factored
in having to pay nearly $2,000 a year to the city of Detroit. The
loan's interest rate was nearly 11 percent, much higher than the 6
percent average on mortgages made that year.[45]

This type of loan, with hidden fees and high interest rates, is also
called a distressed mortgage, or a "high-cost loan." Detroit home
buyers, along with minority home buyers in many other cities,
were much more likely to receive these loans than white home buyers with similar incomes.[46] An analysis done by Local Initiatives
Support Corporation (LISC), an organization that works with disadvantaged communities, found that with the exception of the
midtown, downtown, and nearby areas, nearly half or more of all
mortgages or refinances made in Detroit in 2006 were high-cost
loans. This was also true for many of the inner-ring suburban
areas.[47] Having a high-cost loan is associated with an increased risk
of foreclosure—that is, having one's property returned to the bank
for failure to make mortgage payments. Homes can also be repossessed if the owner does not pay property taxes. In these cases, the
city or the county takes ownership of the home and may try to auction it off to reclaim some of the lost revenue. Detroit's property tax

rates are among the highest in the country; the city has increased them over time to make up revenue as it lost residents.[48]

By 2011, Geneva was more than three months behind in her mortgage payments and technically in foreclosure, although she said that the mortgage company seemed to be willing to work with her to make a plan for her to get back on track with payments. Geneva was not the only one worried about foreclosure. Teresa lost her home, Yvette voluntarily walked away from her home, surrendering it to the bank, and Lorraine's and Charlene's homes were in foreclosure, although, like Geneva, Lorraine was hopeful that her lender would work with her to keep her in the house. She noted that several of her neighbors had been evicted, but said that they had lost their homes due to failure to pay property taxes.

In addition to the bad loan, the high property taxes, and potential foreclosure, Geneva was faced with a leaking roof and old and drafty windows, but she did not have the money to replace anything. Whether to invest money to make needed repairs and upgrade old features was a difficult decision for all of the homeowners in the study, not just those who were having difficulty with their mortgage payments. Beth and her husband owned a home on Detroit's east side that was built in 1941. They were renovating it, and even though they were doing much of the work themselves, there was still a cost. At one point, Beth estimated, between what they had already spent and what they planned to spend, the total cost of renovations would be around $40,000. "It's kinda hard. I mean I eventually . . . we've talked about it, so many times, moving out. We really can't afford it." Unfortunately for Beth, the home's assessed value was only about $45,000, so selling the house would mean taking a large hit financially.

Home mortgage loans account for the largest share of household debt, but if housing prices rise and the homeowner is able to make significant progress on paying down the loan, this debt should be transformed into a source of wealth. And in the early to mid-2000s, housing prices were rising, at accelerated rates. Increasingly, however, lenders were making risky or subprime loans (as well as other nonconventional mortgages, such as those requiring very low down payments or little to no documentation of income and ability to pay). Lenders were also offering mortgages with adjustable rates—that is, loans in which interest rate changes periodically, sometimes to a much higher rate. Borrowers were often promised that they would be able to refinance to a loan with better terms once the value of their house had appreciated.

When housing prices stopped going up, many holders of adjustable rate mortgages found themselves both unable to refinance and unable to make their now high monthly mortgage payments. Charlene found herself in this bind. Charlene and her husband owned the property across the street from their home and, until their tenants stopped paying, rented it out for enough to cover the mortgage payment and a little extra. Charlene later regretted this move. In 2008 she said of the mortgage company:

> They ripped us off, you know. People financed, and they financed, refinanced they homes. Everybody was doing it, you know. They [the mortgage company] gave us such, you know, leeway, [saying] that, you know, "Anybody can get financed. Anybody. I don't care how bad the credit was.". . . You started off paying, making payments of five hundred dollars a month, it was affordable, whether or not you lost your job, you could still afford it. . . . But you didn't know that, its interest rate was going skyrocket and they were gonna up your mortgage from five to seven [hundred], or, from five [hundred] to a thousand dollars, you know. And pretty much just yanked your house from you. . . . I'm not living it yet, but it's scary that I have to.

By 2010 Charlene's monthly mortgage payment, as she had predicted, had gone up quite a bit, rising from the initial $500 to $600 and then finally $900. When she and her husband got behind on the payments, she worried that they would become one of those families who was "yanked from your house" through foreclosure.

Many homeowners across the country defaulted on their loans, and their homes were foreclosed, including a number of homeowners in this study. Yvette "walked away" from her house, but she did so through foreclosure. Teresa lost not only her own home in a downriver community but a home she had been persuaded to purchase after the death of the owner, a member of her family. Debbie's house was foreclosed when the family with whom they had an informal arrangement to buy the property stopped paying the mortgage. Geneva had just started receiving foreclosure notices on her home, but she was hopeful that the bank would work with her so that she would not lose the house. Public and real estate records indicate, however, that Geneva eventually was foreclosed on. Since 2011, a number of other women in the study have lost their homes. Carol's beautiful brick home was foreclosed in 2013. In 2011 she had been talking about the house being too large for just her once her daughter left for college. Perhaps she tried to sell it and could not. Sandra's house was listed for sale multiple times in 2013 and 2014 and was finally foreclosed in 2015. In 2011 her husband had been able to find work only out of state, and she was talking about joining him. Cynthia's house and Tanya's house also were foreclosed, according to public records.[49] None of the contact information I had for them had remained up to date, so I do not know what happened. I do know that Charlene was able to work out a repayment schedule with her lender and avoided foreclosure.

Among those who managed to hold on to their home, many ended up owing more than their home was now worth. Although the overall U.S. housing market is in recovery, prices are still below their peak levels, and in some cities, such as Detroit, prices remain quite low.[50]

## Accruing Debt Instead of Building Wealth

To build wealth, families need to have positive net worth; their assets need to be greater than their debts. Assets are resources with intrinsic cash value. Money in a savings account is an asset, as is a home worth more than its mortgage balance, even if it must be sold or refinanced to obtain cash. Other common assets are retirement accounts, pensions, and stocks and bonds. Wealth, and not just income, is a very important indicator of well-being. Having wealth means that families have a "nest egg" and can finance higher education, without going into significant debt, they can live in better neighborhoods where home values do not depreciate (or if they do, prices rebound), they can weather spells of unemployment without sinking into deep debt, and they have money to use in retirement.[51] The disparity in wealth between African American and white households has been well documented.[52] At all income and education levels, African Americans hold less wealth than whites, and the gap is quite large. In 2010 the median white household had a net worth of just under $139,000, while the median African American's net worth was about $17,000.[53] One factor behind this gap is that while whites hold more debt than African Americans, their assets, such as houses, are worth so much more.[54]

For whites, on average, achieving the American Dream of homeownership builds wealth, but for African Americans homeownership too often strips them of wealth. Residential segregation, although at an extreme in the Detroit area, is a fact of life in many major metropolitan areas, and homes in white neighborhoods are valued higher than comparable homes in similar black neighborhoods. Add to this the targeting of African Americans for subprime loans, which put them at much higher risk for foreclosure, in the years leading up to the financial crisis of 2007–2008. Even those who weathered the foreclosure crisis were spending more money on their homes—instead of being able to save that money—if they had a loan with high or adjustable interest rates. Between 2007 and 2009, equity (the difference between what is owed on a home and the value of the home) for white homeowners declined 9 percent, whereas for blacks the decline was 12 percent. Those declines have slowed, but from 2009 to 2011 white equity was down only 2 percent, while for African Americans that figure was close to 6 percent.[55]

Housing values across the country collapsed, but the situation in Detroit and the surrounding suburbs was particularly dismal. Although housing in Detroit is quite cheap compared to other parts of the country, prices peaked in early 2006. These prices were over-inflated, the result of the lending boom and the increased demand for housing (itself often fueled by investors as opposed to potential homeowners). When the market crashed, housing prices plummeted. In Detroit, prices bottomed out in 2011, with value dropping almost 50 percent. The market has recovered somewhat, but an average home in Detroit purchased in 2006 was still down in value by 23 percent in 2014.[56] Kendra's west side home (technically owned by her sister, but Kendra paid the mortgage) was purchased for $85,000 in 2006. Its value hit bottom in 2011 and has stayed at around $36,000. Geri's home, which she and her partner purchased in 2005 for $75,000, was only worth $50,000 by 2009. Its value continued to drop, and by the end of 2015 it was worth $45,000.

Besides the homes they purchased as residences, a couple of families had investment properties. These investments had become money pits. Carol bought a house in Detroit through a county auction, paying only $500 for it in 2005. After she made improvements, she said, it was appraised for $65,000. She started renting out the property, which was located in a neighborhood some distance from where she lived. Tenant after tenant left the house a mess when they moved out. Finally, in 2010, Carol had had enough. She had gone over to the house to check on it after some tenants moved out and found it in even worse condition than it had been when other tenants moved out. She said, "They stole my windows. They stole all the electrical stuff. I said, hell with this." Carol decided, in her words, to "give up" the property, in effect abandoning it. I asked her if she was worried that the city would come after her since she hadn't paid the property taxes, and she admitted that at first she hadn't even thought about it, but once she did, she became a little concerned. Moreover, she didn't seem to know what consequences she might face for walking away from her mortgage. She said:

> Well, I wonder, because everybody, you know, you see so many houses [abandoned], and I've seen people walk away from their houses. Like my sister, her neighbor across the street from her, she was an older lady, and she had a house I think she owed the note [mortgage] on. She just walked away. And I wonder, what they do to you. She said she just don't care. She just couldn't take it no more, so she, you know, but it looked like it had to be something you have to face. You just can't walk away from your house, but so many people doing it.

The last sentence was posed like a question, as if Carol wanted to know what the potential consequences of walking away might be. So I told her, "Yeah, usually your credit score goes into the toilet." At that time I didn't know who "they" might be; I assumed she was talking about the city and her unpaid taxes. Only later in the conversation did I learn that she had taken out a $50,000 mortgage resulting in an initial monthly mortgage payment of $500. She charged $700 a month in rent, so she was able to put all of the rent money toward the mortgage and have a couple hundred left over. But her mortgage was one with an adjustable rate, and quickly her monthly payment went up to $700, an amount that the rent just covered. She stopped paying the mortgage completely after the house was stripped of its windows and other fixtures. I asked if she had checked her credit score recently, and she said that it had been a while, but at that time her score was somewhere in the 500s, making her rating quite poor even before she stopped paying the mortgage. Carol did not lose a lot of her own money, but her investment potentially damaged her credit—although, she reasoned, her score could not get much worse—and any wealth-building potential of that investment was gone.

More education is supposed to result in improved earnings over the course of one's time in the labor market. Six years—the time over which we followed these women—may not be long enough to determine whether postsecondary education was a worthy investment for these families. The value of additional education may also not be fully realized until many years after graduation. Since few of the women had entered a postsecondary program directly after high school, most of their degrees and certificates were still fairly new, so they might not have seen yet the earnings potential of those new credentials. However, we generally do not think that getting more education will make someone worse off financially. Earlier in the chapter, I highlighted Geneva's experience with attending a for-profit school for a program in medical billing. Not only did that program leave her owing $10,000 in student loans, but she was unable to find a job in her field. The low-wage job she did take paid just enough to make her ineligible for several public programs and left her worse off financially compared to the income she previously received from disability and food stamps.

Not only did these households have negative equity in their homes (or no equity if they were not homeowners), but they generally lacked any other asset. Only ten households had savings or retirement accounts (including pensions). With the exception of Beth, who was able to save and keep $4,000 in an account over the course of the study, the amounts they managed to save were quite low, ranging from $20 to $200. Most of those who had retirement accounts had not accumulated a great deal in savings either. Sharon once had a significant amount of money in her savings account but went through all of it when she was unemployed. She estimated that she had about $25 in the account after that. Sharon also had a 401(k), an employer-sponsored retirement account, from a previous job. However, she was no longer making any contributions, nor was her employer. Leah and her husband both had employer-sponsored retirement accounts, but both had taken cash out of the accounts on several occasions. Neither of them were yet fifty-nine and a half years old, the age at which there is no penalty for withdrawing money. Because contributions to employer retirement accounts are made on before-tax income (in effect lowering taxable income), the Internal Revenue Service treats withdrawals from these accounts differently. With a few exceptions, any money withdrawn early is taxed, and a 10 percent penalty is also assessed.

We did not ask the women in the study for the current balances on their retirement accounts, so I cannot directly calculate net worth. However, it is unlikely that any household was doing well in terms of asset accumulation, even those who were teetering on the edge of the middle class. Gwen, in her early fifties, was one of the highest-earning women we interviewed, making about $90,000 a year. As a longtime federal employee, Gwen would receive a pension when she retired that would be worth, she estimated, about $3,500 a month—or a little less than half of what she was currently making. Her husband was retired but not yet collecting Social Security benefits. They had no savings. Gwen owned a home on the west side of Detroit in a neighborhood that was once fairly stable but had rapidly declined after the housing crisis began. She bought the house in the early 1980s for about $24,000 and in 2004 was just a few years away from paying off the mortgage when she decided to do a cash-out refinance of the mortgage so that she could get money to pay bills and replace her roof. In these types of refinances, the balance of the original mortgage and the amount of cash the owner receives are packaged together in a new loan. For example, if a home is valued at $100,000, and the balance on the mortgage payment is $40,000, the owner has $60,000 in equity. If the owner wants to receive $50,000 of that equity in cash, the new mortgage will be $90,000 (the balance of $40,000 on the original mortgage plus the $50,000 cash-out). I did not know exactly how much equity Gwen extracted, but it must have been substantial. I knew her current monthly mortgage payment was about $700, including property taxes, and in 2011 she still had more than twenty years of mortgage payments to make. (The interest rate on the refinanced mortgage was also higher than what was charged to the original loan.) In 2004 her home would have been near its peak value — about $90,000, according to the real estate website Zillow. Her home's value in 2015 (according to Zillow and other real estate websites) was about $57,000, but in reality, homes in her neighborhood were routinely selling for much less. The likelihood that Gwen would have any equity built up in her house was very slim. Add to that the $15,000 of credit card and other debt that she had, and Gwen's net worth was probably negative.

## Conclusion

Overall, the assets of households in this study were paltry to nonexistent. For African Americans trying to build wealth through homeownership, history may be repeating itself. The writer Ta-Nehisi Coates has documented the systematic theft in the 1960s from African Americans who were pursuing the American Dream and attempting to buy homes.[57] Like the strivers of today, they were pulled into predatory arrangements with white businessmen and offered land contracts that kept them from accruing equity and allowed the holder of the deed to quickly repossess the property for any missed payments. Coupled with federal and local discriminatory housing and lending policies, sellers and their agents were able to reap a profit at the expense of African Americans, who often wound up out of money and out of a house, unable to build wealth. The system that emerged in the 1990s had many of the same features: predatory lending that targeted high-cost mortgages to minorities (including higher-income African Americans who could have received prime mortgages).[58] The run-up of housing prices went hand in hand with subprime lending, with the result that many of these home buyers were purchasing their homes at their peak price, a level that was not sustainable. Those who have remained in their homes may have negative equity, and those who were foreclosed upon lost not only equity but their homes.

Less attention has been paid to the ways in which the postsecondary education system, as encountered by strivers, operates in a similar fashion. For-profit schools charge high tuition and fees that financial aid may not fully cover, leaving students no choice but to take out loans. The jobs they subsequently find—if they are able to complete their degree—often do not put them on a path of greater prosperity. Strivers who participate in online education, working alone, often late into the night, frequently end up with the same results: student loans and a low-paying job. Students using the community college system may not experience anywhere near the same levels of debt, but public investment in higher education has not kept pace with increased demand, and many community colleges are struggling. Wealthier students who are much more likely to attend four-year institutions are the beneficiaries of funding formulas that give their schools more money per student, while community colleges, which disproportionately serve more disadvantaged students and more students of color, receive substantially less. The women in the study who enrolled in community colleges invested much of their time in courses, only to languish in developmental education course work and start and stop different programs, particularly when financial and other challenges arose.

With the abandonment of the promise that middle-class status can be secured through investments in higher education and home-ownership, there is little hope that these households will attain any wealth. Rather, they have been stripped of wealth by the very institutions that are supposed to bolster it.

# ↭ CHAPTER 5 ↭

## ABANDONED BY THE SAFETY NET:
## CONTESTATIONS, DENIALS, AND
## INCOMPETENCE IN BENEFIT PROCESSING

A leta worked on the assembly line at an auto supply company where she had been employed for more than five years. One day at work, as she recalled, "I was packaging parts in a large container, and when I turned my back to put the parts in a smaller container, the large container was broken, and I didn't know it. And it fell on me and it hit me across the back of my head, the back of my shoulders, and I have been out of work since September."

Her balance was thrown off by her injuries, after which, she said, the two sides of her body would not function in tandem. She had been referred to a neurologist and had completed physical therapy, but she still was having great difficulty bending and lifting. She had tried to go back to work, but after the third day she was in so much pain that her coworkers had to take over for her. Since she was injured on the job, Aleta had filed for worker's compensation, a program designed to help workers with the costs of rehabilitation after an injury and replace lost wages. Aleta had a sinking feeling, however, that obtaining benefits was not going to be easy. Private employers generally purchase insurance to cover worker's compensation claims, and Aleta was led to believe by the insurance claims investigator that her condition was considered preexisting and therefore not covered by worker's compensation. Aleta also worried that the claims investigator did not have her best interests in mind. She said, "After talking with the [investigator], I realized she was not really trying to help me. She was working against me, because she mentioned to me that she was the one who would tell the insurance company, 'Unfortunately, we have to pay this client.' See, so it turned out she was an independent operator. She told me she worked for several insurance companies. So she wasn't doing anything to, you know, help me get the right medical attention." While Aleta waited for assistance, her elderly mother was paying her gas and electric bill, and her daughter was helping out financially as best she could. As someone who was used to being the family member who provided help, being on the receiving end was very uncomfortable for her. Aleta eventually received about $150 in food stamps and $260 from a small, state-funded disability program. The injury occurred in 2005; Aleta finally received the money she was owed from her employer in 2009.

Rhonda, a single mother of four, lost her home health care job in February 2010. She had actually left three different jobs over the course of the previous twelve months, for various reasons—once because she thought she was going to be fired, once because she thought the company was going to go out of business, and once because the company had her caring for more clients than was legally allowed. Her low income qualified her for federal food stamp benefits, which were supposed to increase to account for the loss of earnings. In March, however, instead of going up, her benefits actually stopped.

Rhonda's affect was usually very even-keeled; she typically did not show anger or any other emotion during her interviews. But in recounting this story, Rhonda raised her voice and became more animated than she ever had been. Her welfare caseworker promised to correct the mistake, and Rhonda ended up receiving food stamps later in the month. But in April her benefits ceased again. She called her caseworker—repeatedly—but the caseworker never returned her calls. Rhonda eventually got in touch with a supervisor in the welfare office, and her food stamp benefits returned in May, but then stopped again in June. In July, she was receiving them again. Her caseworker claimed that the problem was caused by a glitch in the state's computer system and she was unable to figure how to fix it. The onus of monitoring her food stamp case was placed entirely upon Rhonda, and Rhonda reported that her caseworker, instead of apologizing, took Rhonda to task for not letting the situation drop.

When people lose jobs, the United States has a number of safety net programs in place that are supposed to help buffer them against hardship during unemployment. These include Unemployment Insurance (UI), old-age benefits, and disability benefits through the Social Security system. These programs are all social insurance programs, meaning that they are tied to past work in the formal labor market, financed in part by workers' tax contributions (for old-age and disability benefits), and available to workers regardless of income. By contrast, social welfare programs, such as cash assistance or food stamps, are means-tested (an applicant's income must be below a certain amount in order to be eligible) and financed through general revenue streams. For decades, social insurance programs were generally viewed in a more positive light, largely because these benefits were perceived to be "earned" and available to deserving families who just happened to have hit a spell of bad luck. By contrast, a certain level of stigma is attached to social welfare programs, owing in part to a perception that recipients have "caused" their own poverty by choosing not to work or by having children outside of marriage.

When William Julius Wilson was writing in the 1980s, welfare programs that provided cash assistance—in particular, the Aid to Families with Dependent Children (AFDC) program—were under fire for encouraging "dependency" and providing an alternative to work and self-reliance. Welfare was also blamed for the increase in the number of births outside of marriage and in the number of single-parent households, the argument being that welfare provided more benefits to a poor woman than she would get from being married to a man working a low-wage job. Welfare is perceived by some as diverting taxpayer dollars from hardworking families to those living off the government dole, some of whom may be committing fraud. Finally, stereotypes about welfare are highly racialized in the United States. In the 1970s, as "welfare" increasingly became associated with the image of an African American, usually a woman, living in an urban "slum," the word began to convey damaging racial stereotypes.[1]

The 2008 Great Recession led to record numbers of Americans receiving public benefits. Food stamp caseloads rose from about 26 million individuals in 2007, prior to the recession, to more than 40 million in 2010.[2] The number of weekly UI claims went from about 3 million in 2007 to a peak of just under 12 million in 2009.[3] The number of families receiving cash assistance from the Temporary Assistance for Needy Families (TANF) program, which replaced AFDC, remained relatively stable, and in some states it declined.

Aside from the TANF figures, a look at the numbers of people receiving benefits would seem to contradict a story about abandonment. However, the difficulty of the process through which these women tried to apply for and use public programs demonstrates the declining public commitment to help. Just securing benefits, regardless of type, and then receiving them on a timely and regular basis were time- and energy-consuming processes, fraught with roadblocks throughout. When striving women were out of a job and needed money, they could not count on the programs that were supposed to help them. Obtaining benefits often entailed fighting with lawyers, employers, and bureaucrats. Globalization has weakened the connections between employers and employees, but employers and their lawyers, perhaps logically, also contested filings for UI benefits and other work-related benefits because these programs could negatively affect their bottom line. Welfare caseworkers repeatedly made mistakes that caused disruptions to benefits that had been difficult to obtain in the first place. Women in the study received conflicting information about the status of their cases—that is, when they were able to find a live person with whom to speak. Given declines in public-sector employment, including specific efforts in Michigan to downsize state government staff (including caseworkers), these consequences are perhaps not surprising. Regardless of the underlying causes, delays in benefits or an inability to receive needed assistance at all during times of unemployment and low income contributed to a great deal of hardship for these families and left them feeling abandoned by the safety net.

## Abandoned by Employers

During the Great Depression, President Franklin D. Roosevelt implemented the Social Security Act, which provided unemployment and old-age benefit programs and a small cash welfare program for widows and their children (who presumably lost a wage-earning spouse). Over time programs providing payments to people who had become disabled were added, as was the food stamp program to help low-income families purchase groceries, and cash welfare benefits were expanded to cover more poor families, including families headed by divorced or never-married mothers. (Married-couple families and single-father families may also be eligible, but the majority of families receiving cash welfare are those headed by single mothers).

Some of these programs are more generous than others. The current UI program replaces a portion of workers' wages — on average about 47 percent — up to a maximum amount, for up to twenty-six weeks, or longer when the economy is poor.[4] Workers who are injured on the job are eligible for worker's compensation benefits and, if they are permanently disabled, for benefits from either the Social Security Disability Insurance (SSDI) program or the Supplemental Security Income (SSI) program. SSDI payments are based on past earnings.[5] The federal government sets maximum SSI benefit levels, which were just a little over $600 in 2006 and $674 in 2011.[6]

To receive UI benefits, a worker who is laid off can file a claim with the state agency that administers the UI program, while a worker who is injured on the job can notify the employer and then file a claim for worker's compensation benefits. UI is funded by taxes paid by employers on behalf of their employees; for worker's compensation benefits, employers typically purchase private insurance that covers these claims, but states designate an agency or board to oversee administration. While the process in both cases seems to be straightforward, a worker cannot receive these benefits without the employer's cooperation. The employer must agree that the employee has lost her job through no fault of her own (for UI) or that she was injured while working (for worker's compensation).

The women in this study were not always able to secure these agreements.

Aleta attempted to return to work, but she found it difficult to perform her tasks. She could not take any more time off, since she had exhausted all of her leave when first injured. Subsequently fired, she hired an attorney to litigate the worker's compensation denial. Geneva experienced a similar fate when she slipped and fell in her company's parking lot, breaking several vertebrae. Her employer fought her claims for several years, and she too needed to hire an attorney. The state of Michigan's handbook on worker's compensation states that cases like Aleta's and Geneva's are atypical. Yet the manual also says that approximately 25 percent of claims are litigated or otherwise disputed.[7]

The same holds true for Unemployment Insurance. In 2011 Tamara sustained a back injury, most likely, she and her doctor believed, because of all the heavy lifting required in her job as a nurse's aide. Tamara thought that she had been laid off, since her injury left her unable to work and her employer did not have other work she could perform. She applied for UI benefits but was told that she was ineligible because she was still on the facility's payroll. Shortly thereafter, she received notice that she had been fired. Workers who are fired for cause are generally not eligible for unemployment benefits. In Sharon's case, being laid off by her employer should have qualified her for UI benefits. But like Tamara, her employer disputed the application, saying that Sharon had been given a severance package; in fact, she had been promised one, but never received it. Like worker's compensation, an estimated 25 percent of unemployment filings are contested by employers.[8]

Why would an employer fight a claim? The bottom line is certainly one reason. In the United States, Unemployment Insurance is financed by taxes paid by employers, at rates determined by an employer's "experience rating." The more "experience" an employer has with the UI system—that is, the more claims have been paid out to its former workers—the more the employer pays in taxes.[9] Employers thus have an incentive to keep their experience rating as low as possible. One way to do that is to never lay off any workers.

Another way is to fight the claims of workers who try to obtain UI benefits when laid off. In 2010 the *New York Times* ran an article about Talx, a firm specializing in helping employers process, and also dispute, UI claims. Part of Talx's strategy, advocates for workers claimed, was to contest a certain number of claims, regardless of each case's merits. As one advocate noted, "It's sort of a war of attrition. If you appeal a certain percentage of cases, there are going to be those workers who give up."[10] Similarly, employers have an incentive to keep worker's compensation claims to a minimum, since premiums on the insurance they purchase are likely to increase the more claims are paid out. And some employers claim that too many compensation claims are fraudulent, costing them thousands of dollars.[11]

At the heart of this phenomenon of contestation is the changed nature of the social contract between employers and employees. In the decades following World War II, a worker might expect to stay with the same employer for his or her entire career. Manufacturing was the dominant U.S. industry, and firms and the "company towns" in which they were located often maintained strong relationships. In addition, labor unions lobbied to ensure that workers were generally well compensated. Beginning in the 1970s, a series of institutional and economic shifts marked the end of that era. Manufacturers began moving operations overseas in search of cheaper labor and fewer workplace regulations. Technological advances led to the automation of many jobs, thus reducing the number of employees a firm needed. Increasingly, employers wanted "flexible" employment arrangements so that they would be able to quickly trim their workforce when demand was low. As a result, more workers became temporary or contract employees, and lifetime employment with the same firm became a thing of the past. Employers pointed to globalization and competition from abroad as reasons to keep wages low for so-called lower-skilled workers (usually workers without a postsecondary degree). Some researchers and social commentators have noted that as companies became more mobile and global, the importance of satisfying employees in particular local communities gave way to an increased interest in pleasing shareholders. Squeezing workers, whether through lower wages, decreased benefits, or layoffs, was one way firms could cut costs and improve profits. In the face of these challenges, unions saw the erosion of their power to negotiate over pay, benefits, and working conditions, and overall union membership dropped. Any notion that employers had an obligation to ensure that their workers were fairly compensated, or were even part of the company "family," was largely abandoned.[12]

Perhaps nowhere are these trends more evident than in the Detroit metropolitan area. Once the center of automobile production and a hub for manufacturing innovation more generally, the industry was battered in the 1970s and 1980s by competition from foreign auto companies. In efforts to cut costs, employers moved some production to Mexico. With production offshored, there were fewer factory jobs in Detroit, and what had been an important pathway into the middle class was increasingly cut off. Moreover, workers who were hired for the relatively few remaining factory jobs were often paid much lower wages than their predecessors. In 2011 the United Auto Workers (UAW) negotiated a contract with the "Big Three" automakers (Ford, Chrysler, and General Motors) that allowed new hires to be paid at a rate that was more than $10 an hour less than what workers who came in under previous contracts earned, solidifying a practice that had begun during the Great Recession.[13]

Despite the weakening of the sector overall, having ties to the auto industry did seem to facilitate a worker's receipt of benefits when unemployed. Temporary layoffs have long been common in this industry, where production may go in fits and starts and there is an expectation that workers will collect UI benefits. Until he retired, Mona's husband had worked for a company that supplied the auto industry. He periodically was laid off for as little as a week or for as long as several months, and during those times he collected UI benefits. Geri was laid off from her job at an auto parts supplier when the factory closed its doors during the height of the Great Recession. She began collecting unemployment benefits soon after the layoff. Her firm also filed a petition with the U.S. Department of Labor on behalf of its employees so that they could take advantage of the Trade Adjustment Assistance (TAA) program.

TAA provides job training, relocation assistance, and other services to workers who have lost or are at risk of losing their jobs owing to "foreign trade," as happens with outsourcing jobs overseas or simply with foreign competition. With help from TAA, Geri was able to enroll in community college. Adrienne also worked for an auto supplier, and her company frequently laid off its employees temporarily when business was slow. The money she received from UI was not enough to pay all of her bills, but she had no difficulty obtaining the benefit.

The experiences of Mona's husband, Geri, and Adrienne were not, however, the norm. Most of the women did not work in the auto industry, and the number of Detroit jobs in auto and related manufacturing continues to shrink. Once she was permanently laid off, Adrienne was never able to find another job in that sector and moved downward into the low-paying field of home health care. No one in the study besides Geri received assistance through TAA, and most did not qualify for UI benefits when they lost their jobs. The circumstances of their employment left them abandoned by this important part of the safety net. Shanice, when asked in 2006 if she had ever received UI, replied, "I never had a job long enough to collect unemployment." Shanice believed that one needed to be in a job for at least one year before being eligible for UI. While this assumption was not quite accurate, Shanice was correct in thinking that workers must log a certain amount of time in the labor market before they can claim benefits. Specifically, a worker must accumulate a minimum level of earnings over a base period before the date the claim is filed. The UI system uses what it calls the "standard base period" in considering earnings accumulated over the first four of the last five completed quarters prior to the date of filing. Let's assume that Shanice had tried to apply for UI after her most recent job loss. Shanice started a temp job in January 2011 and was let go in April because work slowed down. Her last completed quarter of work would have been January to March 2011. To determine whether she qualified for UI, the UI office would look at her earnings over the period January 2010 to December 2010—the four quarters prior to her last completed quarter of work. Except for the first three months of that year, Shanice spent all of 2010 unemployed and would not have reached the minimum amount of earnings needed to qualify. A problem with the standard base period is that it does not consider a worker's most recent earnings (for Shanice, what she earned from January to March 2011) when computing eligibility for the program. For workers with low earnings and short spells of employment, like Shanice, the use of the standard base period may render them ineligible for benefits.

Michigan, like many other states, has moved to using an "alternative base period" for workers who do not qualify under the standard base period; the alternative base period considers earnings for the four most recently completed quarters. While the use of alternative base periods has been shown to increase UI receipt for some low-earning workers, many part-time employees or those who end up working part-time hours may still not meet the minimum earnings requirements.[14] Even if they meet the requirements, lack of information about the rules may lead these workers to believe that they are ineligible. Alix Gould-Werth and Luke Shaefer have found that among unemployed workers who did not apply for UI, those with less education (those with a high school degree or less) were more likely than their college-educated counterparts to believe that they had not earned or worked enough to qualify.[15]

Another stipulation for receiving UI benefits is that a worker must have lost her job through no fault of her own. Although that was the case for her most recent job loss, other times, Shanice said, her jobs had ended because "I'd quit, get fired, something like that." Being fired for cause or quitting without good cause can render an individual ineligible. In practice, however, it is difficult to determine what "good cause" means. Rhonda quit three different home health aide jobs in the course of a year. As discussed in chapter 3, at the first job, her supervisor alleged that Rhonda had withheld food from her elderly patients. Rhonda explained that she had merely not given them fruit with their breakfast. Fearing that the incident with the breakfast fruit would lead to an allegation of abuse, Rhonda quit lest she be fired. At the next job, Rhonda was asked to care for more patients than was legally allowed. She worried that if something happened to one of the patients, she would be liable. The next employer also engaged in practices that Rhonda found

121

problematic. She was asked to take on duties for which she had not received any training, namely passing out medications. The company kept promising to send her to classes but never did. Once she started hearing rumors that the company was on the verge of going out of business, she quit and found another home health care job. In Rhonda's mind, she preemptively quit under threats to her and her reputation; she did not believe that her employer had her best interest in mind. But if she had applied for unemployment, it is not clear that her reasons for quitting would have been viewed as "good cause."

Erica also quit a job rather than get fired, but she went ahead and applied for UI benefits even though she knew she was not technically eligible. Like Rhonda, she said that she was continually being written up for infractions she did not commit. In our interviews, Erica always talked about herself as a middle-class girl who had to learn the ways of the street after she left her abusive husband and found herself without any income. When Erica's electricity was cut off because she had not paid the bill, a neighbor showed her how to turn it back on illegally. Like Rhonda, Erica believed that her employer was looking for reasons to fire her. Erica eventually quit her job preemptively out of frustration; when a friend informed her that it might be possible to collect unemployment, Erica signed up and starting receiving UI benefits. She believed that she would only be able to receive benefits for two months before the state figured out that she had quit—and she was correct in this prediction. Further, she had to pay back the money she received, but for those two months she had had income coming in while she looked for another job. Erica believed that she was "owed" this benefit after being subjected to hassles from her employer and threats of being fired.

Among the women who should have received benefits but did not and those whose benefits were delayed because of employer contestations, disbelief was the common emotion. Sharon said that after her employer failed to pay her severance and contested her unemployment filing, her employer fled the state with money he had embezzled from a client. However, she felt as if she was being punished for his misdeeds, since she was the one without any income. Geneva, who had worked at a telecommunications firm, owed money to that company as a customer but refused to pay. Although the bill was small (and nonpayment was hurting her credit more than the loss of money was hurting the firm), not paying was the only way Geneva could express her anger at the company for the way it treated her. Tamara had worked in some sort of job since she was thirteen years old. To her, all of those years of work should have meant that there was something for her if she got injured. She said:

> I have been working at a job for five years, for six years rather, and look at what happened to me. There should be a policy as far as unemployment where, you know, it shouldn't have to happen like that. There should be exceptions ... with unemployment where you should be able to collect unemployment if you're injured. If you can't work. It should be a policy of the states. If you're injured, you might can't get the full amount of what you're asking for or whatever, but you should be able to collect something.

Instead, Tamara was left with nothing but unpaid bills.

## Work First Doesn't Work

Another set of benefits is designed to help lower-income people during periods of unemployment or when income is very low. These include cash payments, food assistance, housing assistance, help paying heating bills, a separate disability program, and public health insurance, to name a few. Collectively, we have come to call these benefits "welfare," even though very few families receive help from all of the various programs that fall under this imprecise heading. For many years, the welfare program that received the most attention was AFDC, which primarily served poor single mothers and their minor children and provided them with a small (or stingy, depending on one's state of residence) check to help pay rent, utilities, and other nonfood expenses. For food, these families could use the food stamp program. Even in the most generous states, AFDC and food stamps never covered all of a family's costs.[16]

States set payment levels for cash welfare; in 2010, for example, Michigan paid a maximum of $492 a month to a single parent with two children, an amount that is just above the average benefit across all states. (Alaska, a state with a very high cost of living, sets maximum benefits at $923, while a family of the same size would receive a maximum amount of $170 a month in Mississippi.[17]) Yet in the later part of the twentieth century, public discourse about welfare portrayed recipients as fraudsters who through their unwillingness to work were bilking taxpayers out of millions of dollars. Candidate Bill Clinton's pledge to "end welfare as we know it" strongly resonated with these voters in the 1992 presidential campaign.[18]

In 1996, President Clinton and Congress ended welfare as we knew it. Aid to Families with Dependent Children, a name that might suggest that helping children was a public priority, became Temporary Assistance for Needy Families, which implies that even the most destitute are deserving of only "temporary," not unconditional, support. The "temporary" in TANF is operationalized through a time limit on assistance. Eligible families may receive federal cash payments for only sixty months total in their lifetimes, regardless of their financial circumstances; under AFDC, families could receive benefits for as long as they remained financially eligible and had a minor child. States have the option of setting lower limits, and some have done that.[19] Michigan was unique in never formally setting a time limit during the first ten years after welfare reform. However, welfare caseworkers were often heard saying that welfare could "end in five years" — perhaps a reference to the five years that welfare reform was initially authorized by Congress.

Of more immediate concern to recipients and state administrators were the law's work requirements. The law stated that a certain proportion of recipients must be working or participating in a work-related activity (for example, looking for a job, receiving short-term training in how to find a job, or, on a limited basis, participating in a short-term training program for a specific job). Initially, 25 percent of adults receiving TANF had to meet the work requirements; that proportion increased to 50 percent in 2002.

A great deal of debate surrounds the question of whether these reforms to welfare have been successful. Supporters point to the dramatic declines in the number of families receiving cash assistance benefits as AFDC transitioned to TANF. Between 1993 and 1999, caseloads fell by 56 percent, from 5 million families in 1993 to about 2.6 million families in 1999.[20] Others note that despite falling caseloads, the poverty rate among U.S. families went down only slightly. Another complicating factor is that welfare reform was first implemented during one of the strongest economies in recent U.S. history.[21] Unemployment rates in the late 1990s were below 5 percent, levels that had not been seen since the 1950s. But what would happen when the economy slowed down and low-wage workers—the very people who might not qualify for unemployment benefits—lost jobs?

The short answer is that, by and large, they would not return to the welfare rolls. "Welfare Is Dead" is a chapter title in Kathryn Edin and Luke Shaefer's book *$2.00 a Day*, which documents the dramatic rise in the number of families surviving in the United States on less than $2 per person per day, a benchmark typically used to measure poverty in the developing world.[22] A large factor driving $2 a day poverty, Edin and Shaefer argue, is that welfare reform did not just replace AFDC with TANF, but "killed it." TANF has become such a small program that some of the women interviewed by Edin and Shaefer were not aware of its existence, while others thought that the government was not giving out the benefit any longer. Unlike Edin and Shaefer's respondents, the women in this study knew about TANF and how to apply for the program if they chose, but they rarely used it. When working, their income was slightly too high to qualify for TANF benefits, although many of those who lost their jobs probably could have received these benefits.

Even in the face of a climbing unemployment rate, TANF continued to emphasize work and meeting participation requirements rather than providing assistance to poor families.[23] In Michigan, the program intended to provide employment assistance to TANF recipients during the study period was called "Work First." The underlying message of the program was that, above all else, work comes first. But in putting Work First into practice, it was unclear whether staff were more concerned about people finding jobs or ensuring that they strictly followed the rules. Judy was a casualty of such a mind-set. A forty-year-old mother of four with an extensive work history, Judy at one point in her life lived in New York City and had a job with a financial services firm. When she moved back to Michigan, all she could find were low-paying service-sector jobs. After losing a job in 2001, she applied for TANF and was sent to Work First. She was participating in Work First when she found a job at a retail chain. On her first day of work she reported to the job and not to the Work First site, since she needed to leave her house at 6:00 AM to catch a bus and did not have time to do both. Instead of congratulating Judy for achieving what the program in theory was promoting—getting a job—the Work First staff told her that they had reported her lack of attendance to the welfare office. Judy was about to lose part of her benefits for "noncompliance" with program rules, as staff called it, even though she had obtained a job. However, if she had not taken the job, Judy could also have faced a reduction in her TANF benefits, since failure to take offered employment was also considered noncompliance. At the end of re-telling this story, Judy exclaimed, "It's not rational thinking. . . . Even a child would see that that's not rational!" With no income coming in until she got her first paycheck, Judy could have used another month or two of TANF benefits as well as other types of assistance that Work First was supposed to provide—such as help with obtaining work clothes and tickets for the bus—but instead she walked away from the program. When she was laid off in 2006, she did not even bother to apply.

Nichelle also could not make sense of the program's rules. While driving, she was rear-ended and suffered a fairly serious injury and lost her job. She went to the welfare office to apply for cash assistance but was told that to receive benefits she would need to participate in the Work First program. When she replied that her injury and her thrice weekly physical therapy appointments would make it impossible to do so, the caseworker did not budge. No Work First meant no benefits. Tamara's caseworker went one step further than Nichelle's. While Tamara's dispute with her employer over unemployment benefits continued, Tamara tried to apply for TANF benefits. Like Judy and Nichelle, she was told that not only would she have to report to the Work First program, but she would also be required to take any available job. Tamara was willing to work, but her back injury had left her unable to lift more than a small bag of groceries. If a job required lifting and Tamara did not accept the position, her benefits would be stopped.

Neither Tamara nor Nichelle was injured enough to qualify for disability benefits, and in fact they did not consider themselves disabled—they were simply unable to work temporarily, but there was no safety net for them to use. By contrast, Annette would have taken any job offered to her. When we met her in 2006, she had been unemployed for a year. At first she received unemployment benefits, but then her eligibility ended. She wanted to attend Work First in the hopes that the program would find her a job, but Annette's children were all adults, and she was not eligible for TANF. Because the Work First program was funded through TANF dollars, Annette was not allowed to attend.

According to women who were in Work First programs in Detroit, Annette may not have been missing much. "Useless" and "a waste of time" were the typical responses I got when I asked women about their experiences with Work First. Judy believed that the skills the program taught, such as preparing a résumé, practicing being interviewed, and searching for work using online resources, were helpful only "for those that have absolutely no skills." Once those skills were gained, the program did not offer much more. The women in the study noted that they did not need to be in a program to sit in front of a computer and apply for jobs; they could do this on their own without traveling to an office that might be a couple of bus rides away. Occasionally programs sent Work First participants off-site to perform temporary jobs. A few women reported that Work First had sent them on job interviews with employers who were ostensibly hiring. But rather than send Work First participants who were interested in or qualified for the job that was posted, the program sent everyone to compete with each other for the position. Usually, none of the participants would be hired, but even if a participant did get hired, the job often did not last. Tykia and a number of other people from her Work First program were hired by a Mc-

Donald's restaurant. Tykia almost always had an upbeat and positive disposition, but she said that as soon as she started the job she figured it would not last:

> There were so many people working and I just looked, you know, there was a lot of, there was a lot of girls, you know, from Work First, because we all got hired at the same time. I just was looking like, "Hmmm, I don't think this is going to last, because it looks like a lot of people." McDonald's, I mean it's a very popular fast-food chain, but some of them do slow down, you know, from time to time, because people don't have money to eat out. So, when I saw it I just said, "I'm going to work as long as I can work." I think I worked there for about a week and a half and they was like, "We're going to put you on call," and I said, "Wow." I just took a deep breath, I said, "Back to Work First I go."

By 2010, Tykia had been through this cycle at least six times.

The quality of the Work First programs varied tremendously across the state. In the late 1990s, I spent a great deal of time interviewing Work First staff and observing these programs. Some staff and programs were heavily invested in helping TANF recipients obtain not just jobs but also other services they might need. In other programs, staff stood at the front of a classroom and lectured in a monotone voice while participants dozed off. Some programs may have had well-meaning staff, but they seemed ill prepared to run a program to help welfare recipients find jobs and did not seem to understand the rules that they were supposed to be enforcing. I once observed a Work First staff member tell participants that when they went to work they would immediately lose their benefits (not necessarily true, and certainly not true for benefits from other programs they may have been receiving). A few programs engaged in some questionable practices. In front of me and another researcher, one staff person advised clients about how to pass a drug test even when they knew that they would "drop dirty."

Based on how she described her experience with Work First, Rae-anne seemed to have gone to one of those questionable programs. She was fired from her custodial job at a shopping mall when she and a coworker (her niece) were charged with shoplifting from one of the stores. Raeanne said that she was unaware that the shopping bags her niece asked her to carry contained stolen merchandise. She spent some time in jail and then was released on probation. Needing money, she applied for TANF and was sent to Work First. Raeanne did not know exactly what being on probation meant for her job prospects. She asked one of the staff what she should write on applications that asked for the reason her last job ended. To her surprise, the Work First staff said that she should just write "company downsized" rather than admit that she had been fired under less than ideal circumstances. Raeanne knew that a quick background check run by a potential employer would show her record, so she was perplexed as to why the staff person told her to lie.

This suggestion probably would not have surprised Erica, who found the entire Work First enterprise to be a bit suspect. Like many states, Michigan contracted out the operation of Work First to nonprofits as well as for-profit companies, some of which received limited oversight. Jason DeParle, in his book *American Dream*, chronicles the shortcomings of the privatized welfare system in Milwaukee.[24] At best, these welfare-to-work providers offered limited services, while pocketing the money they would have spent had they delivered all of the services that recipients needed. After DeParle's book was published, an audit of one of the providers uncovered highly questionable and even illegal uses of public funds, including the use of state TANF dollars to solicit business in other states and to pay for the singer Melba Moore to provide entertainment at an office holiday party.[25]

While Erica never alleged financial malfeasance, she believed that the incentives under which these providers were operating did not benefit clients. She said that if welfare reform was successful and people found jobs, the various Work First contractors might find themselves out of work. In her mind, it was to the benefit of the Work First providers to make sure that people never found stable jobs. She noted, "A lot of the Work First contractors, they're making money off the people being on welfare and not getting off. If they get people off welfare every time, then you won't have any more people trying to work to get people off and everything, basically.

Because most people that usually go to Work First, they usually go through there like five or six times. It will be the exact same people going through there all the time." Erica was pointing out the phenomenon of churning—the same people cycling through a program over and over, just as Tykia did for several years.

Despite Erica's suspicions, in the years after welfare reform's passage, many recipients left the program's rolls and found jobs, albeit jobs that tended to be unstable, low-paying, and not long-lasting. Or they just left welfare without any employment; the research on the factors contributing to the large drop in welfare caseloads has been unable to pinpoint the exact underlying causes.[26] By the 2000s, many within the welfare policy community were beginning to say that caseloads were becoming "harder to serve," meaning that the people who were most likely to get and keep jobs had left welfare and not returned. Those who remained on TANF were believed to face more challenges, such as low education and literacy levels, chronic health conditions, and substance abuse problems.[27] Some states began offering alternatives to employment programs. In 2000, Michigan embarked upon what it called the "Summer Project," the ultimate goal of which was to have more welfare recipients get jobs by offering participants literacy classes, counseling, parenting classes, and other social services.[28]

States could do these types of activities because while caseloads had declined, funding had not: many states had a surplus of TANF funds. Additionally, a provision in the original law allowed states to lower their work participation rate through a "caseload reduction credit." This credit reduced required work participation rates based on how much the TANF caseload had declined since 1995. So instead of needing to place 50 percent of adults in work activities, as the law mandated, a state that had greatly reduced the number of families on welfare might now need to achieve a participation rate much lower than 50 percent. In fact, Michigan's effective participation rate in 1999 was zero, once caseload reduction credits were factored into the equation.[29] But after Congress passed the 2005 Deficit Reduction Act (DRA), programs were required to return to maintaining work requirements at a high level; moreover, the caseload reduction credit was recalibrated, making it difficult

130

for states to achieve the low participation rates of earlier years. The DRA also emphasized job-related activities and restricted the types of activities in which TANF recipients could engage and count toward the work participation rate. Sending welfare recipients to substance abuse treatment programs or providing other social services were not widespread practices, but some states had set up programs to help people with so-called "barriers to employment."[30] Under the DRA, such practices would count as "participation" only under very limited circumstances.

With this singular focus on work, the welfare system essentially abandoned people like Marie, who might have benefited from more services. In 2009, Marie was on the brink of losing her home, her children had been removed from her custody by Child Protective Services (CPS), she had just gotten out of jail (for driving under the influence) and was anticipating getting locked up again because she missed a probation meeting, and she was treating her depression with a combination of Paxil and alcohol. Marie had attended Work First a couple of times, but then her caseworker excused her from the program when Marie disclosed that she was in an abusive relationship. Advocates for domestic violence victims had pushed for this rule, called the Family Violence Option (FVO), so that women in abusive relationships could receive alternative services or be exempted from participating in work activities if there was reason to believe that doing so would put them at risk.[31] Given all that was going on in her life, Marie was probably not going to be able to get a job. Even if her life had been more stable, she still would have faced challenges. She had never finished high school, and her prior work experience was limited. Removing her and others like her from the pool of people required to be in Work First could help local offices meet their work participation rates. But being exempted also left Marie to fend for herself. When she missed an appointment with a caseworker because she was in jail, her benefits were simply cut off.

Of the ten women who had used TANF for any period of time, most were younger and had very little to say about the program, either positive or negative. (In addition to these ten, Dorothy received a TANF check on behalf of her granddaughter when the granddaughter lived with her, and Miss Price received TANF benefits while waiting to be approved for SSI, but neither was subject to the state's work requirement.) Unlike older women who may have received cash benefits under AFDC, these women had known no other regime and had very limited expectations for what the welfare office should or could do for them. Shanice said that when she used TANF, she just "did what they [the welfare office] tell me," and as long as she followed the rules, money was deposited on her electronic benefits card. (Welfare offices no longer issue paper checks; instead, they deposit benefits onto a card that functions like a debit card.) And unlike Judy, Shanice did not question the rules. She took the rules for what they were, saying, "If you're the type of person to where, like, you know you gonna go to Work First, you know you supposed to do this, if and you not following the rules, then of course you're gonna be cut off, or penalized, or whatever. So me, I just, make sure that I follow the rules, because if I don't have that, what am I gonna do?" However, her last statement indicates the bind she faced. When she was not working, she had nowhere else to turn for help. Her mother, Aleta, lived on a fixed income from Social Security. (After having no income for several years, she was finally deemed eligible for the Social Security disability benefit.) Shanice's boyfriend was unemployed, and her children's father had never paid child support. Her choice was either follow the rules or have no cash coming into the house.

Determining eligibility for a public program like TANF involves many steps, such as calculating income, assets, other financial resources, and the number of people living in the household. Although it is not possible to say with certainty who might have been able to receive TANF but did not, the information we gathered about women's earnings and other household income leads us to believe that between four and nine women might have been eligible for the benefit in a given year but did not receive it. Karla did not use TANF when she was not working, even though she was probably eligible. She applied for the benefit only when she stayed in a homeless shelter that required residents to obtain aid. After she left the shelter, she lived with friends, and the welfare office wanted information about those friends' financial circumstances. She said,

"The Department of Human Services wanted their information, and that's just, it's just . . . [*pauses*] I don't mind if it's just my business, but it's other people's business that I do mind. You know, I don't mind telling [DHS], you know, what I need to tell them in order for them to do something for me, but. . . ." Karla's voice trailed off at that point. She was willing to subject herself to the scrutiny of the welfare office, but not her friends, who were providing her with a place to stay but were unable to offer any other kind of financial help. She could purchase food with her food stamps, but she could not pay any other bills.

Danielle's experience with the Work First program led her to take herself off of TANF. She and others in her Work First cohort were sent to clean Ford Field (where the Detroit Lions football team plays) the day after an event. She described the day as follows:

> Okay, it comes the day to go to work. Now mind you, you have to [show up] at eleven AM. They provide transportation for you to get to Ford Field. You can't get there on your own. They take seven dollars out your check for that, every day that you go to Ford Field. Then, that day when I got there at eleven o'clock, they get to explaining what we gonna be doing. You have to clean the bathrooms, you have to sweep this street — whiles they sleep. Oh, you might have to clean up poop. Then he [the crew leader] say, "You might have to clean up human spills." I'm like this [*makes a face*], because I don't know what that is. "What is human spills?" He say, "Throw-up." I say, "If I see throw-up, I'm gonna throw up." My stomach is sensitive like that. He all cocky, smart: "Well this might not be the job for you."

After that, Danielle refused to return to Work First and lost her benefits.

By not applying for TANF after a job loss, or forgoing it altogether, Karla and Danielle entered the ranks of the "disconnected," a term that researchers and policymakers began using to describe the growing number of single-mother families who, with no earnings and no cash assistance, were disconnected from both the labor market and part of the safety net. Research on the disconnected has found that some families survive through help from relatives, friends, and children's fathers, but other families face great difficulty making ends meet and are compelled to double up with others to afford housing or engage in off-the-books or illegal work.[32] A subset of the disconnected are those living on less than $2 per person a day, a level of extreme financial deprivation that would put an individual or family well below the federal poverty line; in 2010 the poverty threshold for a single mother with two children was about $16 per person per day. In months during which Danielle was unable to earn any money doing hair, she and her children were among the $2 a day poor. The family lived in public housing, so when her earnings were zero, so was her rent. But in those months Danielle would not pay her utility bill, and she sometimes used some of her food stamps to buy snacks, which she would mark up and have her children sell to other kids at school. Karla moved into government-subsidized housing in 2008, but before that she moved in with one family member after another when she was "disconnected" and living on less than $2 a day.

The term "disconnected" is sometimes used in policy discourse in ways that seem to imply that this status is the result of a choice. If single mothers would just get a job, they would be connected to the labor market (and thus would not need to be connected to the cash welfare system). If they would follow the rules or take the time to learn about TANF, they might be connected to that program during times of need. What these assumptions about the "disconnected" ignore are the very processes by which this phenomenon occurs—namely, the social abandonment of work as a pathway to inclusion, stability, and mobility accompanied by the abandonment of a commitment to a functioning safety net.

## The Workers Don't Answer Their Phones

In contrast to TANF, nearly all of the women who were eligible received benefits through the Supplemental Nutrition Assistance Program (SNAP)—or food stamps, as nearly everyone outside of the U.S. Department of Agriculture (the federal agency running the program) calls it. Adults in households with children may face work requirements, but until relatively recently (after 2010) these work requirements were often not strictly enforced. Nevertheless, keeping their food stamp benefits or receiving all of the benefits to which they were entitled still proved challenging for the women and exacted high "transaction costs" — that is, the time spent dealing with the bureaucracy and the stigma associated with these interactions. The women were left to navigate the program on their own, constantly needing to follow up with caseworkers who seemed to have abandoned their posts.

When Michigan changed governors in 2003, the Family Independence Agency (FIA), which oversaw TANF, food stamps, and other programs, became the Department of Human Services. Despite its new name, these women reported fewer and fewer interactions with actual human beings when they needed services. When they did finally reach a caseworker, more problems would ensue. Many of the women in the study were often abandoned by the caseworkers tasked with helping them.

Welfare offices are not usually thought of as places where people want to spend time. At their best, they are impersonal public offices with a sterile waiting room and rows of cubicles where caseworkers sit. At their worst, the waiting rooms are dingy, crowded, and full of people who have been waiting for hours to see a caseworker. If clients are lucky, they are able to find a seat in one of the room's hard plastic chairs. In urban areas such as Detroit, welfare offices often have more of the feel of a correctional facility than that of a place providing social services. The office may employ security guards to watch over the cars in the employee parking lot. Receptionists may sit behind bulletproof glass, and clients are often escorted to the back of the office to see their caseworker. In short, welfare offices are not pleasant places.

However, most of the women I talked to had rarely entered the welfare office, and a couple of them said that they would be hard-pressed to recognize their caseworker in person. If everything was going smoothly, there was no need to see a caseworker. Women on food stamps were mailed forms once a year for their annual "recertification." They would mail back the forms, and the caseworker would schedule an appointment for a phone interview. Of course, recertifying food stamp benefits was not the only reason the women might need to talk to a caseworker. Over the years they recounted numerous stories of benefits being stopped for no apparent reason and then having to try to get them restored, an arduous process that could drag on for months. In these instances, the women tried to reach their caseworkers by phone, often to no avail. Caseworkers reportedly rarely returned phone calls, and many of the women complained that their caseworker's voice-mail boxes were perpetually full, so that they were unable to leave a message. Geneva was once able to leave a voice-mail message regarding a question she had, but it then took three months for the caseworker to call her back. Even if they were able to track down their caseworker and have a conversation, problems might still remain.

Brianna, a young mother with a teenage son, had received health insurance through Medicaid for many years, but owing to a clerical error, her case was mistakenly closed. She tried in vain to contact her caseworker, but her phone calls were never returned. At the end of her rope—and at the end of the bottle of a needed prescription—she called her caseworker's supervisor. The supervisor set up an appointment for Brianna to meet with her caseworker. The meeting resulted in Brianna's Medicaid case being reopened, but at the cost of ill will with her caseworker. Brianna recounted her meeting with the caseworker:

> When I went down there [to the office], she kind of was, I guess, upset because I guess she must have, I don't know, if she got in trouble or what, but she was kind of mad that I went over her head to her supervisor. [But I] was just like, "Well, you know, I have medication I have to get and I couldn't get it, and I had left messages for you for a week, you know, so I think it was time to talk to somebody else." Um, she just, well, she just told me, "You don't have to talk to my supervisor." And I explained to her, "If you answer your phone, I wouldn't, or if you returned calls, I wouldn't have to talk to your supervisor."

When Tamara lost her job, her food stamp payment should have increased to compensate for the loss of income, and she wanted to apply for TANF. She informed her caseworker about her job loss, but weeks went by and nothing happened. Then she called again, but to no avail: "I can't get in touch with my caseworker. I've been looking for her for about a month now. She been on vacation for the last two and a half weeks. She doesn't even come back until the eighth. So, the last time I talked to her she was supposed to be sending me paperwork so that I could apply for cash assistance [TANF]. She never even sent it out to me, and then when I called her, that's when her voice mail said she was on vacation till the eighth. And that was like two and a half weeks ago." Unlike Brianna, Tamara decided not to call her caseworker's supervisor. We spoke during the midst of this confusion, and Tamara, a usually animated and gregarious woman, seemed overwhelmed and at her wit's end, perhaps feeling unable to launch into yet another fight to receive benefits. Without earnings or any welfare or unemployment benefits to replace that income, her car was repossessed when she could not pay her monthly note, and she was worried that her utilities would soon be disconnected.

Raeanne, on the other hand, was not going to wait. In 2007 she recounted an incident with a former caseworker, although it was not clear how long ago the event had occurred. Raeanne's benefits also stopped inexplicably, and this went on for six months. She took herself to the welfare office and demanded to see her caseworker. Raeanne could look very intimidating when she wanted to, and she had a gruff voice that she wasn't afraid to raise if she believed that the situation called for it. She and her caseworker got into an altercation, which may or may not have resulted in the police being called. Raeanne gave a couple of versions of this story, but it always concluded with her saying, "Yeah, I cursed her out, I threatened her. It wasn't a day that I didn't threaten her." In retaliation, Raeanne believed, the caseworker called Child Protective Services to investigate how she was feeding her children and paying the rent without any income. The investigation did not turn up anything that merited opening a case, CPS left, and Raeanne felt vindicated, but she was now in the CPS records as having had a complaint made against her.

The public welfare system has long been a mix of what Vicki Lens calls "social control and social help."[33] The waits associated with

137

receiving benefits or having problems resolved by welfare office staff can be thought of as a mechanism for instilling in recipients the need for compliance and demonstrating the state's ability to assert control.[34] The frontline practices of welfare office staff can serve the same purposes. Long before welfare reform, studies of welfare office staff observed them putting up barriers to program use. Individual caseworkers were able to exercise discretion in their daily routines that could result in some clients being denied services or possibly benefits. For example, limited resources might lead caseworkers to ration services, such as child care. For some clients, this denial of services would lead to difficulties meeting program requirements and subsequent penalties, including reductions in benefits.[35] Welfare reform, by devolving more authority from the federal government to the local level, opened up the possibility for increased levels of discretion by caseworkers, which could be used for either good (such as referring a client to needed services) or questionable purposes, such as threatening to remove a child from the home.[36]

Welfare reform also increased the workload for staff in some offices. Processing and verifying eligibility for benefits can be a time-consuming process for caseworkers, particularly since avoiding errors in overpayment and other inaccuracies is often a key component of caseworkers' performance evaluations.[37] Welfare caseworkers were also asked to take on more of a social work role, since a new component of the job was ostensibly helping clients find jobs and become "self-sufficient," not just determining eligibility for benefits.[38] Yet, not only were many staff not trained as social workers, but the new responsibilities were simply added to their existing work of processing and maintaining eligibility. The result was undertrained staff who frequently felt overburdened.[39]

The increasing workload of welfare caseworkers undoubtedly contributed to some of the delays reported by Geneva, Brianna, Tamara, Raeanne, and others. In the mid-1990s, Governor John Engler embarked on what he termed "rightsizing" the state's public workforce. For a brief period of time, eligible public employees were offered the option of early retirement, which he incentivized with an increase in monthly retirement benefits. More than 5,000 workers—1,500 of whom worked for the Family Independence Agency—accepted this offer. State agencies were only allowed to replace one worker for every four who retired. When another round of early retirements were offered in 2002—this time explicitly for the purpose of cutting costs from the state's budget—about 20 percent of FIA staff retired. The remaining caseworkers and their supervisors were stretched thin. Michigan's original model of post–welfare reform casework called for the creation of a new position called the family independence specialist (FIS, pronounced "fizz"). The FIS was supposed to work with a relatively small number of families, providing them with services tailored to their individual needs. For a short period of time, the average caseload of a FIS was under 100 families. By 2009, however, caseworkers reported handling up to 800 cases at a time. The number of people in Michigan receiving some type of public assistance increased by more than 400,000 between 2008 and 2009, yet the number of staff working in local offices barely budged upward.[40] And while Michigan might have started its downsizing earlier than other states, it is not alone. Across the country, the Great Recession led state and local governments to cut back on their workforces (outside of education), and as of the end of 2014 those losses have not yet been recovered.[41]

Michigan began feeling the effects of an economic downturn prior to the Great Recession; as budget problems continued into the next governor's administration, state workers were mandated to take unpaid furlough days. In the welfare office, work continued to pile up. Caseworkers reported that threats were being made against them, and some had been physically assaulted by clients, suggesting that Raeanne's response to her caseworker was not an isolated incident. In meetings I attended in Lansing, employees talked about increases in the number of stress leaves granted to caseworkers. This left even fewer workers to handle the work.

Caseworkers' stress may have also contributed to terse interactions with their clients or to actions such as Raeanne's worker calling Child Protective Services. Brianna said that her caseworker was snippy the few times she talked to her: "I called her and she answered the phone and said, 'What,' instead of saying, 'Good morning, this is the Department of Human Services.' She said, 'What.'"

Although Brianna was unemployed at the time, she had worked fairly steadily since turning eighteen. She knew the norms of professional behavior and believed that her caseworker should subscribe to them. When asking about interactions with caseworkers, I frequently heard some variation of the phrase "my worker acts like I'm taking money out of his pocket." At first I did not understand what this meant, but Tamara explained it in more detail to me: her caseworker left her feeling like any money she received from the welfare system was money that was coming out of the worker's own bank account rather than from federal tax dollars. To Tamara, this attitude on the part of caseworkers was unwarranted particularly because she, Tamara, was also a taxpayer.

During the 2012 presidential campaign, Mitt Romney was caught on video saying that 47 percent of Americans would vote for Obama because they were dependent on government and paid no income tax. It is true that close to 47 percent of Americans pay no *federal* income tax, and Tamara was one of them. However, this figure is a result of the Earned Income Tax Credit (EITC), which provides low- and moderate-income workers with a refundable credit at tax time. For workers with low wages, the amount of the credit may well exceed what was taken out of their checks as federal withholding. But does this negate Tamara's claim on benefits as a taxpayer? Tamara may not have paid federal income tax, but she paid Social Security taxes, state income taxes, a city income tax, sales tax, and property taxes. Was it her fault that she earned so little that she got a refund on her federal income taxes? The welfare system and its caseworkers seemed not to think of her as a worker who had lost her job.

Waits can also be built into the structure of public benefit programs for seemingly reasonable purposes. As Aleta waited for her worker's compensation claim to be adjudicated, she also applied for Social Security Disability Insurance (SSDI), the federal program funded via workers' payroll taxes and available to workers who become unable to work owing to serious and long-lasting illness or injury. Her initial application for benefits was denied. However, Aleta had expected this outcome. She said, "I've been denied Social Security once, which I understand is a normal procedure, and now they are working on my claim for a second time." Aleta's statement had some basis in fact. According to data from the Social Security Administration (SSA), between 2001 and 2010 about seven in ten disability claims were denied at the initial application stage. Overall, about 45 percent of all claims filed eventually result in the receipt of benefits. Moreover, multiple applications, denials, and appeals may occur before someone is determined eligible, and three to five months may pass at each step in the process.[42]

One reason for these delays is that it takes time to go through the reams of documentation that must be supplied to determine eligibility for a program. Applicants for programs like TANF and food stamps must provide proof of their low income through bank statements, paycheck stubs, tax returns, and other documents. Disability applicants like Aleta must meet other criteria, including providing all medical records and certification from a medical professional that their disability is expected to last at least one year (or result in death). Once submitted, staff must verify the accuracy of the information provided. We want benefits to be given only to those who are eligible, and caseworkers want to avoid errors in overpayment. For the women in this study who were trying to receive benefits, supplying all of this paperwork, abiding by Work First's rules, and doing all the monitoring that was required on their own part to keep their cases open was time-consuming and exhausting. Sometimes people simply give up, an outcome that is perhaps desirable to a strapped state welfare system.

Within this sample, problems receiving benefits, whether from delays, the need to monitor their case, inadvertent case closings, or disputes from employers, were widespread. Table 5.1 shows the number of women who reported receiving a safety net benefit (UI, disability, TANF, food stamps, or public health insurance) for themselves or a member of their household at least once during the study period, and among those the proportion who reported a problem obtaining or receiving that benefit. On the positive side, public health insurance was one of the most widely used benefits (60 percent, twenty-eight families) and the one for which users reported the fewest problems (11 percent, or just three women). But 28 to 42 percent of recipients reported problems with other safety

Table 5.1　Receipt of Safety Net Benefits Among Respondents and Reported Problems in Obtaining or Receiving Those Benefits, 2006–2011

| Type of Benefit | Number Receiving Benefit (Self and Household Members) | Percentage Reporting Problems |
|---|---|---|
| Unemployment Insurance (UI) | 18 | 28 |
| Disability benefits: SSDI, SSI, state program | 9 | 33 |
| TANF | 12 | 42 |
| Food stamps (SNAP) | 32 | 31 |
| Public health insurance: Medicaid, Medicare, state CHIP (Children's Health Insurance Program) | 28 | 11 |

*Source:* Author's calculations.

net programs. This was true of lesser-used programs such as disability (used by nine women, with three reporting problems) and TANF (used by twelve, with five reporting difficulties) as well as for food stamps, a benefit that was used by more than 70 percent of the households at some point in time, with just under one-third reporting problems.

## The Consequences of Abandonment

Losing a job and then having to wait months or even years before receiving benefits contributed to significant economic hardship for these women. While Sharon was waiting for her dispute with the unemployment office to be settled, she spent all but $300 of her once-flush savings account. She sold off some of her possessions and eventually cashed out her 401(k) retirement fund when her unemployment benefits ran out. When those funds were exhausted, her parents liquidated part of their retirement investments and loaned the money to her, about $20,000 in total. Once she got another job, albeit one that paid much less than her previous one, she began making monthly payments on that loan. For all of them, Sharon said, the arrangement made sense. She got a loan from her parents at a lower interest rate than she would have from a commercial financial product, but she was paying them back at an interest rate that was higher than they were receiving by keeping their savings in a traditional account. She said, "It's an investment for them, because the economy is so bad . . . and their investments were like totally takin' a crap so they invested in me. Like withdrew their money markets accounts and stuff like that, because I'd pay them a higher interest rate. So they're making money off me, and I'm paying a lower interest rate than [I would have]." However, the success of this arrangement was contingent upon Sharon keeping a job and her parents not needing to access their money right away.

Tamara didn't have much in the way of reserves, either personally or from family. After she lost her job, she could not make her car loan payments, and her car was repossessed. She was also on the brink of having her electricity turned off. Aleta went the longest period of time without a job and without benefits; it took four years for her worker's compensation case to be resolved. Her telephone was turned off multiple times, her electricity once. When her employer canceled her medical benefits, she was unable to fill many of her prescriptions, since the state-funded health insurance she had paid for only some of her medications. Her car stopped working altogether, and of course she had no money to replace it. She started going to a local church's food pantry and needed to rely on her mother and daughter for money to pay the bills. In 2008 she said she felt "like I'm caught up in the whirlpool and I don't see my way out of it. And my life has never been where it was out of control before. I've never been dependent on other people before."

The stress of not knowing how bills were going to get paid or having to rely on others for money manifested itself in a number of ways. Aleta felt embarrassed that she had to ask her family and friends for money. Sharon said that she gained weight and her hair started going gray. Geneva blamed her injury and subsequent job loss for the breakup of her marriage. She and her husband never formally divorced (filing for divorce was an expense for which they did not have money); nevertheless, she said, he was unable to "take it" any longer. Between Geneva's physical problems and lack of money, he "cracked under the pressure," as she put it, and went to live with his mother. Tamara, like many other women, diagnosed herself with depression after she lost her job. She said that she would often spend days looking out the window and crying. Other days, when she was feeling better, she went online, looking for jobs. But job hunting became just another source of stress. When she was not stressed, she said she felt bored, and her children had "cabin fever" because they had no money to go anywhere or do anything fun. Rhonda felt fortunate that during the time she was without food stamps she had a freezer full of food, but she suffered from high blood pressure and worrying about whether or not her benefits would come each month was not good for her health.

Usually the women eventually received benefits, but only after going without income for many months (or years in Aleta's case). Aleta's worker's compensation case was eventually settled out of court. Her former employer agreed to a $100,000 payout. However, once Aleta paid her attorney, took care of her unpaid medical bills, and reimbursed the state for assistance she had received while waiting for compensation, all that remained was $20,000. And her continued health problems made it unlikely that she would ever be able to return to the labor market. Sharon found another job, but not until 2007. Her pay was $10,000 less than what she had been making before, and she continued to owe her parents money. During Geneva's wait for benefits, she lost nearly everything—her house, her car, and her husband.

# Conclusion

The social insurance programs examined here were inaccessible to many of the women in the study, and the social welfare programs were unreliable. Cases that should have stayed open were closed, paperwork was routinely lost, and calls to the welfare office went unanswered. History may provide some indications of why the modern-day safety net fails so many of the people, like the women in this study, who are entitled to its support.

When today's safety net programs were coming into existence, African Americans were largely kept from using them. Agricultural and domestic workers were initially excluded from the coverage provided by the 1935 Social Security Act's social insurance provisions. Although, numerically, more whites than blacks were in these occupations, proportionally blacks were overrepresented in them; as a result, 65 percent of African Americans workers were unable to access these benefits, compared to 27 percent of white workers.[43] For several decades, African American women living in the Southern states were frequently kept off of welfare rolls so that their labor could be exploited.[44] Although delaying or denying benefits because of bureaucratic problems may on its face seem like a race-neutral situation, in fact actions such as these are embedded within a system that has long considered many public assistance recipients "undeserving" of help and that the public thinks of as being used primarily by single black mothers (Gilens 1999).[45] Moreover, the delays that the women in this study experienced were borderline abusive and left some of the most vulnerable families in continued financial distress, abandoned by the very systems that were ostensibly supposed to help them.

# ❧ CHAPTER 6 ❧

## DEBT: THE NEW SHARECROPPING SYSTEM

Sharon's six-month battle with her former employer to receive unemployment benefits when he laid her off not only left her without any income for those months but also left her deep in debt. She had some savings, but not much. Even without a job or public benefits, she did have access to credit, specifically nine credit cards. Those cards provided her with a lifeline, but as she said, "I have a lot of debt . . . the whole time I was laid off . . . because unemployment got all screwed up, so I wasn't getting any money that way. So I basically lived off of my credit. [I] would do the zero percent interest for the next sixteen months, like those types of credit cards. Well, now all those are expiring and have regular interest rates. And I pretty much lived off of them, so now I have debt." In total, Sharon estimated that between her credit cards and student loans she was at least $20,000 in the red, not counting what she owed for the mortgage on her house.

Unlike Sharon, Cheryl could not use various credit cards to pay the bills when she was unemployed or working only part-time. She had a card but had deliberately stopped using it long ago, not being able to keep up with the payments. She still owed several hundred dollars to the credit card company, but her first priority was to pay her "bills," which in Cheryl's mind were the rent, utilities, groceries, and phone. And if money was really tight, she would stop paying for the phone, let it be disconnected, and then sign up with a new carrier when she had money again. Her history of not making payments or making only partial payments was reflected in the debts listed on her credit report. In addition to the credit card company, she owed money to several phone companies, the local utility provider, and several doctor's offices for medical bills that she had accrued in the past. In total, she estimated that she owed between \$5,000 and \$6,000. While that amount was considerably lower than what Sharon owed, Cheryl was often unemployed or underemployed and in a typical year earned only about \$6,000. (Although Sharon's earnings went down over time, she made about six times that amount.) Of course, Cheryl usually received a sizable tax refund check, but in 2009 her state income tax refund was garnished by the credit card company to retrieve some of the money she owed it.[1]

When striving women were abandoned by the safety net, they took on and maintained debt. Debt accrued when an unexpected expense arose or money was tight for other reasons, and substantial debt arose from their attempts to become upwardly mobile, in the form of student loans and mortgages. In the wake of abandonment by the institutions that should have promoted economic security, encouraged upward mobility, and protected them from labor market vagaries, families were left to finance their survival on their own. Since most did not have extended families who could provide substantial financial support, they used credit cards or did not pay all of their bills. These strategies only temporarily solved financial problems, however, and left families drowning in debt with little prospect of getting out from under it; their earnings were not rising, and their homes were not appreciating in value. Additionally, some of the financial products that the women used had very high interest rates and fees, which only added to the amount owed, since they could rarely make more than the minimum payment on the balance of their debt.

This cycle that these families experienced — not making enough money, losing jobs, not being able to quickly access the safety net, and then going into debt — coupled with the significant debt they took on to finance their attempts at upward mobility in the wake of their social abandonment, has eerie parallels to the sharecropper system in the post–Civil War South. Sharecropping developed as a way to keep a stable supply of labor on plantations after slavery ended. Sharecropping relied on debt peonage — forced labor to pay off debts. Small farmers, or sharecroppers, were allowed to farm plots of land owned by someone else in return for a share of the profits from the crops. But in order to raise a crop, the farmer needed to purchase seeds, supplies, and other items from the landowner on credit. The high interest rates charged by many landowners for these loans and their unscrupulous practices when it came time to "settle up" at the end of the harvest often kept sharecroppers in debt to the landowner, and so they would have to stay on for another season to work off their debt. Meanwhile, the landowner could sell the crop on the market at a higher price than the value credited to the sharecropper. And the cycle continued. Although both whites and blacks were sharecroppers, blacks were overrepresented among the ranks.[2]

For socially abandoned people in Detroit today, the wages they are paid (or the benefits that could replace lost wages) are never enough or are not paid in a timely enough fashion for them to keep up with bill payments. Employers control when and how much they work, the social welfare bureaucracy has a great deal of control over the disbursement of benefits, and the credit card companies set the terms for borrowing; in the end families are left in debt when the money coming in is always less than the money going out. This pattern is much like the pattern under sharecropping: the landowner did the hiring, set the interest rates charged on loans, and decided prices at harvest time when settling up with the farmers, who, like the women in this study, were always left in debt in the end. Families today use debt as a way to manage day to day, just as sharecroppers did when they had to borrow in order to plant, to pay rent, and to purchase food.

Sharecropping was a means of maintaining a system of labor that bore similarities to slavery: African Americans were kept tied to someone else's land, laboring for nothing and then getting into debt. In the modern-day equivalent, debt is the fallout of abandonment, of employment not providing true inclusion, of education and homeownership not providing upward mobility, and of the safety net failing—all of which contribute to the reproduction of existing inequalities between the poor and nonpoor and, importantly, between whites and blacks. If mass incarceration is the "new

Jim Crow" that denies an entire class of citizens (predominantly black males) various human and social rights, perhaps social abandonment is the "new sharecropping" that deprives affected families (who are disproportionately black) of opportunities to better their situation.[3]

Failure to pay debts can lead to bad credit scores, and bad credit scores can haunt families when they try to obtain additional loans. Perhaps even more worrisome is that credit scores are increasingly being used by employers in hiring decisions and by landlords in renting units. A bad credit score, then, is like the mark of a criminal record, making it difficult to secure jobs and housing. Short of declaring bankruptcy, there is no real way for these families to escape debt.

Until relatively recently, much of the debt accrued by these families would not have been possible — credit cards, mortgages, and student loans would have been out of reach because lower-income families would have been deemed too much of a credit risk. Access to credit is crucial for most Americans; it can be impossible to finance the purchase of larger goods (appliances, cars, and homes, for example) without credit. From this standpoint, the opening up of credit to families who had previously been locked out can be viewed as a form of financial inclusion. But the substandard loans that these families received and their need to finance basic needs through debt instead trapped them, excluding them from opportunity.

## Borrowing and Debt: A Quick Overview

Debt can play a number of roles in a household. As discussed in chapter 4, taking on debt can promote upward mobility through education financed by student loans or homeownership paid for via a mortgage. Debt also allows an individual or household to support levels of consumption (the purchase of goods and services) that would not otherwise be possible at a given income, and debt may function as a way to smooth consumption during periods when income falls.[4] That is, households may go into debt during a spell of unemployment because they are trying to maintain the standard of living they achieved on their previous income (or some standard close to it). They may use credit cards to pay for bills that they previously paid for with cash, and then they may not pay down the balance on those cards.

Going into debt is not, however, the only way to smooth consumption — households can draw down savings, they can apply for public benefits to replace lost income, and they can borrow money from friends and family.[5] The research that examines how well these approaches work to smooth consumption shows mixed results. Using personal savings is the least effective way to smooth consumption, since the median household with a working-age adult does not have enough savings to cover a month of consumption at previous levels.[6] Likewise, extended families in the United States are rarely able to extend significant financial help.[7] Unemployment Insurance, the social program designed explicitly to replace (at least partially) wages after job loss, has been found to play an extremely important role in consumption smoothing for households that receive it.[8] Recall, however, that not every worker who loses a job is eligible, and the experiences of the women in this study show how difficult it can be to obtain UI benefits.

For much of the twentieth century, low-income borrowers and single women of any income level were locked out of the mainstream credit card market, but lending practices changed in the 1970s with the deregulation of the financial sector as well as technological innovations. Previously, caps on the interest rates that lenders could charge for loans protected consumers from predatory lending. That changed in the late 1970s.[9] While competition for consumers with strong credit histories kept credit card interest rates and fees at reasonable levels for that segment of the market, deregulation allowed the industry to tap into new markets, such as lower-income consumers and students, who could be charged higher rates to compensate for the increased risk associated with lending to these populations. Moreover, technological advances and the plethora of personal data that became available made it easier for companies to examine a person's finances, determine his or her risk, and tailor a credit product to take that risk into account;

as a result, lenders were able to expand credit card markets even further into low-income communities.[10]

Broadening access to credit cards can provide many benefits. Credit cards not only provide a convenience to holders — particularly in a place like Detroit where ATM machines are not found in certain neighborhoods — but also are useful during emergencies, for example, when cash is not on hand for a needed car repair. Lower-income households responded to the increasing availability of credit cards: the share of low-earning households with credit card debt grew by 40 percent over the period 1989 to 2004. Among families earning between $10,000 and $25,000 a year, the proportion holding credit cards increased from 52 percent in 1989 to nearly 60 percent in 2001. Among those with even lower incomes (less than $10,000 a year), the proportion holding cards rose from just over one-quarter to more than one-third of these households.[11] The catch is that the products available to these groups often carry quite high interest rates, significant penalties for late payment, and other fees. The rationale behind these charges is that since this group of cardholders is at a greater risk for nonpayment, issuers must find other ways to collect revenue.[12]

Overall, about 80 percent of all Americans hold some type of debt. Whites hold more debt than blacks ($41,500 versus $18,950), but again, much of that disparity is driven by higher rates of homeownership (and thus mortgages) among whites. Among households earning $40,000 or less, there is less racial difference in debt levels: $8,660 for whites and $7,120 for blacks).[13]

## Carrying Debt in Detroit

All households in this study, at some point in time, carried debt. Low wages, unstable employment, difficulties gaining access to and receiving public benefits in a timely manner, and the limited assistance available to families through private safety nets and nonprofit agencies resulted in many of the women borrowing to make ends meet. Additionally, just under half of all the households across all income levels took out student loans or home mortgages. Table

6.1 provides a more detailed look at the types of debt owed, gives an approximate range of the amounts owed, and displays the median amount owed across different categories of debt. Families are counted as having a type of debt if they ever reported it between 2006 and 2011. The amount of debt by type represents the women's report of the amount owed by the household the first time the debt was mentioned. I derived this amount by taking the median of the total debt reported at each interview wave (2006 to 2011). Much of what is reported in this table is based on estimates. The women in the study tended to report their debt in round numbers or in ranges. Sometimes they did not know the exact amount owed and instead would give a ballpark estimate, such as saying that their credit card debt "wasn't more than $5,000." Others would reach for a stack of bills during the interview and cite the balances owed on each.

Owing money to one or more utility providers was the most common type of debt, reported by almost three-quarters of respondents at some point; most had owed this money for three years or more and were unable to pay down their balances in full. (See discussion later for details on how the women sustained this debt without loss of services.) Two-thirds of respondents reported credit card debt, either for cards currently in use or for cards they had stopped using (and on which they typically had stopped making payments). Most reported credit card debt of $5,000 or less, but as noted earlier, one of them, Sharon, owed $20,000. Just under half had medical debts; some were quite small (about $50) and represented copayments for doctors' visits, but several households carried substantial medical debt that had been incurred when they were uninsured. (Of course, medical debt can also be incurred when insurance does not cover certain procedures or requires the policyholder to pay a deductible before covering services.) As noted in chapter 4, four in ten households had student loan debt, and most were in a state of deferment—that is, they were temporarily exempt from making payments because they were still in school or their incomes were low enough to qualify them for a temporary exemption from payment. Debts to cable companies or cell-phone providers, mortgages or other home-related debt, and car notes were each held by one-third or fewer households. More households, nineteen in total, reported

Table 6.1    Types and Amounts of Debt Held by Respondents, 2006–2011

| Type of Debt[a] | Percentage of Women Ever Reporting (n = 45) | Amount Owed[b] |
|---|---|---|
| Utility company | 73 | $270–$10,000 |
| Credit card | 67 | $150–$20,000 |
| Medical | 47 | $50–$12,000 |
| Student loan | 40 | $700–$200,000 |
| Cable or phone service | 33 | $50–$350 |
| Car note | 27 | —[c] |
| Other[d] | 42 | $350–$10,000 |
| Median total amount owed[e] | | $2,500 ($279–80,000) |
| Median debt-to-income ratio[e] | | 0.17 (0.01–4.0) |

*Source:* Author's calculations.

[a]The types of debt are not mutually exclusive, that is, respondents often held more than one kind of debt.

[b]The amount owed on individual debts is based on the first instance the debt was reported. Total amount owed is derived by taking the median amount owed by each respondent across the six waves of interviews.

[c]We did not ask about the total amount owed on cars; getting behind on payments resulted in repossession.

[d]Other debts included bank overdrafts, parking tickets and moving violation fines, court-related payments, and personal loans.

[e]Owing to large amounts of missing data (we did not ask about car note debt amounts, and most homeowners did not know the balance of their mortgages), the amount owed and the debt-to-income ratio excludes car note and mortgage debt.

"other" kinds of debt, which included bank overdrafts, parking tickets and moving violation fines, court-related payments, and personal loans.

The amount of debt held by these families overall was slightly lower than national averages. The median amount of housing-related debt nationwide falls between $109,000 and $123,000, average educational loans are about $13,000, and credit card debt averages $2,000.[14] Housing prices in Detroit are below national averages, so the largest mortgage held by a woman in this study was below the national median. The range of credit card debt and student loan debt held by respondents encompassed the national median. (Given the imprecision with which the women reported their debts and their tendency to know how much they owed for one or two categories of debt but not others, I do not present median debt amounts in table 6.1).

Households were often in debt to a variety of different creditors at one time. The women might be enrolled in school and have a student loan, owe on current credit cards that they were using to pay other bills, and owe money on an old phone bill as a result of not making payments during an earlier period of financial difficulty. The median reported debt for these households was about $2,500 at any given time, which does not necessarily seem insurmountable. But for some households, the amount of debt they held relative to their annual income was quite large. Half of the households held debt that amounted to about 20 percent of their income during the study period, and ten of those households had debt that was equivalent to half or more of their income. Some women had given up making monthly payments toward some of their debt, believing (perhaps rightly) that a $20 minimum payment to a credit card company made little to no dent in the balance they owed. Finally, considering that most of the women did not know the exact amount of all their debts, a simple report of debt relative to income may obscure the extent of financial distress in these households.

## Origins of Debt

For households in this study, debt was most often incurred because of a need to smooth consumption when the household's basic expenses exceeded income. Fewer households took on debt as a means of investing in the future, but when they did, the mortgages and student loans they held were significant sources of debt. Few reported having debt as the result of spending beyond their means; those who did often reported that they had accrued this debt when they were younger.

Some of the women used credit cards to cover their basic expenses (such as groceries or fuel for their cars) when they experienced drops in income. This strategy was slightly more common for women like Sharon and Yvette, who had relatively higher incomes when working. Yvette's salary at a telecommunications firm was based on commissions, which decreased as the slowing economy led to fewer people wanting to purchase new services. At the same time, she had some unexpected expenses, and her child support payments were not timely. To pay her bills, she used her credit cards. She said, "I basically, like, used the credit cards for gas, groceries, um, you know, just things like, living things that I didn't have the money on my paycheck to pay it because I had to pay bills. And so, then I had got just too dependent on my credit cards being there to get me out of the bind every two weeks when my paycheck wasn't stretching." At one point, she was carrying balances totaling just under $14,000 on her various credit cards.

As discussed earlier, Sharon had been a salaried employee making $36,000, but she was laid off in 2006. She filed for UI benefits, but her employer contested the claim, and for several months she had no income. She went through her savings. She began to rely on credit cards for everyday purchases, such as food, and also as a means of paying her mortgage. Her method of consumption smoothing entailed the management of about a dozen credit cards and was so complex that she maintained an Excel spreadsheet to keep track of the balances. In order to use so many cards without paying enormous finance charges, she sought out cards with a 0 percent finance rate. When the card's rate began to rise, she found a better deal and moved her balance to the new card. At any one time she was juggling at least ten different credit cards. Showing me the complicated spreadsheet she maintained, Sharon explained how she kept track:

> What I did last week was, I called the credit cards I already have. I called and said, "Hey, you know, I'll transfer this balance over here if you give me this rate for this period of time." And they seem to be buying onto that. . . . This is my July bills. [*referring to her spreadsheet*] Like these ones are zeroed out. But they're being real sticklers on the interest rate, so I'm not using

them. But this one . . . I only got a two-dollar balance on there. But I just worked out a promotional interest rate with them and took out a cash advance on that one. So I'm not going to pay any interest on that one until August '09, and I had to pay thirty-five bucks to transfer the balance.

Using all of these cards had led to Sharon's credit card debt of $20,000.

Households with lower income also used credit cards extensively. Charlene relied heavily on her credit cards when her hours at work were cut from full-time to part-time, using the cards to pay bills and to purchase food. She said that when she was working more, she only used the credit card for convenience, paying off the balance each month. But with less income coming in, she used the cards to replace the cash she did not have; she had quickly hit the limit of her card, $5,000.

As a consumption-smoothing strategy, women more commonly borrowed against one bill to pay another, or, as the women colloquially termed it, "robbing Peter to pay Paul."[15] This form of consumption smoothing—which was used by women at all income levels—entailed paying all or part of a bill one month, then putting nothing toward it another month (robbing Peter) so that funds could go toward paying another bill or keeping current on other expenses (paying Paul). In 2007, Mary's daughter was diagnosed with a serious medical condition, and Mary stopped working at a child care center in order to care for her. Although Mary, who always had very low income, often characterized herself as having poor money management skills, no one would have been able to cover expenses on the limited income she had from welfare (about $300 a month, and that stopped once her daughter turned eighteen) and food stamps (about $200 a month). She deliberately made partial payments on her bills, putting $100 toward a $200 utility bill, for instance, and "worry[ing] about the other hundred later." However, the "other hundred," when it came in, usually went toward other bills. Mary was caught in a constant cycle of juggling payments, borrowing from one bill to pay another, and being left in debt to everyone.

Using credit cards resulted in debt because these women lacked the funds to pay down balances. They were using cards not as a convenient substitution for cash but rather in place of cash they did not have. Borrowing from one bill to pay another resulted in balances that were not paid down. And "robbing Peter to pay Paul" could also bring significant risks, depending on the type of debt held. Debt generated through credit cards is considered "unsecured" in that there is no particular item attached to it as collateral. The credit card issuer can send a collection agency after the holder if she is not making minimum payments (or take other actions), but otherwise, the interest on the charges accumulates. Medical debt and student loans are also unsecured. Mortgages and car loans are "secured" debt because the loan is tied directly to the property. Lack of payment can result in foreclosure or repossession, so those who find themselves behind on payments run the risk of losing their home or car. Debt owed to utility companies and phone companies is generally considered unsecured in that there is no property to repossess, but providers can and do disconnect services for unpaid bills, making the consequences of nonpayment or underpayment similar to those of secured debt.

Tamara always had credit card debt, but she had long ago stopped making payments toward that debt, seemingly with no consequences. But her secured debt caused her difficulties when she lost her job in 2011. Tamara stopped making payments on her car loan in order to use that money for other bills. A few months later, her car was repossessed, leaving her reliant on others or the spotty Detroit bus system to take her where she needed to go. She also received a shut-off notice from the power company when she got too far behind on that bill.

The women also held what many called "back debt," that is, older debts incurred from earlier periods of consumption smoothing. Common forms of "back debt" were old cell phones that they had stopped paying for when finances were particularly tight, or credit cards they had ceased using because they had reached the maximum allowed by the card issuer (usually $500 or less). Sometimes they initially did not list back debt in response to our question, "Tell me about the debt you have," perhaps in part because they typically were not making payments toward that debt. As Tamara said, "Honestly, back debt I don't even care about right now. . . . I gotta keep my lights on, I gotta keep my gas on, I gotta keep my water on. Everything else, that stuff that I owe back in the day, I don't even care about, it's gonna be there." Tamara's back debt was mostly old credit card debt. Categorizing certain old bills as back debt allowed families to prioritize payments when juggling their bills and smoothing consumption.

As discussed in chapter 4, families attempting upward mobility also took out student loans and mortgages, but sometimes used these loans as consumption-smoothing tools as well. The house in which Charlene lived (as opposed to her rental property) was a family home: owned by her husband's grandparents, it was completely paid off. When they needed more cash, however, they took out an adjustable rate mortgage on the home in 2004. Eighteen households held one or more student loans, which, like mortgages, can also be used to smooth consumption. Brianna stopped working when she was in an associate's degree program. Initially, she and her son were able to survive on the Pell grant and the federal work-study money that was left over after she finished paying for tuition and books. But by her last semester she felt stretched very thin financially. She took out a federally subsidized student loan so that she would have some money if unexpected expenses arose—in other words, if she needed to smooth consumption.

But loans need to be repaid. For four of the eighteen households with student loans, repayment had been temporarily suspended because of either deferment or forbearance for at least some period of time (see chapter 4). Erica had massive amounts of student loan debt—about $130,000 in total—from both her undergraduate years at a private college and a professional school she attended for two years, although she did not complete the degree. Yet she never made a payment during the time I knew her. Enrolling in graduate school, having very low income, and experiencing frequent bouts of unemployment allowed her to avoid payments. In 2006 she explained: "When I got out of college, I wasn't able to find a job, so I used my little forbearance time. Then when I was working, I was able to pay on some [loans]. And then I had got—since I stopped working I been trying to stay in school, so I'm going to have to pay them. So that's another reason why I'm working on my master's degree. So I deferred that some more, a little longer." But by 2007 she had stopped attending school and had requested and received deferments. However, she was quickly reaching the deferment limits (three years for economic hardship and three years for unemployment).

Those who were not in school and not in deferment status were making payments on their loans, although most were not making much headway. Tykia and Judy were able to pay off their loans, but their loan amounts had been relatively small ($3,000 and $4,500, respectively), whereas other women owed anywhere from $10,000 to more than $100,000.

Finally, these women had debt due to encounters with public systems that levied fees and fines on them. This debt was completely unplanned and certainly did not serve as a way to smooth consumption or as an investment in their future. This debt was usually (although not always) the result of breaking a law or municipal code, but the regressive nature of these fees effectively penalized those who could least afford to pay. When Brianna was pulled over for speeding, she expected that she would get a ticket and a fine, but what caught her off guard was the "driver's responsibility fee" assessed over and above the speeding fine.[16] Other women owed money for multiple parking tickets, sometimes several hundred dollars. Miss Price's car was impounded owing to parking ticket debt, and as a result, she had to rely on family members to take her where she needed to go. One of Nichelle's teenage sons got in trouble and spent a short amount of time in a juvenile facility. The trauma of this experience was only made worse when Nichelle learned that she was expected to pay $7,000 to the state for having "housed" her son. Unemployed and homeless at the time, Nichelle was unsure where she would get the money.

As states have become more reluctant to raise taxes and localities face budget shortfalls due to declining property values, increased pension payouts, decreased revenue sharing from the state, or some combination of these factors, policymakers have turned to levying fees as a way to make up the difference.[17] For those with little to no extra money on hand, something as seemingly innocuous as a parking ticket or moving violation can turn into hundreds of dollars of debt if the fine is steep and other charges are added. The "driver's responsibility fee," which was levied against several women in this study, is an example of such a revenue-generating scheme. The fee was put into place in 2003 as a way to provide funding to local governments and their police departments. It is an additional fee tacked on to the regular penalties for speeding and other driving violations.[18] Public outcry over the law's regressive nature and its impact on lower-income drivers led to a replacement of fees with community service and an eventual phaseout of the law entirely by 2019.[19] In addition to the regressiveness of such fees and fines, they always had a sudden and unexpected impact on the women in this study, disrupting their already precarious financial situation. The penalties for not paying could be severe, such as losing a driver's license, having a car impounded, or having wages withheld for payment.

Little is yet known about how widespread such practices are. The U.S. Department of Justice's report on policing practices in Ferguson, Missouri, recently brought a national spotlight to the use of fees, fines, and other monetary penalties as a means of generating revenue at the state and local levels.[20] Although not as common as credit card debt, debt resulting from being assessed such penalties caused significant financial stress for certain women in this study. This debt served no purpose but to penalize women severely for rather minor infractions. Moreover, with some individuals who are unable to pay even facing possible jail time, the "debtors' prisons" that were disbanded in the 1800s have effectively been resurrected in some circumstances and localities.

## Paying Down or Taking on More Debt: Modern-Day Sharecropping?

Table 6.1 provides an overview of the types and amounts of debt held by families, but it does not show if they were able to pay it down over time. Between 2006 and 2011, more than half of the households in the study (twenty-four) took on additional debt.

Nine of those households added more debt to preexisting debt without paying down the latter, and ten households made progress on paying down some debt but then took on more. Five households declared bankruptcy, but then subsequently took out new debt. The other households (twenty-one in total) avoided taking on new debt. Eleven of those were able to pay down some of their debt without taking on more, but they still owed money to other creditors. Nine carried roughly the same debts throughout the study period. Some of the married-couple households were able to make payments toward some debt because they had two incomes, while a couple of the single mothers paid off smaller debts. However, it is important to note that nearly all of the debt that was paid down was collected through garnishment, a claim that creditors can make on wages or other income to receive payment. Only Annette was able to clear all of her debt and remain debt-free through the end of the study. Everyone else was trapped by their debt and tied to their creditors — like sharecroppers to landowners.

The volatility of their employment and earnings and their difficulties replacing that income when unemployed, coupled with their fixed expenses (rent or mortgage, utilities, food, and limited other expenses), left many of the women engaged in constant consumption smoothing. Like sharecroppers in the post–Civil War South, the money they earned was rarely equal to (let alone exceeded) the money going out. And when households had a little extra money, it was not enough to make a dent in their existing debt. As Geneva said, "My overhead is just, well, last month, when I didn't pay the mortgage, we had exactly $104 left over. And that's because I didn't pay the mortgage. Usually I'll have about $18 left for the whole month. That's for the toilet paper, that's for the gas, that's for anything that the food stamps don't cover. So it's usually like that. So I can't make any payment arrangements."

At a theoretical level, consumption smoothing assumes that there is some "permanent" income or equilibrium around which year-to-year income varies and that households consume goods at a level equivalent to their permanent income, regardless of income in any particular year. In years when income is higher than their permanent income, households save (or pay off debt); in years when income is lower, they spend their savings (or take on debt). What this model requires is that households experience periods of time when they can recover from whatever downward "shocks" they experience, such as a job loss or a pay cut. But for these women, there were no recovery periods. With the disruptions in their receipt of benefits, the instability in the number of hours they worked from week to week, and their periods of unemployment, these families never experienced "equilibrium." There was no money to put toward paying down existing debt, and some families had to take on more.

Among other debt, Rhonda owed about $5,000 to various credit card companies. She had obtained these cards more than ten years earlier and said that when she was working steadily and receiving child support, she had been able to manage the payments. When Rhonda's oldest child turned eighteen, her child support payments decreased. She was working only twenty-five hours a week in 2006, and when she lost that job, she was unemployed for several months. She started working in home health care and was getting lots of overtime, but the company switched management, her overtime hours were eliminated, and her regular hours were reduced from forty to thirty-two per week. Every year of the study she talked about her credit card debt, and for several years she talked about wanting to pay it down. In 2009, for example, she said, "I haven't paid them yet, but I am planning on paying them next year. That's what I'm going to do with my income taxes [tax refund], start paying off some of my bills." But 2010 and 2011 were particularly difficult years for Rhonda. Fearing that she would be fired because of a disagreement with her supervisor, Rhonda quit her job, was unemployed for about four months, and then cycled through a series of different jobs before finding one that was more stable. Her children's father also lost his job, and child support payments stopped. In addition, Rhonda's food stamp benefits would stop and start again for no apparent reason. Instead of paying the credit card debt, the income tax refund was used to pay the utility bills and other bills she had gotten behind on owing to all the disruptions to her income and the need to smooth consumption by juggling those payments.

Even women with fairly stable income were engaged in constant consumption smoothing. Jen's income of $22,000 a year covered the essential expenses for her, her daughter, and her niece who lived with her, but there was nothing extra to cover the unexpected. When Jen's car broke down, the only way she could pay for the repairs was to "take away from other things." As a result, she was overdue on the payment for her home security system and started carrying a balance. After catching up on that payment several months later, her daughter became ill and needed to go to the emergency room. Paying for the ER visit caused her to get behind on her cable bill. After settling those debts, she was hit with a very large medical bill for using a provider who was not in her health care network. So the cycle continued.

When I asked the women to describe their monthly bills, the response I got from Brianna provided a fairly representative listing of the types of bills they paid. "I think each month it's [the electric bill] only like $130. Yeah, it's like $130. Rent is $800. The water bill will probably be like fifty or sixty dollars. Phone bill like $70. . . . Whew, cable will be like $100 and something—$130 monthly or something like that. Well, it's cable, and then you know you got the cable and Internet. I got car insurance . . . it's like $200." Brianna paid more rent than the average woman in this study, but her utility bill was lower than average. For a short amount of time, she paid for an alarm system at her home but gave that up. She did have a cell phone, but like nearly everyone else in the study, she had no land line. Her cable bill included an Internet connection, which she needed in order to complete assignments and access materials for the courses she was taking online at a community college.

One of the challenges with any discussion about debt is that people's spending decisions are called into question. Could Brianna and the other women have paid down their debt if they had given up cable, the Internet, and their cell phones? Possibly, but women have good reasons for considering these expenses part of their basic set of bills. Cell phones provide people with a connection to employers (some of whom called with scheduling changes) and to families. Most public libraries offer computers and Internet access to people without those services at home, but libraries have limited hours, and Detroit's financial difficulties have led to the closing of neighborhood branch libraries. When money got extremely tight, these families dropped cable and often car insurance (if they had it in the first place). Nichelle, who at one point was carrying more than $10,000 in debt, dropped cable in 2007 and car insurance in 2009; by 2011 she had reduced her monthly expenses down to rent, utilities, and $50 for her cell phone. Erica always dropped cable service when she was unemployed (and often went without it when she was working). Dorothy had cable when she was living with her adult children, who could help pay the bill, but when she was on her own she didn't have a television, let alone cable.

# Principal Versus Interest

In the parlance of credit card companies, people who carry balances on their cards but pay only the minimum monthly payment (or some other amount lower than the balance) are referred to as "revolvers." Companies charging high interest rates on their cards can make money from revolvers because these customers let interest compound on their balances. For example, assume a person has a $500 balance on a credit card with an 18 percent interest rate. If that person makes payments of $20 a month, she can pay off the balance in about two and a half years, but she will have also paid the credit card company more than $130 in interest.[21] Someone who pays off her credit card balance in full each month is not as profitable for the credit card company, since she does not let interest accrue on the account.

Gwen fit the model of the revolver, because on all of her credit cards she paid "just the minimum" required each month. Gwen was still using her cards, increasing the principal owed and not just the interest. But the women who had stopped using their credit cards were also caught in this trap. Tanya described her use of credit cards as having been driven by irresponsible spending, but the high interest rates and other fees caused her to stop using them. "The interest rate was so high," she said, "and it was like a $35 late fee, a $35 over-the-limit fee, so every month they was charging like an extra $70. And yeah, I had them, I still owe them, the bill was going up higher and higher, and it's hard for me to get caught up."

For a time Tanya stopped paying even the minimum, but interest and other nonpayment penalties continued to accumulate, increasing her debt.

Charlene also voiced frustration that any money she sent to her credit card companies did not seem to make a dent on the balance she owed. She said, "What I'm paying 'em now, it's not even touching my money [principal] at all." She was hoping to enter a credit card hardship program. Most credit card companies have programs that allow cardholders to negotiate temporary, short-term changes to the terms of their cards, such as a lowered interest rate and the suspension of fees. The goal is to keep the cardholder afloat by providing a payment plan that is workable, given their financial circumstances. Such programs are not well advertised and have some potential drawbacks, such as a risk of a lowered credit score for participating.[22] Charlene hoped that by entering such a program, the interest rate on her card would be lowered and she would make some progress toward paying down the principal. Unfortunately, the credit card companies were unwilling to work with Charlene (perhaps because by then she had been laid off and was judged unable to make steady payments). She stopped sending payments and said, "Let them sue me."

In addition to credit cards, most households with utility debt were also facing the challenge of being "revolvers." The regulation of utility services and their practices vary by state, but many states have passed laws that limit the ability of utility providers to disconnect services for nonpayment, particularly in the winter months. In southeast Michigan, households can participate in the local utility company's "shut-off protection plan." Typically, households sign up for this plan when they are overdue on payments and facing a loss of services. Estimated costs for future bills are spread out over twelve equal monthly payments plus equal payments on any unpaid balances, with the goal of paying down the balance while keeping up with current payments. In theory, this plan is very helpful in that families do not have to worry about losing their gas and electricity. However, the reality for the thirty-three households in this study that were in debt to the utility company (most in excess of $1,000) was that increases in rates or higher-than-expected levels of use (for example, during a particularly cold winter) usually prevented them from fully paying off balances by the end of the year. For some of the women, this payment plan did not seem to make any difference in what they owed. Tamara owed $1,800 to the utility company, a large proportion of her income, which was usually $8,000 a year. She said, "It seem like the more and more I pay, it seem like my gas bill just keep going up higher. Don't matter how much I pay, it still just never seems to go down. . . . It seem like when I make a payment, they send me a bill, and it's just like right where [it was]." On the other hand, Tamara never lost service, and she knew exactly how much money she needed to pay each month.

Another form of borrowing that can easily lead to a continuous cycle of debt is the use of payday loans. This type of loan is not offered through a bank but rather by a retailer who provides a borrower with quick cash with an expectation of quick repayment, such as within two weeks (a standard pay period). These loans are usually small (several hundred dollars) and are advertised as useful for people who need money to tide them over until their next paycheck comes. However, payday loans come with exorbitantly high interest rates, typically 391 to 521 percent.[23] For example, an individual might receive a loan for $400 and then two weeks later have to repay the $400 along with a $54 borrowing "fee." Annualized, that $54 comes out to an interest rate on the loan of just under 352 percent. By contrast, the average interest rate for a thirty-year fixed-rate mortgage in 2010 was just under 4.7 percent.[24] If a payday loan cannot be repaid at its due date, the borrower may be able to "roll over" the loan, which essentially is an extension of the loan, with interest being charged until the loan is paid off. (Some states either do not allow this practice or place limits on it.)

Payday loans are one of several products and services that are part of the so-called alternative or fringe financial services sector — "alternative" because this sector is thought to provide an option to people who have difficulty accessing loans through mainstream institutions (for example, because they have poor credit histories), and "fringe" because this sector operates outside of the regulatory framework that governs banks and other financial intuitions. Fringe financial services are not a new phenomenon. In the 1800s and early

1900s, neighborhood "loan sharks" flourished in many communities, lending small amounts of money at very high rates to those who needed cash quickly and were unable to access other forms of credit.[25] Other modern-day fringe services include check-cashing outlets, pawnshops, and rent-to-own retailers.

Payday loans may be used when people need quick cash but lack the credit necessary to take out a loan from a bank or credit union. These loans are fast and convenient: often located in lower-income neighborhoods, they stay open longer hours than banks. The majority of the women in the study said that they never used payday loans, primarily because they understood the cost associated with these financial products, but also because it had never occurred to them to go to such a place. Seven women, however, reported using payday loans; their attitudes about the loans and their experience with them were quite varied. Both Lorraine and Leah had taken out payday loans; Leah had done so multiple times. They said that getting the loan was easy, and they believed that the payday lender was an important institution that was available to them in emergencies. Leah was slightly more ambivalent about the payday loans, in part because she feared getting herself into a cycle of constant use. She said, "I think that you can get caught up in a trap with that—with those payday advances, you know. And then, I—I just don't like being caught up in the traps like that." But she still used payday loans, sometimes to help one of her adult children pay the rent, sometimes for a car repair, and once so that she and her daughter could get their hair done. A couple of times she reported difficulty paying back the loans.

Interestingly, both Leah and Lorraine consistently used the terms "cash advance" or "paycheck advance" rather than "payday loan," despite the fact that we always asked about "payday lenders." Both women were in professional jobs and seemed to view this product as a way to tap into their next paycheck early, rather than as a fringe loan with a very high interest rate. Leah was paid biweekly and said she always got her "cash advance" on the "off weeks" in between paychecks. Further, neither Leah nor Lorraine seemed to realize just how high the interest rate was. In explaining one of her experiences, Leah said, "So I took a $400 loan out, and I have to pay

$54 back interest on that in two weeks. Which, you know, is not bad." In fact, that interest rate, as shown in the example earlier, was more than 350 percent. Leah seemed to think that this was reasonable, however, because Michigan had put in place some regulations of the industry.[26] She said, "The rates are standardized now in Michigan, because the state took control over those places. Because I guess they were charging people too much money. And each [lender] varied. So now it's more controlled, and it is controlled by the state." Leah was right, but the rate cap still left her with an interest rate of 350 percent.

Jen, on the other hand, reported that her experience with a payday lender was "horrible." Jen had been late making her car payment and did not have money in the bank to cover it. So she used a payday lender. She said that the lender subsequently took money directly out of her checking account when she received her next paycheck.

> When the money [paycheck] went in the bank, the payday loan people took my money. I needed to pay my bills, you know, [but] they took my money. So I had to stop my direct deposit just so I could catch up on my bills from the payday loan. Because they come and get that money, oh my goodness, they come and get it. . . . So I had to stop getting the direct deposit, so I could get a [pay-] check to catch up on the little stuff that I couldn't pay because [the payday lenders] were getting they money. And then I got behind with them, and then they started adding fees. And they just started, just kept adding fees.

The lender was not claiming the full amount of her paycheck, just some of it, so that Jen's repayment was being dragged out and interest and fees were accumulating. To put an end to this, Jen closed her bank account and eventually paid off the loan directly to the lender.

Being a revolver—whether from making minimum payments on a credit card, being on a payment plan that did not resolve the underlying problem of debt, or taking out a payday loan—only exacerbated the debt problems faced by these families. But there was an exploitative element as well to their experience of debt. Landowners in the South certainly made money off of sharecroppers by valuing crops at low prices and subsequently selling them on the market at a much higher price, but to be "successful" they also charged high interest rates on equipment, supplies, and anything else the sharecropper needed to buy on loan. The sharecropper was left in debt to the landowner and always had to return the following year to supposedly "work off" the debt. Creditors now make these same types of profits by providing credit for people in financial straits, but then setting up the terms so that the borrower is always left owing.

## Voluntary and Involuntary Repayment

Ideally, people should repay their debts. For a system of borrowing and lending to work, there needs to be trust on the part of the lender that the borrower will repay. With a few exceptions related to very specific debts, the women in the study wanted to pay down their debt. Only thirteen of them, however, made some progress toward that goal by voluntarily making payments to some of the companies they owed, although the amounts paid down were not large and they were often still left with substantial amounts of debt. Most reported that they had stopped answering the phone if they did not recognize the number of the caller, knowing that in all likelihood it was a bill collector. Taking those calls was pointless, many said, because they did not have the money to pay, although occasionally they were able to strike a deal for a workable payment plan. But creditors had one other way to force repayment—through garnishing, or laying claim to portions of their paychecks or tax refunds. Garnishment was something the women hoped to avoid, since it could be extremely disruptive to their already precarious financial lives.

The married-couple households, who had higher (and usually two) incomes, were the most likely to make voluntary payments on their debts. Lisa and her husband had about $26,000 in debt, including student loans, balances on credit cards, and medical bills. In 2008 she paid down the balance on both of her credit cards, but each had only a $500 limit, so the total amount of their debt, at

$25,000, remained basically the same. Tykia, a single mother, was able to pay down her student loans, but the loan was fairly small at $3,000; one year she used her income tax refund to pay off the entire loan. Leah, who was married, had a flexible spending account through her job that allowed her to divert a portion of her paycheck into a fund that she could use to pay for medical expenses not covered by her health insurance. Despite always putting $5,000 in this account each year, Leah was still left with several thousand dollars of medical debt, some of which resulted from paying medical bills for her uninsured young adult children. (This was prior to the implementation of the Affordable Care Act of 2010, which now allows families to keep their children on their health insurance until age twenty-six.) But some of the debt was the result of having to pay for procedures not covered by her health insurance. Unfortunately, she never learned about the lack of coverage until after she had the test done and received the bill.

Setting up a payment plan, as Beth and her husband did with their credit cards, requires that the debtor interact with the business to which she owes money. Some companies collect debts in-house, while others contract with a collection agency that specializes in collecting debts. Typical means of trying to collect include mailing notices to debtors and calling them on the phone. Those who said that they talked with debt collectors on the phone reported varying satisfaction with those calls. The collector who called Brianna about a credit card bill ended up being willing to write off some of her debt, accepting a smaller payment. Carol, who usually did not answer her phone, had a bad experience with a bill collector. She said he "got smart" with her, so she refused to speak with him further. But her next encounter went better. "One day I just answered [the phone]," she said. "I said, 'Let me just get this over with.' He [the bill collector] was decent, and I told him, I said, 'The only reason I'm talking to you is because you're decent.' And I told him the experience I had with their company." In talking further with the collection agent, Carol was able to work out a payment deal. She said, "[The debt] was originally seven hundred some dollars, and I think I had to wind up paying three something. It wasn't much."

Most of the women, however, avoided answering the phone if

they did not recognize the number. Earlier, Carol had told me that she and her daughter had a routine around answering their landline phone: "We just look [at the phone]. Who's that number? If we don't recognize it, we don't answer it. Yeah. Like, you calling me from an 800-number? We don't answer them." Once she told me that, I stopped using the toll-free line I had set up for this project, since my calls would have been showing up on her caller ID as a toll-free number. Occasionally, someone in the house would take a call from an unknown caller, which usually resulted in frustration. Geri said that she often avoided bill collectors, telling them, "Geri is not here," if she answered the phone. Other times, she said, she would tell them that she was not working (which was the truth) and that, as soon as she was, she would start paying. "I'm not working" and "You'll get it [money] when I have it" were common answers from the women when I asked, "What do you tell the collectors?" Tamara once said that she told a creditor, "I can't give you what I don't have," when asked to pay on a bill she owed. The exasperation in her voice as she reenacted this encounter was noticeable. The women wanted bill collectors to show some understanding about their economic circumstances, but the collectors were rarely empathetic and sometimes were rude and sarcastic. Geneva said about collection agencies: "I try not to be rude unless they're rude to me. But usually I tell them, 'When I get it, I'll send it to you.' But if they're really rude, most of the time I'll hang up on them. And that's really unfortunate because I know they just doing their job. But some of them can be really cruel." Lisa tried to get on a payment plan with the holder of her student loan, but they would not take her up on what she offered to pay. She said, "They wouldn't accept [my offer]. Since I'm not working, they wouldn't accept a hundred dollars a month. Well, I think I just got a bad rep [representative] on the phone. One of those, I was like, 'Well, what do you want me to do?' They told me to get a job! I said, 'Okay, I'll call you back when I get a job.'" For the most part, the women reported that bill collectors were like welfare caseworkers. They were unhelpful and failed to understand the circumstances facing families.

Sometimes the women would deliberately not pay a bill. Geri refused to pay an old cell-phone bill because she contended that she had not gone over her allotted minutes, as the bill indicated. And Geneva refused to pay a debt owed to a telecommunications company because that company had been her employer when she was injured on the job. Other studies have found that lower-income households, when faced with choices over which debts to pay with their limited income, will put to the side those that they believe were unfairly assessed or those that arose due to circumstances they deemed unfair.[27] Sometimes, however, women had real reasons to be suspicious. Kendra refused to get on payment plans with two different phone companies, believing that they did not have the correct information about what she owed. Tanya received a phone call from a collection agency regarding a hospital bill from many years earlier. She had no recollection of the charge and thought that it sounded "kind of farfetched to me." She said that the collection agency's claim "didn't sit well with me," and she worried that it was a scam. Tanya might have had good reason to be concerned. Sometimes debtors receive calls, not from their original creditor, and not from a collection agency hired by the creditor, but rather from a representative of a debt-buying company. Debt-buying companies do just what their name implies: they purchase debt from creditors, often credit card companies that have been unable to collect on the debt. The debt-buying company typically purchases the debt for a few cents on the dollar, taking it off of the original creditor's balance sheet. The debt is then owed to the debt-buying company. Instead of continually making calls to those who owe, many debt buyers file suits in small claims court in an effort to collect some or all of the debt. Reviews of some of these cases have found numerous mistakes as well as cases in which the debt was already paid or otherwise discharged. Despite these problems, in the majority of cases the courts find in favor of the debt-buying company, often because the debtor fails to show up in court.[28] Debt buying has become a $100 billion industry.

When a judgment is issued against a debtor, a common way that payment is recouped is through garnishment. Creditors can obtain legal orders allowing them to recover debt from borrowers through the withholding of a portion of the debtor's earnings. The withheld, or garnished, wages go directly to debt repayment. An estimated one in ten working Americans between the ages of thirty-five and forty-four are currently having their wages garnished for debt payment. Further, the majority of requests for judgment come from just a few types of lenders—major credit card companies, large payday loan firms, and debt-buying companies, all of which file thousands of lawsuits at a time.[29] Among the women in this study, having their wages or tax refunds garnished to make repayment or having an item repossessed was as common as paying off a debt voluntarily. Although garnishment certainly helps creditors obtain payment and relieves debtors from some of their debt, it is very disruptive to their financial lives.

Charlene and her family were facing real financial challenges in 2006. As the only people in their network with stable housing, Charlene and her husband housed relatives and friends who had lost their homes. While they had numerous unpaid medical bills and were carrying large credit card balances, Charlene attributed some of her family's debt to having other people living in the house. As she put it, "When people live with you, your light bill get higher, your gas bill get higher, your toilet flush more." In 2008 her paycheck was garnished for an unpaid medical bill from several years earlier when the family was uninsured. She said, "I had doggone near $190 [taken out of each check]. I mean, they took half of my money damn near." To compensate for the lost income, Charlene stopped making payments on certain bills, including her utilities. She said she lived "in fear of any utility truck coming down the street," worrying that her service would be disconnected since she was not on the company's shut-off protection plan. By 2010 her utility debt had skyrocketed and she had lost her job, the family's main source of income. Their power was disconnected and only restored after she paid $800 toward the balance; to pay that $800, she got behind on her mortgage payments. Although other challenges in their lives—job loss, people moving in with them, and lack of health insurance—clearly contributed to their financial distress, Charlene always returned to the garnishment when tracing out the development of their problems, reminding me at every interview, "Remember how I got garnished?"

Nichelle had been through especially hard times over the course of the study. In 2007 she left her abusive husband, fleeing the state. After achieving some stability, Nichelle quit her relatively well-paying job (although prior to that she had feared she would be fired) and struck out on her own by opening her own business. The business quickly ran into difficulties. Nichelle could not pay rent, so in 2009 she decided to move back to Detroit, where a friend offered her a place to stay. She and her three sons moved into an extended-stay hotel when that arrangement did not work out. That summer we met up in her hotel room, which was a small room with two double beds, limited storage space, and a small cooktop and refrigerator. Because Nichelle had worked most of the previous year, she was expecting a rather large tax refund. Her refund was large, but she did not see most of it. As she explained, "I got a refund, but a chunk of it got taken for student loans and then another . . . some more got taken because there was a loan when I was with my ex. So they got me first even though he was the primary person on there. They got me. So what I really had . . . I really had expected for my, um . . . the return to kind of really set things straight, where I could at least have savings in the bank. And it just threw me off." One of the ways in which Nichelle hoped to "set things straight" was to use the refund money to make a security deposit on a rental house. Although the garnishment significantly decreased her student loan debt, Nichelle and her sons ended up staying in the hotel for another year before moving to a shelter.

Some women would check their credit report, not to obtain a credit score (which for nearly all was quite low) but rather to see which outstanding debts were listed on the report. This was a way to keep tabs on which creditors might try to garnish for repayment. Geri owed her bank $700 due to overdrafts and associated fees. In 2007 she was ignoring this debt, saying, "The bank account . . . it ain't went to my bad credit [report] yet. But I know it's coming in the next couple months if I don't get something done. So . . . I know by January, I got until at least [until then] before they put it on my credit report." But even if the debt showed up on their credit report, the women could not predict when garnishment would occur.

The fact that these women faced difficulty in paying down debts because they constantly needed to borrow for everyday expenses, while very frustrating, was not necessarily unexpected. Those who were uninsured but needed medical care knew that going to the doctor would lead to debt. Making partial payments to utility providers, credit card companies, and others that were owed was not their preferred method of budgeting, and they generally knew the consequences of doing so (for example, incurring more debt due to interest). But being garnished took families by surprise and often happened with "back debt" that they had believed they could put aside.

## What Does Bankruptcy Do?

One way to erase debt is to file for bankruptcy. Two types of bankruptcy are available to consumers: In Chapter 7 bankruptcy, or "liquidation," a debtor's assets are sold (with certain exemptions) to pay off creditors, and any remaining debt (again with some exceptions) is discharged, meaning that the debtor is not under obligation to pay it. Chapter 13 bankruptcy, sometimes called "the wage earner's plan," or reorganization, allows those with a steady income to pay back their debts over time, usually five years. It also allows filers to maintain their home (as long as payments are made). A trustee appointed by the court oversees the repayment of debts. Businesses file for Chapter 11 bankruptcy, and cities and municipalities wishing to declare bankruptcy file for Chapter 9.

In part due to concerns about abuse of the bankruptcy code, specifically that too many Chapter 7 bankruptcies were being filed by consumers who had the ability to repay their debts, Congress passed the Bankruptcy Abuse Prevention and Consumer Protection Act (BAPCPA) in 2005. The law includes a "means test" that is intended to limit the ability of higher-income individuals to discharge their debts via Chapter 7.[30] However, other changes may have made bankruptcy more prohibitive for families with very limited income. Filing fees for Chapter 7 bankruptcy were increased, and the law requires that attorneys personally vouch for the accuracy of the information provided by clients. A Government Accountability Office report found that as a result of the changes, attorneys' fees have risen from about $700 to more than $1,000.[31]

Bankruptcy filings dropped immediately after enactment of BAP-CPA. In 2006, the first year of the law's implementation, just under 600,000 nonbusiness Chapter 7 and 13 bankruptcy applications were filed, down from the 1.56 million applications filed in 2004. (Filings in 2005 were even higher, at over 2 million, but some of that increase was likely due to anticipation of the law's passage and the desire to file under the old rules). But by 2011 nonbusiness Chapter 7 and 13 filings were back up, to 1.37 million.[32]

Despite carrying high levels of debt relative to their income, only five of the women — Yvette, Cynthia, Kendra, Jen, and Debbie — had filed for bankruptcy or were still actively in bankruptcy during the time we collected data; another two (Annette and Karla) had filed previously. Their households were not necessarily the ones with the largest amount of debt. Both Cynthia and Marie were carrying about $17,000 in debt, but only Cynthia filed for bankruptcy, while Marie never considered doing so. Kendra had $15,000 of debt, most of which was eliminated after her bankruptcy, but Teresa had $20,000 of debt and never followed through on her plans to file. Similarly, Erica thought about filing for bankruptcy to eliminate the roughly $22,000 of non–student loan debt she held, and she had even gotten as far as filling out some of the paperwork, but other things came up and she never completed the process. Every year we asked the women if they were considering bankruptcy, and the vast majority always said no. Some said that they were "too broke" to file, referring to the fees needed to file and the costs associated with hiring an attorney. And they were correct to be concerned about these costs. When Yvette eventually filed, she reported that, in total, she paid more than $1,200 in various fees and other charges. Debbie's Chapter 13 filing cost even more, at $9,000. Kendra had to borrow money from a friend in order to file. Others thought that the amount of debt they held was not overly large and not enough to justify bankruptcy. And some were adamant that they wanted to be able to pay off their creditors, despite years of being unable to do so.

What can we learn from the experiences of the small number of bankruptcy filers in this study? Previous research that examined more than two thousand bankruptcy filings of middle-class households in the 1990s found that it was precipitated by a major life event, such as divorce, job loss, or a health problem that resulted in a large medical bill.[33] The stories of the women in our study, all of whom were experiencing significant financial distress, help uncover the various events that ultimately result in a decision to file. They made their decision relatively quickly, and some sort of crisis was usually involved, but not of the magnitude of a life event such as divorce. But ultimately, filing for bankruptcy left these families no better off economically than those who did not. Going through bankruptcy offered a temporary reprieve from a backlog of debt, and for some an emotional burden was lifted, but not all debt was erased, and no one saw an improvement in their overall economic situation.

Kendra's debts were not particularly large. She owed money to the utility company and to several phone companies. She also was in debt to an auto dealership for a car that she had purchased six or seven years earlier but that had been repossessed when she missed a number of loan payments. Despite no longer having the use of the car, Kendra remained responsible for the missed payments. She said, "I have to pay that [the car note]. To be totally honest, I do not want to pay it, but I know I have to if I want to get good credit." In 2006 bankruptcy never entered her mind as a possible way to avoid paying off that debt, but then, in 2007, the dealership started garnishing her wages to force repayment. She was also hit with a much larger than usual utility bill at the same time that her paycheck was smaller. When she got behind on those payments, her utilities were eventually disconnected. Then, in addition to garnishing her wages, the dealership went after the little bit of money she had in her checking account: "They [the dealership] also took—not like I had a lot of money in the bank—but they took everything I had in the bank, garnishing it. And I just had no other way to go. At that point, there was nothing. . . . I couldn't have my wages garnishing and, you know, then trying to deal with the lights and gas situation. So there was no other way for me . . . at that point. That's how I felt." Kendra saw no way out of her immediate financial bind. A friend suggested that she talk to a lawyer, who told her that declaring bankruptcy would bring a halt to the garnishment and her utilities would be immediately reconnected. So with money loaned to her by that same friend, Kendra filed for bankruptcy. Within three months her debts were erased, with the exception of the utility bill, but the utility company had put her on a payment plan. Although Kendra was not happy that she had needed to declare bankruptcy, her personal financial crisis was over and the lights were back on.

Yvette's narrative about her bankruptcy filing reveals that the tipping point that precedes a decision to file can be emotional as well as financial. Yvette was deeply in debt, having more than $15,000 in credit card and other debt, a student loan, and a mortgage for a home in a neighborhood where property values were in steep decline. Yet in 2007 she stated that she had not thought about filing for bankruptcy. She was thinking about walking away from her house and letting it go into foreclosure. The house kept her tied to Detroit, and she hoped to leave the state and find new opportunities elsewhere. The expenses associated with the house, such as the homeowner's insurance, the utilities, and the property taxes, were also burdensome. It was the struggle to live on her income, not her debts, that was her biggest financial challenge.

Filing for bankruptcy and letting her house go into foreclosure gave her a way to erase some of this debt, but when she talked about her decision-making process, the difficulties in her home life, rather than her financial life, came to the fore:

> One of the reasons why I decided to—not just the struggle of trying to keep all the bills paid and everything, and keep the house and everything like that—but mentally, I was just exhausted. I have the older boys . . . young men in the city under so much negative influence. The gambling, the drugs, the alcohol, the theft, I mean, you know, just all different kinds of criminal activity. You know, and by me being at work or gone from the house eleven hours out the day, the two or three hours I was able to spend with them and say, "Do the right thing. Do the right thing. Represent me well," it was outweighed by the other eighteen hours of influence that the neighborhood had on the kids. So I was fighting a losing battle.

While Yvette was at work, her older sons, out of school and unemployed, stayed at home, running with a rough crowd. They played dice on the front porch, smoked cigarettes and pot in the house, and managed to break several of her windows and the garage doors while "playing" with some guns. Her sales job was paying her less and less as she struggled to convince people to purchase more services from her employer, even as the economy tanked, and she was tired. She said, "Everything that I had spent all these years struggling as a single parent to try to save up the money to put it into the house, to try to provide [them] with a nice home. . . . At this point I don't have any peace, I'm stressed out, my—I mean, I have to keep my job because there's no other jobs out here, so I have to go through what I'm going through. But I need to downsize these expenses that I have, and get all of this excess baggage and weight off of me." In her mind, however, the "excess baggage" and the expenses she needed to downsize were her sons and the money she spent to repair damage they had done to the house. She ended the story of her bankruptcy and foreclosure by saying, "This [house] isn't even worth me trying to hold on to. It's not worth it. It's not worth it, so I'm just gonna walk away. That's all." With much of her debt eliminated, Yvette moved with her younger children to an apartment in the far northern suburbs of Detroit. She barred her older sons from moving along with her. Yvette felt relief at having the "weight" lifted from her shoulders, yet had to concede that her attempts to better her family's life by providing them with a nice home had come to naught.

When discussing their experience with bankruptcy, both Jen and Debbie said that they had filed in order to "keep a car." Their filings had taken place before the study started, Jen filing for Chapter 7 and Debbie and her husband for Chapter 13. In retelling the circumstances that led up to filing for bankruptcy, Jen said that at the time her hours at work had slowed down and she was having difficulty paying her bills. She was threatened with repossession of her car, so, as she said, "I filed bankruptcy just to keep a car." The handling of vehicles—and indeed, all secured debts—during a Chapter 7 bankruptcy proceeding is complicated; the debtor typically has several options: (1) return the car; (2) pay off the remaining balance of the loan to the creditor; or (3) work out a payment plan with the creditor.[34] Likewise, Debbie and her husband filed for

Chapter 13 bankruptcy when his car was repossessed. Debbie's husband had been unemployed for six months, but with Debbie working numerous part-time jobs, they could keep up with most of their bills, although not his car payment. Just as her husband found a job, his car was repossessed. It was his car payments that became the issue. She said, "But he had to have his car to go back and forth to work. I had, I mean actually at the time of bankruptcy, the only things we were actually even behind on was his car. We were not behind on my vehicle; we were not behind on the house. Our utilities were a little behind, but primarily it was because they took his car." By filing for Chapter 13 bankruptcy, as she explained it, they were able to get the car back and continue making payments on it through their trustee. Debbie did not seem to regret filing for bankruptcy; she saw it as a way to make sure they did not lose one of their financial lifelines, her husband's car.

Cynthia owed money to many different companies—several phone companies, medical providers, and the utility company. She also filed for Chapter 13 in the hopes of being able to stay in her house. Since she could not afford the monthly payments to the trustee, she ended up losing her home anyway. Cynthia said that her debts, including a loan from a local nonprofit and several thousand dollars of medical debt, were "put back on me, so it [filing for bankruptcy] actually didn't resolve anything." Nevertheless, she reported that "I'm still seeing things disappear off my [credit report]. It's just, like it's just being wiped off my credit report." When our interviewer asked her that year how this happened, Cynthia, a deeply religious woman, said, "I don't think I [cleared up the debt]. I think Jesus did. Because a lot of things that I owed came to me as paid in full. I had a $2,000 gas bill, gas and light bill. When I called to set up my gas and light bill before I moved over here, I was calling to set up payment arrangements so I could get my gas and light bill, and when I called I didn't owe them anything. So I think a lot to do with prayer and Jesus was clearing up my debt." However much prayer and faith may have helped Cynthia get through difficult times, the larger debts in her bankruptcy filing were still there. And she was engaged. Not wanting to enter her marriage being in debt, she filed for Chapter 7 bankruptcy in 2008. In 2011 she characterized herself as "debt-free," even though she had subsequently taken out $20,000 in student loans for her online course work and would need to start making payments soon.

Bankruptcy, at least in theory, is supposed to provide filers with a "fresh start" or a "clean slate" financially, but for those with unstable incomes or ongoing financial challenges, the fresh start may never happen.[35] Kendra, Yvette, Jen, and Debbie certainly were not much better off financially in the years after bankruptcy. Cynthia's financial situation was perhaps somewhat improved, but she had gotten married to someone who worked or received UI benefits when he was not working. And bankruptcy did not eliminate all debt. Federal student loans, for example, are very difficult to discharge through bankruptcy; the filer must demonstrate that repayment of the loan will cause undue hardship. Cynthia still had $20,000 in student loans. She had graduated in 2011 and had not yet started making payments, but presumably she would need to do so in the future. Yvette had been making steady payments of $250 a month on her student loan, but she still owed more than $26,000. Debbie went back to school in 2010 and took out loans to supplement the financial aid she was receiving. By 2011, she estimated, she had $10,000 in loans and she had not yet finished her bachelor's degree. Shortly after discharging her debts, Kendra received a credit card application. Individuals who have gone through bankruptcy are usually perceived to face difficulty in obtaining credit in the future, but any negative consequences tend to be short-lived.[36] Kendra rapidly accumulated four new credit cards and started carrying balances. While all of the cards had very low credit limits ($300 or less), she admitted that they carried very high interest rates. Kendra said that she used the cards only for emergencies or unexpected expenses, but then quickly noted that occasionally she had to use the cards to pay bills, potentially beginning the cycle of debt accumulation again.

Filing for bankruptcy certainly provided an emotional relief for Kendra and Yvette. Being in bankruptcy got the electricity turned on for Kendra and took a "huge weight" off of her shoulders; it provided a reason for Yvette to walk away from a family situation that was spiraling out of control. But emotions went both ways for

Yvette. She had put time, effort, and money into building a good life for her children, and she had done it on her own, as a single mother. For her, leaving her house and having to declare bankruptcy was a relief but also a letdown. She said, "Just the whole separation issue of walking away from everything that I had invested so many years in trying to build and maintain. So that was—that was just really hard, real emotional." The experience of bankruptcy, Kendra said, made her pay more attention to her finances and budgeting, in part because she never wanted to file again. Having gone through bankruptcy did not seem to leave much of an impression on Cynthia. She was focused on her future, renovating a house she and her husband had purchased and finding a new job. For Debbie, going through bankruptcy was easy compared to what came next for her: realizing that her husband was abusing the children. And once he hit Debbie, she quickly put plans in motion to go. She and the children left in the middle of the night, without any money or identification (her husband had taken all of that away) and just the clothes on their backs. She, too, was focusing on building a new life for herself.

Unfortunately, filing for bankruptcy does have significant repercussions, most notably a negative effect on one's credit score. According to FICO, individuals with very high scores can expect to see a large drop in their score, while those whose scores are already fairly low might see a smaller drop (from an already low base value).[37] Yvette's score plummeted. She said, "Yeah, I think it's like in the 490s or something. It's really low, but then I guess with the bankruptcy on there, then I guess nobody wants to, like, loan you anything or give you any money because they think you don't have a way of paying it back or something." She reasoned, however, that her low score did not matter because she was not trying to obtain any credit cards or take out any loans. Jen said that her score was about 590, an improvement from a low of 550. She had tried to get a loan to buy a car, but was denied because of her low score.

Today credit scores are not just used in the loan business but are increasingly used by landlords when making rental decisions and sometimes by employers before offering jobs. The rationale in the housing market is that the credit score will be a good predictor of the ability to pay rent, while an employer may not want to hire an applicant with financial problems out of concern that he or she might steal from the company. Employers may also use the credit score as a general proxy for responsibility.[38] None of the bankruptcy filers in the study, however, brought up this concern.

Interestingly, Kendra said that her credit score was higher after she had gone through bankruptcy. She did not know why, but perhaps the credit cards she obtained helped boost her score; many online bankruptcy advice sites say that getting a credit card or two post-bankruptcy can help boost a credit score, assuming that the holder pays down the balance every month.

After bankruptcy everyone still had debt, and their prospects for being able to pay down that debt, including large student loan amounts, did not seem good. It may seem somewhat drastic that Jen and Debbie entered into bankruptcy to "save a car." Debbie and her then-husband were not behind on any other payments, and Jen's level of debt was not particularly high (a couple of thousand dollars relative to her $25,000 a year salary). A short-term loan might have helped both families keep their cars. Similarly, Kendra's immediate problem was having her utilities shut off. Federal dollars, distributed via states, are available to help households with their utility payments, but funding levels are low, and many times states run out of money before serving all who need help.[39] More funding for such programs might have helped Kendra avoid bankruptcy, although the wage garnishment would not have been addressed. Bankruptcy might have been the best option for Kendra, but again, she was still left with significant amounts of student debt, as was Cynthia.

During the study, only Annette was able to clear herself of all debt without filing for bankruptcy (although she had filed in the early 2000s), but she paid a steep price in doing so. Annette had been married until 2003, when her husband died. She had always worked, but without his income the bills starting piling up. So she declared Chapter 13 bankruptcy, and the court-appointed trustee was to make monthly payments to her creditors on her behalf. In 2004 she lost her data entry job. She was able to manage for a while by taking on a part-time job she found working at a grocery store.

One day in 2005 Annette came home to find an eviction notice on her door. As she explained it, the trustee had not been paying the property taxes on the house. Annette had been making payments to the trustee, but somehow those payments were not making their way to the City Treasurer's Office. She then lost her part-time job after a customer complained about Annette's behavior, making accusations that Annette said were untrue. Annette was allowed to exit bankruptcy, since she had no income, and in a bid to save her house, she sold it to her daughter and son in-law, who were already living there with Annette. Soon afterward, mother and daughter got into a fight, and Annette was asked to leave.

With no income except a small food stamp benefit, Annette had few options. She moved in with a male friend, someone she had known for a while but with whom she was not particularly close. When I asked her what he did, she said, "I don't get in his, I don't even ask him none of his business. I don't know, he just says he's retired and I leave it at that." In exchange for a roof over her head, Annette purchased their food with her stamps. In 2008 she was able to find a job as a caretaker for a friend's elderly mother. When she filed her taxes, her refund was garnished to pay for an old credit card bill that was not settled during the bankruptcy. Once she started working, she stopped receiving Medicaid, so when she went to the emergency room in 2008 and was admitted to the hospital, she ended up with a $10,000 bill. The hospital eventually wrote off that debt, classifying her as a "hardship" case. In 2011 Annette could say she was "debt free," but she also had very little money to her name, earning just $8.50 an hour in a part-time job and receiving a small amount of food stamps. She had long ago lost all of her possessions when she was unable to pay a storage bill, and she remained dependent on her male friend for housing. For Annette, staying out of debt meant living precariously in the most bare-bones way possible.

# Conclusion

Debt was a fixture of these families' lives. Abandonment by the social safety net contributed to their need to accrue debt just to meet basic needs. They were also shut out of opportunities to use debt as a tool for building wealth. The degrees the women obtained left them deep in debt from student loans but still with jobs that paid little or did not offer the hoped-for improvements in salaries. The mortgages they took out were for homes that plummeted in value. Some of these debts might have not been so large if the financial products offered to these families did not come with high interest rates and other fees. The social abandonment these women experienced left them in the red year after year. And bankruptcy did not wipe the slate clean.

Sharecropping died out when the mechanization of farming greatly reduced the need for human labor and when African Americans headed north as part of the Great Migration, hoping for better opportunities. We do not need to wait, however, for technological change and shifting historical forces to put an end to social abandonment. Remedies exist to undo the damage.

## ✺ CHAPTER 7 ✺

## MAKING ABANDONED FAMILIES
## STRIVING FAMILIES AGAIN

In 2006, when we began interviewing the women profiled in this book, Michigan's unemployment rate was about 7 percent, which was higher than the national average of around 4.7 percent. Most of the women believed that the economy and their own economic circumstances were experiencing a temporary downturn and that their position would improve.

Tamara, perhaps the epitome of a low-wage striver, was working two jobs, one in an assisted living facility and the other as a caretaker for her grandparents. She saw her financial situation as being more difficult in 2006, since she had previously been working in a better-paying job and living with her grandparents, who paid all of the bills. They had moved out of the house, however, leaving Tamara to take care of it and handle the associated expenses. Nevertheless, Tamara was confident that her life was going to get better soon because she was going to school. At that point, she believed that she would be finished eighteen months later. Even Geneva, who had been through so much physically and emotionally, fought to remain upbeat. She said, "Sometimes I feel like life has handed me a really raw deal," but then added, "There's nowhere else to go except up. I've already been down there, and if I have to go back down there, at least I'll know how to deal with it, if I do."

Lisa was actually feeling pretty comfortable in 2006. She said that she could always be doing better, "but I can't complain. I mean, you look at other people's situations and you really can't complain because, you know, I really have to say that I'm blessed that my business has done well. And you know, I had enough money saved to carry at least to this point, so can't complain."

Fast-forward to 2008. This was a presidential election year, and many women were excited about the possibility of either an African American or female president. (Only Sharon said that she was a Republican.) Geneva said that the election in the fall would be one thing that would get her out of the house. She said, "It's amazing for me to see how far the country has come. I know that we have our problems with the economy and everything, but it's amazing to see that an African American may be the next president." Tamara had been getting more hours at work in 2008, and she had received a raise, albeit a small one. Tamara was also having some problems with the welfare office, but she felt confident enough about her situation to say that very soon she was going to ask to be taken off of food stamps.

It was also in 2008 that Lisa's house caught on fire. I found her in a cramped apartment, in a complex where the buildings were so packed together that it felt claustrophobic just walking outside. They had lost everything, including the income from the day care business Lisa had been running out of the home, and were left with only a few possessions. But Lisa was thinking about the future, figuring out what kind of business she might open next and looking at houses they could move into and ones they could use as investment properties. By 2011, Lisa had discovered the real estate guru and was captured by his positive way of thinking and message of hope. She did not want to think about the economy (except to hope that the housing market would be favorable to their plans to start flipping houses). The seminars and the guru's books had helped her through a period of depression, and it was good to see her looking better. She did acknowledge, however, that even positive thinking had its limits: "Every time we try to get ahead, you know, something comes on us."

Therein lay the problem for Lisa, Geneva, Tamara, and all the other women in the study. Despite their best efforts to get ahead or just stay afloat, they never could. By 2011, Tamara had been fired after being injured on the job, and that same employer was trying to make sure she could not collect unemployment. Lisa had poured time and money into learning about real estate, only to find herself owning a home that needed a tremendous amount of work before it could be flipped; with all of her money tied up in that investment, she had been forced to live in the house, which was in a neighborhood she had not realized had a high crime rate. Geneva had tried to follow the recipe for success: go to school, get trained to perform a job for which there is high demand, and buy a home to develop a nest egg for the future. All that had left her with were outstanding student loans, a mortgage she could not afford, and a job that was not what she trained to do, making wages that left her worse off than when she was receiving disability benefits.

These women and their families were not socially isolated. Social isolation implies dislocation from the mainstream. Yes, many received some form of public assistance, but mostly because of the quality of their jobs, and any assistance they received was hard to come by. Otherwise, they were doing everything expected of American citizens who want to get ahead: working, buying homes, becoming more educated. They were striving to achieve the American Dream, but somewhere along the way the promise of these engines for inclusion, upward mobility, and protection was lost, leaving them abandoned.

What is life like if you are part of the abandoned class? You probably work in a job that has no prospect for upward mobility and in an isolating work environment where you are unlikely to come into contact with people who might help you find better jobs. These jobs are also precarious—a term we often hear used in reference to the growth of temporary and contract work and now the rise of the "gig economy." The precariousness you face in these jobs stems not only from their temporary nature but also from working for employers who blatantly violate the few rules still in place that protect workers, who are arbitrary and capricious, and who actively thwart your attempts to receive safety net benefits when you are let go. If you are an abandoned worker like Tamara, you are paid low wages, are not given enough hours on the job to be able to bring home a decent paycheck, and have to spend a great deal of effort getting the public assistance benefits you need because your income is so low. When you are no longer of use to your employer, as happened with Tamara when she was injured, you are tossed to the side. And you are invisible — not just to the larger world but to the employer as well. A worker who an employer has never met is a worker who is much easier to fire.

If jobs are so bad, then why not get more education and get a better job? Because going to school is very challenging when, like Cynthia, you have to keep a job, care for your children, and try to find time to complete course work in the wee hours of the night. Once you have your degree, perhaps from an online-only institution, perhaps from a for-profit school, you find that it is worth very little. What you do have is debt.

You will always have debt. The debt is from student loans, from an underwater mortgage, and from the credit cards you used when there was no safety net to catch you. Some debt might be small and from long ago, but with your low income, you don't have any extra money to pay it off. Then some company decides that it's time for them to get paid, and all of a sudden your paycheck or tax refund is garnished.

You may have wanted to use that tax refund, as Nichelle intended to do, for a deposit on a rental unit for you and your kids, but instead you are living in a hotel room. If you are able to escape to the suburbs, you find yourself hidden away from the rest of the community. If you move a lot, you have had to abandon many of your possessions. If you stay put, you may watch the neighborhood around you slip away, the casualty of a mortgage crisis in which the perpetrators were bailed out but you and your neighbors were not.

And what if you are among the poorest of the poor? The abandonment of the poorest women in this study was profound. In 2006 Marie was quite depressed. She hadn't worked in three years, and she was facing a large bill from years of unpaid property taxes. At one point her electricity was disconnected (but she had "solved" the problem by running an extension cord across the street to a neighbor's house). She had an open case with Child Protective Services, she was on probation, and she had started drinking. She was also being abused by her on-again-off-again boyfriend. She managed to get sober for a time, but by 2011 she was back to drinking and using drugs. Her children had been taken away from her for a year but subsequently returned. We were talking in a park, since by then she was all but homeless—two years earlier she had faced eviction but her house burned to the ground before that happened. She had been deemed eligible for disability benefits, but she was receiving no help for any of her many challenges. The only systems she was attached to—criminal justice and Child Protective Services—were ones she did not want to confide in to get help. If she did, in all likelihood her children would be gone again. If, like Marie, you are truly abandoned, then you have been cast aside, possibly left to collect disability checks, but connected to no institutions that can help you.

By 2011, many of the women recognized this abandonment and were angry about it. Geneva was angry. We were talking about proposed cuts to food stamps and Medicaid, and she said, "I just, I honestly don't understand how, I'm trying to word this in a really nice way, but the ones that are at the top that have the money, why are you, why you feel you should get some additional breaks when down here, it's just, horrible. If we could trade places. . . . I think that that should be a law before cutting [benefits]. All of those people are crying tax breaks, come down here and live for thirty days. That should be, that should be the law. Then you can have your tax breaks." Tamara was similarly outraged about the thought of benefits being cut: "How are you going to cut something [food, medical care] that people can't afford anyway? We can't afford it! And I don't know if they're looking at it from peoples who's making $100,000 to $200,000 a year. Maybe they can afford that. Me personally, I can't afford that."

Others voiced similar concerns. Lorraine wanted to talk about income inequality and tax policy. She said, "So, how can [the government] not raise taxes? The question is, who do you put that burden on? Do you put that burden on people who actually have the money and will not necessarily miss the money? Or do you spread it out equally that we all bear responsibility? So how do you do that? You tax one class heavily, heavier than another class . . . or . . . you tax certain class of people just right out of existence." By certain class, she meant people like herself, who were struggling to get by, despite getting an education and playing by all of the rules. Tanya also reflected on this issue, saying, "So there's no middle class. You're either rich or you're poor." And Tanya considered herself poor.

Women feared that no one cared about them and the issues they faced. They knew they had been abandoned, and it was hurtful. Geneva got tears in her eyes as she talked about what she would tell the country's policymakers if she had the opportunity: "Don't just throw us away. Don't look down on us because [you think we're] always here asking for something." Beth made a plea for government to consider what people's daily lives were really like:

> I think policymakers, a lot of policymakers, they see it from the outside and not in the inside. I think someone should take the experience of seeing what it's really like, you know. You have so many people out there that are rich, and they put Detroit down. But they don't know what it's like. But you don't know what it's like. You don't know that we can't go get a job. Or sometimes, even people that have college degrees, now you can't get a job, in the, you know, the field. So you know, I think they need to, instead of you sitting back and judging or talking, you need to experience what we're experiencing.

Aleta voiced a very similar sentiment: "I think that if policymakers put, put theirselves in other people's position, if they just walked a mile in somebody else's shoes, then they would know how other people feel. And then there would be more attention to the needs of other people. Because a lot of people, a lot of people, are just taken for granted, just because people don't know."

"Walk a mile in my shoes" can sound tired and trite, but there is a reason Aleta used this phrase. The problems and challenges faced by abandoned families are not being addressed. Aleta was charitable to believe that the lack of concern was due more to ignorance of the issues than to not caring, but Geneva believed that at least some of the neglect stemmed from stereotypes held by those in power about people who need help and from a sense that the poor—par-

191

ticularly poor African Americans—are throwaway people, deserving of separate and unequal treatment.

So what can be done to help abandoned families and provide them with the opportunities for inclusion and mobility that everyone deserves, so that their striving is not all for naught? When Wilson was writing *The Truly Disadvantaged,* urban poverty was geographically concentrated and economically isolated from most of the middle class, from jobs, and from opportunity. Some of the policy prescriptions he suggested to help socially isolated individuals included on-the-job training and apprenticeships for youth that would expose them to the world of work and quality child care for single mothers so that they could work. I am simplifying Wilson's recommendations, but his goal was to find a way to incorporate the socially isolated not only into the world of work but into larger U.S. society. Work would be the mechanism for combating social isolation and reconnecting the socially isolated to all of the opportunities available in this country. Additionally, Wilson recommended that policies be "race-neutral." Even though he described social isolation as a problem primarily affecting minority urban poor, he was concerned that interventions targeted to the disadvantaged would not have public support.

Given the social transformations over the last several decades, policies need to go far beyond preparing people for work. Fundamentally, social abandonment supports systems that perpetuate racial inequalities, so perhaps not all should be race-neutral. We need to dismantle the modern-day equivalents of separate and unequal and remove people from the bonds of debt-driven sharecropping.

## A Worker's Bill of Rights

It is difficult to imagine how policy might go about directly dealing with the workplace isolation experienced by some women, but much could be done to better protect workers and shift some of the balance of power away from employers and to employees. The idea of a worker's bill of rights is not original. A number of advocacy organizations working on behalf of certain occupations (such as restaurant employees or domestic workers) have proposed such bills, and San Francisco adopted a bill of rights for retail workers.[1] Provisions in these bills typically include guaranteeing a minimum number of hours a week, giving workers more input in their scheduling, and enabling part-time workers to obtain full-time work if it becomes available.

The ability to organize should also be a fundamental right of workers. Collective bargaining provides the power in numbers that can help workers improve their wages, hours, and working conditions. Worker organizations can also provide a vehicle for enforcement of existing rights by making sure that laws such as the Americans with Disabilities Act are followed and serving as an intermediary when employees have grievances. Although efforts have been made here and there to organize Walmart workers, fast-food workers, and others in the service sector, existing unions have not placed very much emphasis on incorporating these workers into their membership. A greater push in this area is particularly needed since many states, including Michigan, have passed "right to work" laws. These laws ostensibly offer workers more choice by banning compulsory payment of union dues for classes of jobs covered by collective bargaining agreements. But the laws can weaken unions if workers opt out of paying membership and the costs associated with union representation are increasingly borne by fewer and fewer members or the union loses its bargaining power because it simply cannot afford to support the cost.

One other very important right is the right to better pay. One reason work is not a mechanism for social inclusion is that the pay in low-wage jobs is so paltry that it keeps people living in poverty. Most women were making wages low enough that they still qualified for public assistance. The federal minimum wage is only $7.25 an hour, and many workers are trying to support themselves and their families on wages at this level. The current efforts across the country to raise the minimum wage are a step in the right direction. Leaving it to states and localities to make increases on their own will only lead to greater inequality in wages across states. The federal government needs to take action on this issue and follow the lead of states and localities that have implemented $15-an-hour minimum wages.

## Fixing the Safety Net

It seems apparent that the safety net in place for poor families, low-wage workers, and even the middle class is inadequate and sometimes barely functions. Many low-wage workers have difficulty accessing the Unemployment Insurance program because they did not accumulate enough earnings or hours before they lost their jobs. Many states have tried to "modernize" their UI programs—for example, by not excluding the most recent quarter of earnings when determining eligibility (as noted in chapter 5), or by providing benefits to individuals who leave jobs for serious family reasons, which happens more often among low-wage working women than other workers.[2] Low-wage workers are still workers, and some system needs to be in place to help them during times of job loss. Additionally, providing more information to workers about UI and its rules could be beneficial, since many less-educated workers perceive themselves to be ineligible and never apply for these benefits.[3]

The financing of the system also provides incentives to employers to deny their former employees access to UI benefits. Changing the funding of UI would be one way to avoid the kind of contestation of benefits that Sharon and Tamara experienced. Alternatively, a pot of money could be set aside that would provide temporary UI to people whose claims are being disputed. If the claim is found in favor of the employee, the employer would have to pay a fine (in addition to any back benefits). If the claim is found in favor of the employer, the filer would have to pay a fine, which might deter someone like Erica from trying to apply.

Perhaps it is time for a wholesale rethinking of the systems currently in place for assisting families who have real difficulty getting jobs and keeping jobs, as well as those who are not able to work at all—the truly abandoned. TANF might be converted to something like a "temporary and partial work waiver," a program proposed by the economist Rebecca Blank to serve people like Marie who otherwise slip through the cracks. Instead of enforcing a work requirement, the program could focus on providing social services to address the needs of the client. It would provide a way for Marie to get substance abuse treatment without having to go through the criminal justice or child welfare systems. Such a program could help people with more challenges prepare to eventually take jobs, and it could assist those with serious problems, like Dorothy and Miss Price, in moving onto the disability rolls. Once on disability, however, these individuals should not be forgotten.

Altering TANF and expanding UI would need to be accompanied by significant administrative changes in the offices that oversee these and other benefit programs. Nearly all states allow online applications for certain programs, reducing the need for in-person visits.[4] (Although, Nichelle had once filled out an online application but still waited a year to have her case opened.) Public benefit offices should be provided with the means to increase the efficiency and accuracy of their case processing. Given technological advances, this task should be doable, although it would require making funding available and prioritizing efforts to address the problem. Some offices may require additional staff, particularly during times of great economic need. These programs also need greater accountability. Some of the waits for benefits that the women in this study experienced were severely harmful financially, and the stress put on them was sometimes borderline abusive.

More than benefits, these women wanted jobs. That was the number-one request when we asked what they most wanted from the government. We hear so frequently that it is not the government's role to create jobs, that job creation is better left to the private sector. Thus far, however, leaving job creation to the private sector has resulted in sluggish job growth in the aftermath of the Great Recession. Even if the economy roars again, history tells us that periods of slow growth will occur in the future. When jobs are scarce, I would argue, government does have a role in providing employment opportunities. In a city like Detroit, there is a lot of work to be done. Playgrounds could be restored, sidewalks repaired, and recreation centers staffed. We have insisted that parts of our safety net be focused on work, so it only seems fair that when jobs are scarce, offering opportunities to earn a wage and gain or retain skills is the responsibility of government. We did this once before during the Great Depression, and during the Great Recession, Congress authorized the states to use TANF "Emergency Funds" to run supported employment programs. No large-scale evaluation of the effectiveness of these programs was conducted, but the research that does exist shows that participants were later able to find unsubsidized employment, and at wages higher than those of a control group.[5] A program such as this would help low-wage workers who are in between jobs.

# Financial and Educational Inclusion: Regulation and New Programs

Access to credit is an important part of financial inclusion in the twenty-first century, but access via bad financial products can financially cripple a household. Reforms such as capping fees and interest rates and other measures that make credit cards less risky would be one mechanism of protection.[6] The Credit Card Accountability, Responsibility, and Disclosure Act of 2009 makes progress in this regard by limiting fees on the types of low-limit cards that many of the study households held. The act also requires card issuers to state, in "plain" language, the terms of the card and also requires issuers to provide holders with information about how long it would take to pay off the card's balance if only minimum payments are made. However, lack of funds, rather than lack of information, seemed to be a much bigger issue for these families. For families already in debt, providing assistance and advocates who can help them work to arrange reasonable and perhaps flexible payment plans with creditors could help them avoid garnishment, a practice that upset, often unexpectedly, the plans that some women in this study had for their limited finances. Individuals who are being garnished might be referred to legal representatives, since garnishment orders are typically modified or reversed through court proceedings. Community organizations have made great strides in helping low- and moderate-income families to claim EITC benefits at tax time, so perhaps adding debt management services and legal counseling to existing tax preparation services would be beneficial.[7]

The practice of garnishment itself should be much better regulated. Garnishment caught these women by surprise, and a few believed that being garnished was at the root of their financial troubles. Many of the debts for which women were garnished were old and not necessarily ones that they remembered having or were making it a priority to pay. Since the onset of the Great Recession, debt collection through the court system has become increasingly popular. Very frequently, the debtor fails to come to court and a wage or property garnishment is put into place. These sorts of default judgments hurt those who may not understand the process and certainly those who cannot afford representation. And representation should be available since so much of the credit offered to low-income individuals is predatory to begin with. Additionally, with firms sometimes filing thousands of these documents, inaccurate and outdated information is sometimes used, and individuals may be garnished for debts that are not theirs or for amounts that exceed what they owe.[8] More transparency and more accountability over this process is needed.

The next "industry" that needs to be examined for predatory practices is for-profit educational institutions. Are they offering training that is of any value? Do their graduates get better jobs? How much debt do students have after completion? These are questions that are starting to be explored by the federal government, but given the large numbers of disadvantaged students who pass through their halls (sometimes virtual), this is a matter of some urgency. Additionally, we need more research on the effectiveness of online delivery of postsecondary education. Given many of the women's preference for the flexibility offered by online options, we should be doing all we can to understand the best ways to deliver this type of education and the circumstances under which it best works.

Doubts about the benefits of promoting homeownership have been raised in the aftermath of the housing bust. For those who become homeowners, greater regulation of the mortgage industry could help ensure that, like credit cards, the products offered and the means by which they are given are not predatory in nature. But putting all of a family's hope for building wealth into homeownership is not the answer either, particularly since the appreciation of homes seems to have slowed down. As long as patterns of racial and economic segregation continue, inequalities in wealth-building opportunities, and racial wealth inequalities in particular, will persist. Darrick Hamilton and William Darity have proposed that the United States adopt "baby bonds," a type of child savings account available to children whose parents have lower than median levels of wealth.[9] It would be progressive, in that those with lower wealth would receive larger bonds. The bonds could be cashed in at age eighteen and used as a base for further wealth building in the future.

# Reparations

After we make changes to these various institutions so that they do not produce separate and unequal outcomes, it is time to target the larger, underlying structural issue: systemic racism. Of all of the suggested policy reforms, reparations is probably the most controversial. Although this idea received no traction when I raised it with a group of public policy students in 2009, the writer Ta-Nehisi Coates has since brought the discussion of reparations into the mainstream.[10] The problems faced by the urban poor that Wilson described and the continued challenges faced by economically vulnerable African American families today are rooted in the legacy of slavery, according to Coates:

> Having been enslaved for 250 years, black people were not left to their own devices. They were terrorized. In the Deep South, a second slavery ruled. In the North, legislatures, mayors, civic associations, banks, and citizens all colluded to pin black people into ghettos, where they were overcrowded, overcharged, and undereducated. Businesses discriminated against them, awarding them the worst jobs and the worst wages. Police brutalized them in the streets. And the notion that black lives,

black bodies, and black wealth were rightful targets remained deeply rooted in the broader society.[11]

We cannot undo the damage that Coates describes, but we can start to repair it.

Reparations would provide a payment to African Americans in acknowledgment not only of the harm that their ancestors suffered under slavery and Jim Crow but also of the wealth those slaves helped build for the country and the wealth that neither they nor their progeny ever enjoyed. Any wealth blacks in the early- and mid-twentieth century might have accumulated was then stolen through sharecropping, and it continues to be stripped away today through residential segregation, bad mortgages, student loan debt for second-rate education, high-interest credit cards, and the burdens of debt that keep families in a state of always owing and never getting ahead. Reparations would also force this country to grapple with, recognize, and disassemble the systems that have continually emerged here to maintain racial inequality. Darity has laid out various methods for calculating reparations, including using "40 Acres and a Mule" as a baseline for determining the amount that should be distributed.[12] As he points out, this phrase is not just part of folklore but was written into the proposed legislation that would have redistributed land to freed slaves had it passed. Representative John Conyers has been introducing reparations bills in Congress since 1989.

Politically, changes in these directions would require bold thinking and action. And money. Implementing a policy of reparations would require a change in mind-set for this country, where we like to believe that racism does not exist and that our institutions are not separate and unequal. But the imperative is urgent. Perhaps more than we realize, we are becoming a country where not just urban dwellers with very low incomes are locked out of opportunity, but middle-class families are denied opportunity as well. Although families of all races and ethnicities have experienced social abandonment, it is particularly a problem in black communities. The very institutions that once promoted opportunity and inclusion have changed in ways that have left too many families abandoned, lacking in hope, and convinced that those in power care little about their plight.

However, social abandonment can be undone. Individuals and families are not meant to be "thrown away," as Geneva said, and we as a nation need to find the will to bring abandoned families back into the fold.

# METHODOLOGICAL APPENDIX

This study did not start out with a focus on social abandonment but rather evolved over time in terms of both its focus and the sampling decisions, the women who were recruited, the interviewers who were involved, and the questions that we asked. Before discussing those decisions, I believe it is important to recognize my position and how that may influence what is presented in these pages. Although I am trained in quantitative methods and have been and continue to be involved in studies that use survey data sets for analyses, one of the aspects of qualitative work that I have always been drawn to is the research process itself, which allows me to uncover topics and phenomena that I might not otherwise have thought about, or thought important. I also enjoy the opportunity that qualitative research provides to bridge at least some of the distance between the people participating in the study and the researcher. That said, as a white woman who lives in the affluent city of Ann Arbor, Michigan, is a highly educated and well-compensated researcher, and has personally experienced only a very few of the challenges the respondents discussed, I naturally come to these types of interviews from a position of privilege. In the end, I will never know exactly how that affected my interactions with the women in this study and what they did or did not talk about with me and with the other researchers who worked on this study. I discuss this issue in more detail later in the appendix. Additionally, my position relative to the women in the study affects how I interpret what they told us. Although I believe that our repeated interactions over the course of six years helped me better understand their situations, as well as how they thought about their circumstances, I also know that I am likely to have sometimes misinterpreted what they said or analyzed it through a lens that they might not think appropriate.

I have tried to use the framework of "cultural humility" in my approach to this kind of work (and also to my teaching). To be culturally humble is to be committed to lifelong learning as well as to the practice of continual self-evaluation and reflection. In striving to be culturally humble, I recognize that I do not know everything and that I need to figure out what I do not know and commit myself to learning what I need to know. Cultural humility also calls me to recognize that power imbalances exist in relationships and to try to find ways to restore that balance, even knowing that I will sometimes fail. As a person of privilege who enters disadvantaged communities, I try to take the view that in these contexts I am not the expert. I need to listen, and listen hard. And I also need to continually think about my own identity and biases and how they shape the work I do and my interactions with people who are generous enough to participate in the studies I conduct. But I fully recognize that I sometimes fail. Cynthia, for example, was a very religious person. Her beliefs and her faith were clearly important to her. When I look back at the interviews I did with her, I see that my own biases about religion and, frankly, my lack of interest in this issue prevented me from really hearing her and recognizing the importance of what she was saying. I was not culturally humble in Cynthia's presence, and that is probably why our interviews were always a bit uncomfortable.

## The Journey of This Study

I did not start this project thinking that I would be attempting to understand the ways in which so many families are socially abandoned and what that means for their chances at economic security and upward mobility. Too often we social policy researchers look at issues through a single lens. Some of us study housing policy, others employment and training, and still others access to education. I approached this project as someone interested in issues related to welfare reform. It took me some time, but with the help of the women who over six years generously shared their experiences, both the good and the sometimes quite bad, I came to see that something more than the fallout of welfare reform was at work.

Once I got past seeing this study through a welfare reform lens, I thought I could make a contribution by gaining more understanding of how low- and moderate-income women make decisions about which avenues of support to pursue (or not), how to maintain their family's living standards, which items they are willing to forgo, how much debt they will accrue, and how to manage once those decisions are made. At moments when I was feeling particularly confident about the study, I thought of it as a "mini" *Making Ends Meet* (Edin and Lein) — that is, a project that would provide insight into the economic coping strategies of lower-income women post–welfare reform and post–economic boom. Over the course of six rounds of interviews, however, it became clearer to me that these women's economic coping strategies were only part of the story.

## The Sample

Originally, I wanted to recruit only women for the study, because they are the ones who are most likely to have been affected by the 1996 welfare reform law. However, I did not want a sample of welfare mothers only. The women participating in this study were identified through two processes. First, in early 2006, we conducted a pilot version of this study with eleven women. Flyers were distributed at several charter schools serving low-income children in the Detroit area and sent home with children in the elementary grades. The mothers or grandmothers of eight children responded to these flyers. Two other women were recruited by these women (one was Shanice, the daughter of Aleta, and Erica recruited her cousin Danisha). Another woman received a flyer from a nonprofit social service agency. Nine of the initial eleven women continued to participate in later stages of the study.

I wanted a larger sample, and one that was more diverse, particularly since some of the people in the sample I started with in the pilot had ties to each other. Michael Barr, a law professor at the

*Appendix*

University of Michigan, let me select cases from his recently completed survey of one thousand households in the Detroit metropolitan area, the Detroit Area Study on Financial Services (DAS-FS). His focus was on low- and moderate-income families' access to financial services, so it would not necessarily have seemed strange if I contacted these participants again to conduct further interviews on their financial coping strategies. Once we obtained permission from our institutional review board, I was set to select a sample.

The DAS-FS sample was intended to be representative of households living in relatively poor and near-poor areas of the Detroit metropolitan area. DAS-FS sample members were selected based on a stratified random sample of the metro area, which includes Wayne, Oakland, and Macomb Counties. To generate a qualitative sample from the DAS-FS, I chose eighty non-elderly households with children and forty non-elderly households without children, for a total of 120 households. Since older African American women living alone were overrepresented in the survey sample, I tried to oversample younger African American mothers for the qualitative study. I also included working-age men in the sample, although the DAS-FS contained relatively few.

Contact via mail was attempted with eighty-six of the 120 individuals selected from the survey sample. Of the eighty-six we contacted, only forty-one were located and completed the first round of interviews. At the second round of interviews, five of the forty-one were not located and could not be found for the remainder of the study. The entire sample for this analysis thus consists of the nine women initially recruited for the pilot and the thirty-six women from the survey who completed at least two rounds of qualitative interviews, for a total sample of forty-five.

I had wanted to interview sixty survey respondents, but the high levels of mobility among Detroit residents made it difficult. Of the remaining forty-five respondents whom we attempted to contact but who did not participate, almost half had moved since the DAS-FS survey was conducted, and we had no additional way of finding them, despite repeated attempts using multiple approaches. We did not make an attempt to contact all 120 people on the subsample list because I was concerned about overrepresentation of higher-income individuals. On average, higher-income sample members were much easier to reach, since they tended to own their own homes and to be listed in telephone directories with current numbers. In addition, my efforts to include men in the study failed. We were saddened to learn that at least three of the men we tried to contact had died. Others were impossible to find. We interviewed one young man, but in the end I did not use his interviews because demographically he was so different from everyone else in the study, and not just by gender.

The qualitative sample was not intended to resemble the survey sample, nor should it be characterized as embedded or nested within a larger survey sample. Rather, the DAS-FS sample made it easier to find participants, in part because they had already established a relationship with University of Michigan interviewers. However, because the majority of them were originally part of a random sample, some common concerns that arise in qualitative research were avoided.[1] For example, if I had relied only on word of mouth to recruit respondents, I would have been concerned about my sample consisting mainly of women who were in similar economic situations or who were embedded within the same social networks, which was already the case with several of the pilot sample members. Likewise, if I had found respondents through social service agencies or welfare offices, I would have captured women who, by definition, used these sources of support. The sample is not diverse on some demographic dimensions, primarily race, but I am not sure it mattered as much as I thought it might. In the end, it was the ways in which people were cut off from various forms of opportunity and support that constituted the overarching narrative.

# Interviews

After recruiting our sample, we then set out to interview the people we could find. A team of graduate students (whose participation changed over the course of the study) and I conducted the interviews, which typically took place in the respondents' homes and lasted, on average, seventy-five minutes. A research staff member of the National Poverty Center and I did all of the interviews in 2010, and I conducted all of the interviews in 2011. A semistructured interview guide was used with specific questions as well as follow-ups that served as cues for the interviewers. The general guide appears at the end of this appendix. Some questions were added or subtracted, depending on the year (for example, in 2008 we asked about the presidential election), but the core set of topics and questions remained the same. The guide was flexible enough to allow interviewers to follow up on areas of interest related to the study. Interviews were audio-recorded using digital recording devices and subsequently transcribed. Respondents were paid $40 at each interview for their participation.

Although in-person interviews are the primary source of data, with repeated interviews, the research team spent significant amounts of time in the women's homes, both before and after the interviews. Each interviewer wrote or recorded observations about the interior of the home, any interactions that would not have been picked up by the recording, and any other relevant information. These field notes supplement the transcripts. This process was repeated six times: interviews were conducted annually from 2006 to 2011, typically in the spring and summer.

## Analysis of the Data

Analyzing the data was a daunting task. Each transcript was approximately forty pages, so multiplying that by forty-five respondents and again by six gave us roughly ten thousand to eleven thousand pages of data. I originally tried using a qualitative software analysis package, but I found that the approach did not work well for these data. Instead, I used Excel and Word. I made spreadsheets to keep track of demographic data and changes in employment, use of benefits, attendance at school, debt, and other pieces of information that were easier to see in a tabular format. I selected segments of text related to particular topical areas I was interested in, such as experiences with using public benefits, what the respondents said about their debt, why they were going to school, and some of the other major topics covered in the interview guide. For some of these topics, I coded the data line by line, as suggested by Kathy Charmaz.[2] I wrote a lot of memos to myself, trying to figure out what these codes meant and how they hung together. I wrote up the story of each woman in the sample by pulling all of the interview transcripts together, attempting to trace out each woman's trajectory, including information about her life prior to the start of the study. I read the transcripts over and over again, looking for (and coding) issues they raised that I had not really thought about. Garnishment is an example of such an issue. Then I wrote more memos, trying to figure out what the underlying story line might be. This cumulative process took place over the years of gathering the data, although I pursued it with much more intensity after I stopped collecting data.

"Figuring out the story" was a long and challenging process for me. I originally thought that I was going to study how families coped in an economic downturn in an era of a changed safety net. Then I thought it was going to be a study of how vulnerable families managed during the recession and the recovery. The Great Recession and the mortgage lending crisis certainly played a role in the lives of most of these women, but no one's life really changed because of the *event* of the recession. Rather, it was people's interactions with the various institutions I discuss in the book that produced many of the outcomes they experienced. For example, what happened on people's jobs and in the immediate aftermath of losing them was more important than a single experience of job loss because of the recession. People's routine interactions with the welfare office, not the reforms that passed in 1996, were the problem. So I tried to focus on these interactions, document them, and then make some meaning out of what the women told us.

I also read a lot of books and news articles about Detroit. Even though I believe that socially abandoned families are not a Detroit-specific phenomenon, understanding respondents' lives and the challenges they were facing required learning about as many of the contextual nuances of the city as possible. I do not live in Detroit, and I did not relocate there while I was conducting the study. I thought about it, but such a move seemed too challenging given my family situation, my work as a researcher at the University of Michigan, and the fact that in 2006 I was also starting a doctoral program. That said, each summer I spent two to three days a week, on average, in the city and its suburbs. When I was not conducting interviews, I was trying to find people who had moved or changed phone numbers. I drove around the city quite a bit, trying to get a better feel for various neighborhoods. I spent time in parks and restaurants when I had time in between interviews. But I am not an ethnographer, and this study was never intended to be a study of Detroit.

As is the case with projects of this nature, I did not use all of the data that were available. I did not focus on issues such as health problems and health care access (although almost no one thought access was an issue). Some of the women are featured in the book more prominently than others. I did this deliberately so that readers would not have to constantly think, *Who is that?* The stories of Tamara, Geneva, Aleta, Lisa, Yvette, and several other women are highlighted more frequently because aspects of their experiences were fairly representative. These women also provided quite a bit of detail in their answers. The lack of detail about the women whose stories are not featured as prominently—but who were dealing with many of the same issues—was a choice made for readability, not because their voices do not need to be heard. That said, in table A.1, I have tried to give the reader some sense of each of the women in the study.

Table A.1    Personal, Family, and Financial Characteristics
of Participants in the Study

| Pseudo-nym | Age | Family | Jobs and Income |
|---|---|---|---|
| Tamara | Late twenties | Two children. Single. Lives in Detroit | Nurse's aide until fired. Average income $8,000 (below poverty line). |
| Lisa | Early thirties | Two children. Married. Lives in Detroit, although spent two years in a suburb. | Self-employed. Husband is a pipe fitter. Average income $70,000 (over three times the poverty line). |
| Geneva | Early forties | Three children, one autistic. Married, but then separated from husband. Lives in Detroit. | Worked in customer service; injured on the job and subsequently disabled. Average income $17,000 (below poverty line). |
| Marie | Late thirties | Latino. Three children. Single. Lives in Detroit. | Unemployed. Average income $5,000 (below poverty line). |
| Annette | Early fifties | Two adult children who live on their own. Widowed. Lives in a friend's house in Detroit. | Home health care worker after long spell of unemployment. Average income $11,000 (below poverty line). |
| Erica | Late twenties | Four children. Separated from husband. Lived in Detroit, but has moved to the South. | Contract IT jobs and other sporadic work. Average income $20,000 a year (below poverty line). |
| Miss Price | Early forties | One adult child and one minor child. Adult child sometimes lives with her. Single, but lives with children's father in Detroit. | Disabled. Children's father does odd jobs. Average income $12,600 (below poverty line). |

Table A.1    (*cont.*)

| Pseudonym | Age | Family | Jobs and Income |
|---|---|---|---|
| Tykia | Late twenties | One child. Single. Lived in public housing in Detroit, but has moved to a suburb. | Retail and security. Average income $11,000 a year (below poverty line). |
| Judy | Early forties | Four children; one lives with a grandmother. Divorced. Lives in Detroit. | Nurse's aide until laid off. Average income $20,000 a year (slightly above poverty line). |
| Sandra | Late thirties | One adult child living on her own; one child and grandchild living with her. Married. Lives in Detroit. | Clerical worker. Husband frequently unemployed. Average income $40,000 (almost twice the poverty line). |
| Tanya | Early thirties | Two children. Single. Lives in Detroit. | Teacher's aide. Average income $32,000 (just over twice the poverty line). |
| Geri | Early forties | Two adult children living on their own; five minor children primarily living with their father, though she helps support them. Lives with partner and partner's four children and one grandchild. Lives in Detroit. | Various factory work, then student. Average income $17,000 (below poverty line). |
| Cynthia | Early thirties | Three children and two stepchildren. Got married during the study. Lives in Detroit. | Various jobs. Husband is factory worker who is often unemployed. Average income $29,000 (just over the poverty line). |
| Carol | Early fifties | Two adult children who live on their own and one minor child. Single. Lives in Detroit. | Stocker. Average income $13,000 a year (below poverty line). |

Table A.1     (*cont.*)

| Pseudo-nym | Age | Family | Jobs and Income |
|---|---|---|---|
| Dorothy | Late forties | Three adult children who sometimes live with her. Has had custody of a grandchild for several years. Married, then divorced. Lives in Detroit but moves frequently. | Disabled. Average income $8,500 (below poverty line). |
| Karla | Midforties | Two adult children and one minor child. One adult child sometimes lives with her. Divorced. Lived in a suburb, but has moved to Detroit. | Temporary factory work, student. Average income $10,000 (below poverty line). |
| Aleta | Late forties | Three adult children, one of whom sometimes stays with her. Has had custody of a grandchild for several years. Divorced. Lives in Detroit. | Worked in factory; injured on the job and subsequently disabled. Average income $22,000 (slightly above poverty line). |
| Sheila | Early fifties | Two adult children who live on their own. One grandchild occasionally stays with her. Single. Lives in suburb. | Unionized service worker. Average income $26,000 (two and a half times the poverty line). |
| Sharon | Late twenties | White. One child. Divorced. Lives in a suburb. | Accounting. Average income $40,000 (just under three times the poverty line). |
| Debbie | Late thirties | White. One adult child and two minor children. Married and moved to the South, but has returned to southeast Michigan and divorced. Lives in public housing. | Various retail, then student. Husband was a truck driver, but often unemployed. Average income $15,000 (below poverty line). |

Table A. 1　　(*cont.*)

| Pseudo-nym | Age | Family | Jobs and Income |
|---|---|---|---|
| Teresa | Midfifties | White. Two adult children who live with her. Married and then widowed. Lives in suburbs. | Does not work. Husband was retired. Average income $25,000 (about two and a half times the poverty line). |
| Brianna | Midtwenties | One child. Single. Lives in a suburb. | Nurse's aide, student. Average income $10,000 a year (below poverty line). |
| Layla | Midthirties | Lebanese. Two children. Married. Lives in a suburb. | Student, then unemployed. Husband works as a cook. Average income $17,000 (below poverty line). |
| Amala | Late forties | Lebanese. One adult child and three minor children, all of whom live with her. Married. Lives in suburb. | Does not work. Husband works as a cook. Average income $13,000 (below poverty line). |
| Pamela | Midfifties | Two adult children; one sometimes stays with her along with his two sons (her grandchildren). Single. Lives in suburb. | Factory work, then retired. Average income $33,000 (nearly twice the poverty line). |
| Leah | Late forties | Two adult children and two minor children. Adult children (and grandchild) sometimes live with her. Married. Lives in suburb. | Social worker. Husband works in real estate. Average income $118,000 (more than four times the poverty line). |
| Danielle | Midtwenties | Two children. Single. Lived in public housing in a suburb, but has moved to Detroit. | Unemployed, but sometimes works under the table. Average income $5,000 (below poverty line). |

Table A.1     (*cont.*)

| Pseudo-nym | Age | Family | Jobs and Income |
|---|---|---|---|
| Mary | Early thirties | One child. Single. Lives in suburb. | Day care worker, although often not working. Average income $19,000 (just over the poverty line). |
| Beth | Early thirties | White. Three children and one stepchild. Married. Lives in Detroit. | Hotel clerk, fast-food worker. Husband works in higher-end retail. Average income $50,000 (almost two and a half times the poverty line). |
| Yvette | Midthirties | Five children; one lives with father. Divorced. Lived in Detroit, then moved to suburbs; has moved back to one of the cities within the Detroit area. | Sales. Average income $48,000 (nearly twice the poverty line). |
| Janelle | Early twenties | Two children. Single. Lives in Detroit, although spent two years in a suburb. | Nurse's aide. Average income $20,000 (just over the poverty line). |
| Cheryl | Midtwenties | Two children. Single. Lived in Detroit with father and siblings, but has moved on her own to a suburb. | Various service-sector jobs. Average income $5,000 (below poverty line). |
| Mona | Early sixties | Two adult children who live on their own. Grandson lives with her. Married. Lives in Detroit. | Does not work. Husband was auto worker before retiring. Average income $40,000 (just over twice the poverty line). |

Table A.1     (*cont.*)

| Pseudo-nym | Age | Family | Jobs and Income |
|---|---|---|---|
| Lorraine | Midfifties | One child. Married. Lives in Detroit. | Teacher at several different schools. Husband was technician at hospital until laid off. Average income $91,000 (more than five times the poverty line). |
| Rhonda | Late thirties | Four children. Single. Lives in Detroit . | Janitor, home health aide. Average income $10,000 a year (below poverty line). |
| Shanice | Early twenties | Two children. Single. One of Aleta's adult children. Lives in public housing in one of the cities located within Detroit. | Home health worker for several different employers. Average income $18,000 a year (slightly above poverty line). |
| Nichelle | Early thirties | Three children, one disabled. Married, but left husband and moved out of state. Returned to Detroit. Now lives in a suburb. | Various jobs and self-employed. Average income $17,000 (below poverty line). |
| Tasha | Midthirties | One child. Single. Lives in Detroit with her mother. | Stocker until fired. Average income $21,000 (about one and a half times the poverty line). |
| Jen | Late twenties | One child and has custody of niece. Single. Lives in Detroit. | Clerical work until she was fired. Average income $28,000 a year (50 percent above poverty line). |
| Adrienne | Early forties | Two adult children who live on their own and one minor child. Single. Lives in Detroit. | Factory work, nurse's aide. Average income $15,000 (below poverty line). |

Table A.1    (*cont.*)

| Pseudo-nym | Age | Family | Jobs and Income |
|---|---|---|---|
| Raeanne | Early thirties | Four children. Single. Lived in Detroit. Died in 2009. | Janitor until fired. Average income $5,000 (below poverty line). |
| Danisha | Late twenties | Three children (gave birth to twins during study). Single. Lives in public housing in Detroit. | Various jobs, but often unemployed. Average income $11,000 (below poverty line). |
| Charlene | Late forties | Three children. Married. Lives in Detroit. Friends and family members often stay with them. | Retail worker, student. Husband is disabled. Average income $20,000 (below poverty line). |
| Kendra | Early thirties | Three children and has custody of niece. Mother and uncle also have moved in. Single. Lives in Detroit. | Clerical work. Average income $22,000 (below poverty line). |

*Source:* Author's calculations.

# Interview Topics and Questions
## Introduction and Overview

1. We last talked with you about a year ago. . . . Have there been any major changes in terms of your work situation, your family, your housing, your health, or other important issues that we should make sure to cover in this interview?

## Employment

1. Please look over this calendar. Can you tell me in which months you worked, where you worked, how many hours you worked each week, and how much you were paid?
   a. Do you get benefits? If so, what are the benefits (health, dental, sick days, retirement plan/401k, etc.)?
   b. Would you work more hours if you could? Explain.

2. What do you do on your job? (*Get descriptions for each different job – as detailed as possible.*)

3. How much supervision do you get? What is your relationship like with your supervisor? With your coworker(s)?

4. At your current/most recent job, are there opportunities for advancement?
   a. How do people get promoted? Or does this not happen?
   b. Do you know anyone that could help you get a new job or move up at a job?

5. (*If changed jobs/got new job*) What led to you changing jobs? How did you find your new job(s)?

6. (*If any spells of unemployment*) What happened that this job ended?

7. Do you ever/did you ever worry about losing your job?

8. Do you work any side jobs or do you ever take on additional work? (*If yes*) What do you do?
   a. How long have you been doing this?

    b.  Why did you start doing this?

    c.  What types of things do you use the money for?

9.  *(If any spells of unemployment)* How did you manage financially during the times you weren't working?

    a.  Did you receive Unemployment Insurance? *(If yes)* When and for how long? How easy or difficult was it for you to get UI? Explain. *(If no)* Did you apply for UI? If so, what happened? If not, why not?

10.  Are other people in the house working? *(If yes)* What kinds of jobs do they do and how much do they make? *(If no)* Are other people in the house currently unemployed? Are they getting UI? Explain.

11.  *(If respondent owns her own business)*

    a.  What do you see as the benefits of operating your own business? What are the downsides? Why?

    b.  How are you making sure that your customers pay?

    c.  Have you had issues with collection of due payments? Explain. How do you handle these issues?

    d.  Do you have a separate account for your business finances or do you use your personal checking account and/or credit card?

## Income

1.  What was your household's approximate income in [*year*]? What do you expect it to be for [*next year*]? Explain any differences. *(Probe for expected versus unexpected income shocks.)*

2.  In the past twelve months, has your income gone up and down month to month or stayed about the same? Please explain. *(Probe for reasons behind fluctuations – job loss, seasonal employment, returns to school, health problems, etc.)* How do you manage these changes in terms of paying bills, budgeting, etc.?

3.  Did you file your taxes? *(If yes)* How did you file them (prepared by self, with friend/family, tax preparer, etc.)? *(If tax preparer)* Did you get a refund anticipation loan? Why/why not?

4. Did you receive or will you receive a tax refund through the Earned Income Tax Credit (EITC) or some other refund? *(If yes)* What will you do/did you do with this money? Explain.

## Managing Expenses

Let's talk about your monthly expenses now.

1. Can you tell me *exactly* what bills, including rent, mortgages, utilities, food, credit cards, or any other bills, you have to pay each month. Walk me through this past month.
   a. Which bills do you get when, and how do you decide what to pay when?
   b. Are there any that you postponed payment on? How did you decide?
   c. When you are done paying bills, how much is left over?

2. Do you have any debt or bills that you are paying on? *(If yes):*
   a. How much is owed to each company? *(Get amounts, even if approximate.)*
   b. How long have these debts been accumulating?
   c. Are you actively paying on them? Why or why not?
   d. Do you have a formal payment plan in place? *(If yes)* How did you work this out?
   e. Is your paycheck being garnished or has it been in the past? Do you think it might be garnished in the future?
   f. Are debt collectors calling? *(If yes)* Which ones and how often? What do you do?
   g. How did you first get this debt? Can you tell me what was happening? *(Ask particularly about credit cards.)*

3. Are there any bills that you are ignoring or not making any payment on? Explain. *(Get amounts for each bill, even if approximate.)*

4. Do you own your own car(s)? *(If yes)* How many? Do they run well?

# Financial Services

1. Do you have a bank account? *(If no)* Why not? Did you ever have one? What happened? *(If not already discussed)* Do you have a credit card? *(If yes)* How many? How much do you owe on your credit cards?

2. Do you have a savings account or a savings account for any of your children? *(If yes)* How much is in that account?

3. In the past twelve months, have you filed or have you considered filing for bankruptcy? *(If yes)* Can you tell me a little more about what happened and why you made this decision [to file/ not to file]?

4. Do you ever use payday lenders/check cashers? *(If yes)* How was the experience? Would you do it again?

5. Do you ever borrow money from family or friends? Explain. Do friends or family ever borrow money from you? *(If yes)* How does that affect your relationships?

6. More generally, do you have family or friends who rely on you to help them out? *(If yes)* In what ways? Explain. *(Probe for how regular or frequent this help is.)* How does the fact that you help out in these ways affect you? *(Probe for financial or emotional stress, notions like, "that is what family does," etc.)*

7. Do you have family or friends you could turn or have turned to when things get tough? Explain. *(Probe for whether or not respondent uses friends/family on a regular basis or just occasionally, and why.)*

8. How easy or difficult is it for you and your family to manage your expenses? Why do you say that? *(Probe for what respondent thinks her options are.)*

9. How easy or difficult is it for you to live on your income? Explain.

## Housing and Neighborhood

1. Can you remind me if you rent or own this home or if you have some other arrangement. How long have you lived in this house/apartment? *(If own home)* We hear a lot in the news these days about foreclosures and people losing their homes because of their mortgages and other issues. How much of a concern is this for you? Explain.
   a. How much of an issue are foreclosures in your neighborhood? Explain.
   b. Are there major repairs or other renovations you need or want to make to your house? *(If yes)* Will you be able to afford these? Explain.
   c. What type of mortgage do you have? Have you ever refinanced? Explain.
   d. How much are your property taxes? How easy or difficult is it for you to pay these taxes?

   *(If rent)* Who is your landlord? *(Probe for friend, public housing authority, family member, rental company, etc.)*
   e. What is your relationship with your landlord like? Explain. *(Probe for issues with fixing problems, hassles with rent, any types of housing scams, etc.)*
   f. Have you ever gotten behind on the rent? *(If yes)* What happened and how was it resolved?
   g. How much of a problem is it to keep up with rent payments? Explain.
   h. Are there major repairs that are needed to this house/apartment? *(If yes)* Will your landlord make them?

   *(If some other arrangement)* What is your housing situation? Explain.

2. *(If respondent is living in a new location)* Why did you decide to move? How did you pick this location? *(If respondent is a former homeowner, probe for what happened.)*

3. In the last year, has anyone stayed with you who didn't have any other housing? *(If yes)* Explain. What was this like for you and your family?

4. In the last year, have you had to stay somewhere else because you didn't have housing?

## Use of Public Assistance/Food

1. In the past twelve months, have *you or anyone living with you* received welfare, such as public assistance, food stamps, medical assistance, child care, SSI, disability, or any other type of assistance from the Department of Human Services/Family Independence Agency . . . or did you try to apply for benefits? *(Go through each benefit.)* *(If yes)* What are the different types of assistance you have received or applied for and are currently receiving? *(Probe for welfare, food stamps, SSI, Medicaid, WIC, child care, any others.)* How many months/years have you been receiving these benefits? How much are you receiving for each benefit?
   a. Tell me about the last time you talked to a welfare caseworker. What did you talk about? What was the experience like for you? Was this a typical experience? Why or why not?
   b. How easy or difficult was it for you to get the types of assistance you need? Explain.

   *(If no)* Do you think you are eligible for any assistance programs? Why or why not? Would you ever use public assistance? Why or why not? *(Probe for whether respondent thinks differently about welfare generically or about individual programs like food stamps and Medicaid.)* Did you try and apply? What happened?

## Health Care Access

1. Could you please remind me, what kind of health insurance coverage do you have, and your children if that is different? Has this changed at all in the last year? Explain.
2. Was there a time in the past twelve months when you needed to see a doctor but could not because of cost? Explain.

3. When was the last time you had a checkup? When was the last time you went to the dentist? Do you have prescriptions that you don't fill because of the expense?

4. Do you or any of your family members have health problems? *(If yes)* What are they? Are they affecting your ability to work or do other activities? Explain. *(Probe for supportiveness of employers to take time off for sick children – including those who don't have chronic/severe problems.)*

## Family

1. Who currently lives with you? You don't need to tell me their names, just their ages and relationship to you.

2. Do you have any other children who are not living with you?

3. How old were you when you had your first child? Some women we've talked to say that they wish they had waited until they were older to start having children. How do you feel about this issue?

4. *(If applicable)* Does your child/children's father(s) help out, either financially or in other ways? Explain. Do your children see their father(s)?

5. *(If applicable)* Where do your children stay when you are working? How did you find this person/center? How much do you have to pay out of pocket?

## Education

1. Have you ever attended college or community college? *(If yes)* Where? When? For what type of program? How did you pay for it?

2. Have you ever attended any kind of training program or high school completion program? *(If yes)* Where? When? For what type of program? How did you pay for it?

3. Are you enrolled in any educational/training program right now? Explain.

## Wrap-up Questions

1. We've talked to you like this for a few years now. If you had to summarize your financial status since 2005, what would you say? For example, have things stayed the same, gotten worse, gotten better, gone up and down? Why do you say that? Are there particular events that you think made a difference, either positively or negatively? Explain.

2. Given everything we've talked about, as well as the continuing problems with the economy, what else do we need to know in order to understand your situation and in order to tell policy-makers how they can help families like yours?

# NOTES

## Chapter 1: From Social
## Isolation to Social Abandonment

1. Wilson 1987.
2. Ibid., 7. In debates about urban social problems, Wilson and others referred to this group of urban poor as the "underclass." The term has generally fallen out of favor, and I do not use it.
3. Ibid., 134.
4. Alexander 2010; Pager 2007.
5. U.S. census, undated. On the 2010 unemployment figures, see U.S. Bureau of Labor Statistics 2016; "Detroit's Unemployment Rate Is Nearly 50%, According to the *Detroit News*," *Huffington Post*, May 25, 2011.
6. Jargowsky 2015.
7. Reardon, Fox, and Townsend 2015.
8. Massey and Denton 1993.
9. Pattillo 1999.
10. Mazumder 2014.
11. Anderson 2000.
12. Landry and Marsh 2011.
13. Lambert 2008; O'Brien 2008; Zuberi 2006.
14. Seefeldt 2008.
15. Tüzemen and Willis 2013.
16. Coates 2014.
17. Ibid.; Sharkey 2013.
18. Edin and Lein 1997.
19. Gordon 2014.
20. Hamilton et al. 2015.
21. Sharkey 2013.
22. Chetty and Hendren 2015; David Leonhardt, Amanda Cox, and Claire Cain Miller, "An Atlas of Upward Mobility Shows Paths Out of Poverty," *New York Times*, May 4, 2015.
23. On women being targeted for subprime housing loans, see Castro Baker 2014.

24. DeNavas-Walt and Proctor 2015.
25. Lacy 2007.
26. Wilson 1987, 80.
27. Edin and Kefalas 2005.
28. Author's calculations based on U.S. Census Bureau, "Living Arrangements of Children," available at: http://www.census.gov/hhes/families/data/children.html (accessed August 24, 2016). On children living in two-parent families, see Livingston 2014.

## Chapter 2: Abandoned Detroit

1. John Gallagher, "Survey Finds Third of Detroit Lots Vacant," *Detroit Free Press*, February 20, 2010.
2. For the 2000 data, see Jargowsky 2015; for the 1980 data, see Sugrue 2005, 180.
3. Sampson 2012.
4. Jargowsky 2015.
5. The website Detroit Memories (detroitmemories.com/) serves as a hub where former and presumably white Detroit residents can reminisce about their time in Detroit in the 1950s to 1970s; the site highlights restaurants, stores, and other places that no longer exist and that may not have been welcoming to African Americans.
6. Sugrue 2005.
7. Joel Kurth, Mike Wilkinson, and Louis Aguilar, "Six Decades in Detroit: How Abandonment, Racial Tensions, and Financial Missteps Bankrupted the City," *Detroit News*, October 4, 2013; Maynard 2013.
8. Rebecca Williams, "Number of Detroit Kids with Elevated Lead Levels Drops, but Problems Remain," Michigan Public Radio, March 5, 2013.
9. Data Driven Detroit, "Detroit Residential Parcel Survey," February 2010, available at: http://datadrivendetroit.org/files/DRPS/Detroit%20Residential%20Parcel%20Survey%20OVERVIEW.pdf (accessed August 24, 2016).
10. Kurth et al., "Six Decades in Detroit."
11. Sugrue 2005.
12. Desjarlais and Rauhauser 2011.
13. Galster 2012.
14. McQuade 2014.
15. John Gallagher, "Downtown Detroit Has More Wealth, Diversity Than City as Whole, Report Says," *Detroit Free Press*, February 18, 2013.

16. Data Driven Detroit, "Detroit Residential Parcel Survey," 1.
17. Author's tabulations using American Fact Finder at census.gov.
18. Alex Kellogg, "Detroit Shrinks Itself, Historic Homes and All," *Wall Street Journal*, May 14, 2010.
19. "Vacant Detroit Becomes Dumping Ground for the Dead," Associated Press, August 2, 2012.
20. John Eligon, "Crackdown in a Detroit Stripped of Metal Parts," *New York Times*, March 15, 2015; Heidi Ewing and Rachel Grady, "Dismantling Detroit," *New York Times*, January 18, 2012. Scrappers have also pulled down telephone and utility poles for the copper wire, causing power outages.
21. Burnett, Hull, and Kussainov 2014.
22. "Enter at Your Own Risk: Police Union Says 'War-Like' Detroit Is Unsafe for Visitors," CBSDetroit, October 6, 2012.
23. Essley Whyte 2014.
24. Laura Gottesdiener, "This Is the Part of Detroit That Most People Are Not Aware Of." *Mother Jones*, November 17, 2014.
25. "Rising Number of Squatters in Detroit," UPI, August 23, 2011.
26. Khalil AlHajal, "Detroit Looks to Alert Property Owners, Trespassers to New Anti-Squatting Laws," Mlive, October 13, 2014.
27. "Welfare Recipients Taking Over Foreclosed Homes," CBSDetroit, May 9, 2012.
28. Legal Services of Northern Michigan, "Land Contract Information," available at: http://lsnm.org/landcontract.html (accessed August 24, 2016); Rural Law Center of New York, Inc., "Buying a Home on a Land Contract," available at: http://www.rurallawcenter.org/docs/Buying%20a%20Home%20on%20a%20Land%20Contract.pdf (accessed August 24, 2016).
29. Steve Neavling, "Detroit Arson a Persistent Problem as City Services Decline," *Huffington Post*, July 13, 2013; Joel Kurth and Louis Aguilar, "Inside Arson Squad: Hectic Days, Senseless Fires," *Detroit News*, February 18, 2015.
30. Thomas 1997; Metzger and Booza 2002; Gordon Trowbridge and Oralandar Brand-Williams, "The Cost of Segregation," *Detroit News*, January 14, 2002.
31. Audrey J. Lambert, "Eastpointe: A Wonderful Place to Live," 2012, available at: http://www.ajlambert.com/history/hst_epwp.pdf (accessed August 24, 2016).
32. I determined this by looking at listings on Zillow for a number of inner-ring suburbs, including Garden City, Warren, Taylor, East-

pointe, and Allen Park. Maps color-code listings that are foreclosures in blue and regular sales in red. Only in Warren was the number of foreclosures small, in both absolute and relative terms.
33. De Souza Briggs et al. 2008.
34. Chetty, Hendren, and Katz 2015.
35. Land annexation began in the early 1800s, but the bulk of the land that would make up Detroit was added from about 1900 to 1926. For maps showing this annexation, see Hill (2013).
36. Monica Davey, "Darker Nights as Some Cities Turn Off the Lights," *New York Times,* December 29, 2011.
37. Galster 2012; Sarah Hullett, "Hamtramck Inches Closer to Closing Ugly Chapter," Michigan Public Radio, November 13, 2012.
38. Recent research by Matthew Desmond (2016) finds that some landlords use nuisance complaints, such as noise, as a reason to evict tenants.
39. Murphy, forthcoming.
40. Peter Rossi (1955) was the first scholar to discuss life course models of mobility.
41. Cohen and Wardrip 2011.
42. Burgard, Seefeldt, and Zelner 2012; Desmond and Shollenberger 2015.
43. Cohen and Wardrip 2011.
44. Burgard, Seefeldt, and Zelner 2012; Kerbow, Azcoitia, and Buell 2003.
45. For different perspectives on the revitalization of Detroit, see Ben Austen, "The Post-Post-Apocalyptic Detroit," *New York Times,* July 13, 2014; Alex Halperin, "How Motor City Came Back from the Brink . . . and Left Most Detroiters Behind," *Mother Jones,* July 6, 2015; Tom Rowley, "For Downtrodden Detroit, Hopes of Revitalization Ride Streetcar Rails," *Washington Post,* July 31, 2015; Donna Terek and David Guralnick, "Against the Tide, Newcomers Move into Detroit," *Detroit News,* September 16, 2014.
46. Emily Badger, "The White Population Is Growing in Many U.S. Cities for the First Time in Years," *Washington Post,* September 24, 2015.

# Chapter 3: Abandoned by Institutions of Inclusion and Stability: The Failed Promise of Employment

1. Trisi 2012.
2. Kalleberg 2011.
3. U.S. Bureau of Labor Statistics 2013.
4. Hilton 2008.

5. Alan Flippen, "When Union Membership Was Rising," *New York Times,* May 29, 2014; Luo, Mann, and Holden 2010.
6. Landry and Marsh 2011.
7. Henly and Lambert 2014.
8. Craft Morgan, Dill, and Kalleberg 2013.
9. U.S. Bureau of Labor Statistics 2015.
10. On low-wage work, see Levine 2013.
11. Alina Tugend, "It's Unclearly Defined, but Telecommuting Is Fast on the Rise," *New York Times,* March 8, 2014.
12. Spinuzzi 2012.
13. Stacey 2011.
14. U.S. Bureau of Labor Statistics 2015.
15. Hodson 2001.
16. Hirsch, Fiss, and Hoel-Green 2008; Newman 2008.
17. Richardson 2008, 70.
18. Deming 2015.
19. Small 2009.
20. It is important to note that these reports of workplace interaction come from interviews with Yvette and Judy and not from observations of how they acted at work. Alexandra Murphy (forthcoming) finds that residents in low-income communities often say that they "keep to themselves," but that they can be observed regularly engaging with each other in daily life. For the purposes of my argument, however, how the women in my study perceived their relationship with their coworkers is important. If they viewed their coworkers as distractions or potential sources of "drama," then they may have been less likely to form bonds.
21. Levine 2013.
22. U.S. Equal Employment Opportunity Commission, "Facts About Race/Color Discrimination," available at: https://www.eeoc.gov/eeoc/publications/fs-race.cfm (accessed August 24, 2016).
23. U.S. Equal Employment Opportunity Commission, "EEOC Enforcement and Litigation Statistics, Charge Statistics, National, FY 1997 Through FY 2014; Charge Receipts by State (Includes U.S. Territories); and Bases by Issue [2010]," available at: https://www.eeoc.gov/eeoc/statistics/enforcement/ (accessed August 24, 2016).
24. Werhane, Radin, and Bowie 2004.
25. Wilson 1987, 57.
26. Granovetter 1995; see also Smith 2007.

27. Stevenson 2009. For a more detailed accounting of the online application process for low-wage jobs, see Edin and Shaefer 2015.
28. Harvey 2005.
29. Small Business Administration 2014.
30. Bates and Robb 2014.
31. Austen, "The Post-Post-Apocalyptic Detroit."

# Chapter 4: Abandoned by Institutions of Mobility: The Failed Promise of Postsecondary Education and Homeownership

1. Pew Research Center 2012.
2. On homeownership promotion in low-income communities, see, for example, Retsinas and Belsky 2002.
3. Shan Carter and Kevin Quealy, "Home Prices in 20 Cities," *New York Times,* August 26, 2014.
4. U.S. Department of Treasury with U.S. Department of Education 2012.
5. For a review of these debates, see Dowd 2003.
6. Fain 2011.
7. Center for Community College Policy 2000.
8. Kahlenberg 2015.
9. Susan Dynarski, "How to Improve Graduation Rates at Community Colleges," *New York Times,* March 11, 2015.
10. Iloh and Toldson 2013.
11. Richard Perez-Pena, "The New Community College Try," *New York Times,* July 20, 2012.
12. Marcus 2012.
13. Bailey 2009; Bailey and Cho 2010; National Council of State Legislatures, "Hot Topics in Higher Education: Reforming Remedial Education," available at: http://www.ncsl.org/research/education/improving-college-completion-reforming-remedial.aspx (accessed August 24, 2016).
14. U.S. Department of Education, Federal Student Aid, "If You Want to Keep Receiving Your Federal Student Aid, Make Sure You Stay Eligible," available at: https://studentaid.ed.gov/sa/eligibility/staying-eligible (accessed August 24, 2016).
15. National Center for Education Statistics 2016.
16. Wilson 2010.
17. Deming, Goldin, and Katz 2013.
18. McGuire 2012.

19. Aud, Fox, and KewalRamani 2010.
20. Hart 2012.
21. Jaggars 2011.
22. Deming et al. 2014.
23. Fry 2014.
24. Deming, Goldin, and Katz 2013.
25. Miller 2014.
26. St. Louis Federal Reserve Bank 2013.
27. Dynarski and Scott-Clayton 2013.
28. Based on author's calculations using Wayne County Community College's "Net Price Calculator," available at: http://www.wcccd.edu/dept/FinancialAid_calculator.htm (accessed August 24, 2016).
29. Consumer Financial Protection Bureau 2012.
30. Dynarski and Scott-Clayton 2013.
31. Manning and Butera 2010.
32. U.S. Department of Education, "Don't Ignore Your Student Loan Payments or You'll Risk Going into Default," available at: https://studentaid.ed.gov/sa/repay-loans/default (accessed August 24, 2016).
33. U.S. Department of Education, "A Deferment or Forbearance Allows You to Temporarily Postpone Making Your Federal Student Loan Payments or to Temporarily Reduce the Amount You Pay," available at: https://studentaid.ed.gov/sa/repay-loans/deferment-forbearance (accessed August 24, 2016).
34. To be eligible for deferment due to economic hardship, loan holders must demonstrate that they are recipients of benefits from a federal public assistance program, such as food stamps or Temporary Assistance for Needy Families (TANF), or that they are employed at least thirty hours a week but have income below 150 percent of the federal poverty line. Peace Corps volunteers automatically qualify for deferment status while serving. Another option for federal loan holders who are facing financial challenges is to request a forbearance. In this status, loan holders may be able to temporarily suspend or reduce monthly payments for up to twelve months. Interest on the loan, however, will continue to accrue.
35. U.S. Department of Education, "If You Are Employed by a Government or Not-for-Profit Organization, You May Be Able to Receive Loan Forgiveness Under the Public Service Loan Forgiveness Program," available at: https://studentaid.ed.gov/sa/repay-loans/forgiveness-cancellation/public-service (accessed August 24, 2016).

36. I calculated the amount using the loan calculator provided by FinAid .org, a well-known and free website (http://www.finaid.org/calcula tors/scripts/loanpayments.cgi) that provides financial aid informa- tion for students. I assumed a 15 percent interest rate and a 6 percent fee rate, which is what CNN reported as the rates charged for Corin- thian Colleges' loans in 2011.
37. U.S. Department of Education, "For Corinthian Colleges Students: What You Need to Know About Debt Relief," available at: https:// studentaid.ed.gov/sa/about/announcements/corinthian (accessed August 24, 2016).
38. Christine MacDonald, "Study: Taxes Hinder Detroit Comeback," *De- troit News,* November 10, 2015.
39. Farley and Frey 1994; Sugrue 2005.
40. National Fair Housing Alliance 2006.
41. My calculations are based on parcel ownership records maintained by Loveland (https://makeloveland.com/company), a company that compiles ownership data for a number of cities, including Detroit. I determined auction prices by using data kept by BuildingDetroit.org, the city's land bank.
42. On earlier homeownership rates among African Americans, see Segal and Sullivan 1998.
43. Kochhar, Gonzalez-Barrera, and Dockterman 2009. The emergence of mortgage-backed securities was one of the key changes. A home buyer would obtain a mortgage from a bank, but instead of the bank keeping that mortgage on its balance sheet, the mortgage would be packaged together with other mortgages and sold off to a third-party investor, who would collect the monthly payments and interest. Because banks or other mortgage originators (including nonbank mortgage compa- nies such as Detroit-based Quicken Loans) could quickly sell off loans, the incentives were in place to make more loans by tapping into a "riskier" pool of borrowers. Theoretically, simply bundling together high-risk loans with low-risk mortgages would offset possible losses from the riskier loans.
44. See the excellent article by Jacob Rugh and Douglas Massey (2010) for more details.
45. Freddie Mac, "30-Year Fixed-Rate Mortgages Since 1971," available at: http://www.freddiemac.com/pmms/pmms30.htm (accessed Au- gust 24, 2016).
46. Rugh and Massey 2010.
47. LISC 2007.

48. Prashant Gopal, "Another Blight for Detroit: Property Taxes," *Bloomberg News,* March 11, 2015.
49. I checked both public records and multiple real estate listings to confirm addresses and find foreclosures.
50. Shaila Dewan, "Housing Market Shrugging Off Rise in Mortgage Rates," *New York Times,* June 26, 2013.
51. Hamilton and Darity 2010.
52. See, for example, Oliver and Shapiro 1995; Conley 1999.
53. Kochhar and Fry 2014.
54. Chiteji 2010.
55. Burd-Sharps and Rasch 2015.
56. Carter and Quealy, "Home Prices in 20 Cities."
57. Coates 2014.
58. Faber 2013.

## Chapter 5: Abandoned by the Safety Net: Contestations, Denials, and Incompetence in Benefit Processing

1. Gilens 1999; Hancock 2004; Schram, Fording, and Soss 2008.
2. U.S. Department of Agriculture 2016.
3. U.S. Government Accountability Office 2012. Typically, UI claimants can receive benefits for up to twenty-six weeks. When unemployment is high, states may extend benefits through the joint state-federal Extended Benefit (EB) program to provide another thirteen to twenty weeks of benefits. In 2008, during the Great Recession, additional funding was provided through the Emergency Unemployment Compensation (EUC) program. Depending on the state in which a UI claimant resided, he or she could receive up to ninety-nine weeks of benefits. The EUC program expired in 2013.
4. Stone and Chen 2012.
5. AARP Public Policy Institute, "Social Security Disability Insurance: A Primer," available at: http://assets.aarp.org/rgcenter/econ/i28_ssdi .pdf (accessed August 24, 2016).
6. Social Security Administration, "SSI Federal Payment Amounts," available at: https://www.ssa.gov/oact/cola/SSI.html (accessed August 24, 2016).
7. Michigan Department of Consumer and Industry Services 2000.
8. Peter Whoriskey, "More Employers Fight Unemployment Benefits," *Washington Post,* February 12, 2009.

9. Ratner 2013.
10. Jason DeParle, "Contesting Jobless Claims Becomes a Boom Industry," *New York Times,* April 3, 2010.
11. Steven Greenhouse, "In Workplace Injury System, Ill Will on All Sides," *New York Times,* April 1, 2009.
12. Giroux 2008; Kurth, Wilkinson, and Aguilar, "Six Decades in Detroit"; Steven Pearlstein, "How the Cult of Shareholder Value Wrecked American Business," *Washington Post,* September 9, 2013; Reisch 2009; Sugrue 2005.
13. Greg Gardner, "What's at Stake at the UAW Contract Talks," *Detroit Free Press,* July 12, 2015.
14. Gould-Werth and Shaefer 2013.
15. Gould-Werth and Shaefer 2012.
16. Edin and Lein 1997.
17. U.S. House of Representatives 2012.
18. Weaver 2000.
19. Seefeldt 2008.
20. For 1993 data, see U. S. Department of Health and Human Services 2004; for 1999 data, see U.S. Department of Health and Human Services 1999.
21. For example, see the exchange between Danziger et al. (2016a, 2016b) and Haskins (2016a, 2016b).
22. Edin and Shaefer 2015.
23. Schott, Pavetti, and Floyd 2015.
24. DeParle 2004.
25. Reese, Giedraitis, and Vega 2006.
26. Blank 2002.
27. Loprest and Zedlewski 2002.
28. Seefeldt et al. 2001.
29. Seefeldt, Danziger, and Danziger 2003.
30. Pavetti 2002.
31. Raphael 1999.
32. See Seefeldt and Sandstrom 2015.
33. Lens 2012, 270.
34. Auyero 2011; Seefeldt 2015.
35. Brodkin 1997.
36. Brodkin and Majmundar 2010.
37. Watkins-Hayes 2009.
38. Ibid.
39. Meyers, Glaser, and MacDonald 1998.

40. Dee-Ann Durbin (Associated Press), "Early Retirement Could Seriously Affect State Services," *The Argus Press* (Owosso, Mich.), July 1, 2002; Ron French, "Feeling Unloved, Skilled Public Employees Are Hitting the Exit," *Bridge* (Lansing, Mich.), January 26, 2012.
41. Dadayan and Boyd 2015.
42. Social Security Administration, "What You Should Know Before You Apply for Social Security Disability Benefits," available at: https://www.ssa.gov/disability/Documents/Factsheet-AD.pdf; Social Security Administration 2011 (accessed August 24, 2016).
43. DeWitt 2010.
44. Katz 1996.
45. Gilens 1999. More whites receive food stamp benefits, although African Americans are disproportionately represented on the rolls, making up 23 percent of the caseload (U.S. Department of Agriculture 2014) and 31 percent of TANF recipients (U.S. Department of Health and Human Services 2015).

## Chapter 6: Debt: The New Sharecropping System

1. In Michigan, creditors can seek a judgment to garnish state income tax refunds. See Michigan Courts, "Collecting Money from a Garnishment—Self Help," available at: http://courts.mi.gov/self-help/center/collect/pages/garnishing-money.aspx (accessed August 24, 2016).
2. See Daniel 1979; Lemann 1991; Mandle 1978.
3. On the "new Jim Crow," see Alexander 2010.
4. Sullivan 2008.
5. Morduch 1995.
6. Gruber 2001.
7. Sarkisian and Gerstel 2004.
8. Gruber 1997.
9. In 1978 the Supreme Court issued a ruling that allowed lenders to charge whichever interest rate is higher: the rate of the state in which the lender is located or the rate of the state in which the borrower resides. In an effort to lure national banks (or at least their credit card divisions) to locate in their state, several states changed their usury laws, raising the cap and in some cases eliminating any cap on interest rates. For example, Citibank's credit card division is located in South Dakota, and Bank of America's division is in Delaware, two states that have all but eliminated caps on the interest rates that credit cards can levy.

10. For overviews, see Mann 2009; Manning 2000; Hyman 2012.
11. Draut and Silva 2003.
12. The Credit Card Accountability, Responsibility, and Disclosure Act (CARD Act) of 2009 places some limits on fees and requires card issuers to state, in "plain" language, the terms of the card. Early evaluation of the effect of the law finds that the CARD Act has resulted in the elimination of many fees, but also less access to credit for borrowers with lower credit scores (Consumer Financial Protection Bureau 2013).
13. Pew Charitable Trust 2015.
14. Brown et al. 2013.
15. Edin et al. 2013; Halpern-Meekin et al. 2015; Tach and Greene 2014.
16. This law is currently being phased out in Michigan, but New York and Texas have similar laws.
17. Hummel 2014.
18. National Motorists Association, "New Fees Target Michigan Drivers" (press release), September 2003, available at: https://www.motorists .org/press/new-fees-target-michigan-drivers/ (accessed August 24, 2016).
19. Eric Lawrence, "Community Service Can Help Michigan Drivers Waive Fees," *Detroit Free Press,* January 21, 2015.
20. Campbell Robertson, "A City Where Policing, Discrimination, and Raising Revenue Went Hand in Hand," *New York Times,* March 4, 2015.
21. Estimates made using Federal Reserve Bank of Dallas, "Payment Calculator for Credit Cards and Other Revolving Credit Loans," available at: https://www.dallasfed.org/microsites/educate/calculators/open -calc.cfm (accessed August 24, 2016).
22. Bright 2013.
23. Standaert 2014.
24. Freddie Mac, "30-Year Fixed-Rate Mortgages Since 1971."
25. Hyman 2012.
26. See Legislative Council, State of Michigan, Deferred Presentment Service Transactions Act of 2005.
27. Halpern-Meekin et al. 2015; Tach and Greene 2014.
28. Holland 2011.
29. Chris Arnold and Paul Kiel, "Millions of Americans' Wages Seized over Credit Card and Medical Debt," National Public Radio, September 15, 2014.
30. Mann 2009.
31. U.S. Government Accountability Office 2008.
32. Author's calculations based on data reported by U.S. Bankruptcy

Court, 2004, 2005, and 2011 caseload statistics data tables at http://www.uscourts.gov/statistics-reports/caseload-statistics-data-tables.
33. Sullivan, Warren, and Westbrook 2000.
34. Eisenson 2014. Depending on where the bankruptcy case is filed, the debtor may have a fourth option called a "ride through," whereby the original terms of the loan are maintained as long as the debtor continues to make payments (Eisenson 2014).
35. Porter and Thorne 2006.
36. Cohen-Cole, Duygan-Bump, and Montoriol-Garriga 2009.
37. "Credit Report Q&A: Considering Bankruptcy," http://www.myfico.com/crediteducation/questions/bankruptcy-fico-score-considerations.aspx.
38. Nielsen and Kuhn 2008.
39. U.S. Department of Health and Human Services 2012.

## Chapter 7: Making Abandoned Families Striving Families Again

1. Jamieson 2014.
2. Stone, Greenstein, and Coven, 2007.
3. Gould-Werth and Shaefer 2012.
4. Center for Budget and Policy Priorities 2016.
5. Pavetti 2014.
6. Bar-Gill and Warren 2009.
7. Romich et al. 2013.
8. Martin 2010.
9. Hamilton and Darity 2010.
10. Coates 2014.
11. Ibid., 61.
12. Darity 2008.

## Methodological Appendix

1. Babbie 2009.
2. Charmaz 2006.

# REFERENCES

Alexander, Michelle. 2010. *The New Jim Crow: Mass Incarceration in the Age of Colorblindness*. New York: New Press.

Anderson, Elijah. 2000. *Code of the Street: Decency, Violence, and the Moral Life of the Inner City*. New York: W. W. Norton.

Aud, Susan, Mary Ann Fox, and Angelina KewalRamani. 2010. "Status and Trends in the Education of Racial and Ethnic Minorities." NCES 2010-015. Washington, D.C.: Institute of Education Sciences, National Center for Education Statistics (July). Available at: http://nces.ed.gov /pubs2010/2010015.pdf (accessed August 24, 2016).

Auyero, Javier. 2011. "Patients of the State: An Ethnographic Account of Poor People's Waiting." *Latin American Research Review* 46(1): 5–29.

Babbie, Earl. 2009. *The Practice of Social Research*, twelfth edition. Belmont, Calif.: Thomson Wadsworth.

Bailey, Tom. 2009. "Rethinking Developmental Education in Community College." CCRC Brief 40. New York: Community College Research Center (February).

Bailey, Tom, and Sung-Woo Cho. 2010. "Developmental Education in Community Colleges." CCRC Issue Brief prepared for the White House Summit on Community Colleges. New York: Community College Research Center (September).

Bar-Gill, Oren, and Elizabeth Warren. 2009. "Making Credit Safer." *University of Pennsylvania Law Review* 157(1): 1–101.

Bates, Timothy, and Alicia Robb. 2014. "Has the Community Reinvestment Act Increased Loan Availability Among Small Businesses Operating in Minority Neighborhoods?" *Urban Studies* (May 28). doi:10.1177 /0042098014534903.

Blank, Rebecca. 2002. "Evaluating Welfare Reform in the United States." Working Paper 8983. Cambridge, Mass.: National Bureau of Economic Research (June).

Bright, Thomas. 2013. "Using a Credit Card Hardship Program." *The Clearpoint Blog*, November 1. Available at: http://www.clearpoint .org/blog/credit-card-hardship-program/ (accessed August 24, 2016).

# References

Brodkin, Evelyn Z. 1997. "Inside the Welfare Contract: Discretion and Accountability in State Welfare Administration." *Social Service Review* 71(1): 1–33.

Brodkin, Evelyn Z., and Malay Majmundar. 2010. "Administrative Exclusion: Organizations and the Hidden Costs of Welfare Claiming." *Journal of Public Administration Research and Theory: J-PART* 20(4): 827–48.

Brown, Meta, Andrew Haughwout, Donghoon Lee, and Wilbert van der Klaauw. 2013. "The Financial Crisis at the Kitchen Table: Trends in Household Debt and Credit." *Current Issues in Economics and Finance* 19(2): 1–8.

Burd-Sharps, Sarah, and Rebecca Rasch. 2015. "Impact of the U.S. Housing Crisis on the Racial Wealth Gap Across Generations." Washington, D.C.: Social Science Research Council (June).

Burgard, Sarah, Kristin Seefeldt, and Sarah Zelner. 2012. "Housing Instability and Health: Findings from the Michigan Recession and Recovery Study." *Social Science and Medicine* 75(12): 2215–24.

Burnett, Jennifer, Elle Hull, and Nurlan Kussainov. 2014. "Is Scrap Metal Theft Legislation Working for States?" Washington, D.C.: Council of State Governments, Knowledge Center (May).

Castro Baker, Amy. 2014. "Eroding the Wealth of Women: Gender and the Subprime Foreclosure Crisis." *Social Service Review* 88(1): 59–91.

Center for Budget and Policy Priorities. 2016. "Online Services for Key Low-Income Benefit Programs," Washington: Center for Budget and Policy Priorities (July).

Center for Community College Policy. 2000. "State Funding for Community Colleges: A 50-State Survey." Denver, CO: Center for Community College Policy (November).

Charmaz, Kathy. 2006. *Constructing Grounded Theory.* Thousand Oaks, Calif.: Sage Publications.

Chetty, Raj, and Nathaniel Hendren. 2015. "The Impacts of Neighborhoods on Intergenerational Mobility: Childhood Exposure Effects and County-Level Estimates." Cambridge, Mass.: Harvard University and National Bureau of Economic Research (May).

Chetty, Raj, Nathaniel Hendren, and Lawrence Katz. 2015. "The Effects of Exposure to Better Neighborhoods on Children: New Evidence from the Moving to Opportunity Experiment." Working Paper 21156. Cambridge, Mass.: National Bureau of Economic Research.

Chiteji, Ngina. 2010. "The Racial Wealth Gap and the Borrower's Dilemma." *Journal of Black Studies* 41(2): 351–66.

Coates, Ta-Nehisi. 2014. "The Case for Reparations." *The Atlantic Monthly*

June. Available at: http://www.theatlantic.com/magazine/archive /2014/06/the-case-for-reparations/361631/ (accessed August 24, 2016).

Cohen, Rebecca, and Keith Wardrip. 2011. "Should I Stay or Should I Go?" Washington: Center for Housing Policy.

Cohen-Cole, Ethan, Burcu Duygan-Bump, and Judit Montoriol-Garriga. 2009. "Forgive and Forget: Who Gets Access to Credit After Bankruptcy and Why?" Working Paper QAU09-2. Boston: Federal Reserve Bank, Qualitative Analysis Unit.

Conley, Dalton. 1999. *Being Black, Living in the Red: Race, Wealth, and Social Policy in America*. Berkeley: University of California Press.

Consumer Financial Protection Bureau (CFPB). 2012. "Private Student Loans" (report to U.S. Congress). Washington, D.C.: CFPB (July 19; updated August 29). Available at: http://files.consumerfinance.gov/f /201207_cfpb_Reports_Private-Student-Loans.pdf (accessed August 24, 2016).

———. 2013. "CARD Act Report." Washington: CFPB (October). Available at: http://files.consumerfinance.gov/f/201309_cfpb_card-act -report.pdf (accessed August 24, 2016).

Craft Morgan, Jennifer, Janette Dill, and Arne L. Kalleberg. 2013. "The Quality of Healthcare Jobs: Can Intrinsic Rewards Compensate for Low Extrinsic Rewards?" *Work, Employment, and Society* 27(5): 802–22.

Dadayan, Lucy, and Donald J. Boyd. 2015. "Good News for Private Sector Jobs, Bad News for State-Local Government Jobs." Albany: State University of New York, Rockefeller Institute of Government.

Daniel, Pete. 1979. "The Metamorphosis of Slavery, 1865–1900." *Journal of American History* 66(1): 88–99.

Danziger, Sandra, Sheldon Danziger, Kristen Seefeldt, and Luke Shaefer. 2016a. "From Welfare to a Work-Based Safety Net: An Incomplete Transition." *Journal of Policy Analysis and Management* 35(1): 231–38.

———. 2016b. "Increasing Work Opportunities and Reducing Poverty Two Decades After Welfare Reform." *Journal of Policy Analysis and Management* 35(1): 241–44.

Darity, William. 2008. "Forty Acres and a Mule in the 21st Century." *Social Science Quarterly* 89(3): 656–64.

Deming, David. 2015. "The Growing Importance of Social Skills in the Labor Market." Working Paper 21473. Cambridge, Mass.: National Bureau of Economic Research (August).

Deming, David, Claudia Goldin, and Lawrence Katz. 2013. "For-Profit Colleges." *The Future of Children* 23(1): 137–63.

Deming, David, Noam Yuchtman, Amira Abulafi, Claudia Goldin, and

# References

Lawrence F. Katz. 2014. "The Value of Postsecondary Credentials in the Labor Market: An Experimental Study." Working Paper 20528. Cambridge, Mass.: National Bureau of Economic Research (September).

DeNavas-Walt, Carmen, and Bernadette D. Proctor. 2015. "Income and Poverty in the United States: 2014." Washington: U.S. Census Bureau.

DeParle, Jason. 2004. *American Dream: Three Women, Ten Kids, and a Nation's Drive to End Welfare.* New York: Viking.

Desjarlais, Mary, and Bill Rauhauser. 2011. *Beauty on the Streets of Detroit: A History of the Housing Market in Detroit.* Ferndale, Mich.: Cambourne Publishing.

Desmond, Matthew. 2016. *Evicted: Poverty and Profit in the American City.* New York: Crown.

Desmond, Matthew, and Tracey L. Shollenberger. 2015. "Forced Displacement from Rental Housing: Prevalence and Neighborhood Consequences." *Demography* 52: 1751–72.

De Souza Briggs, Xavier, Kadija S. Ferryman, Susan J. Popkin, and María Rendón. 2008. "Why Did the Moving to Opportunity Experiment Not Get Young People into Better Schools?" *Housing Policy Debate* 19(1): 53–91.

DeWitt, Larry. 2010. "The Decision to Exclude Agricultural and Domestic Workers from the 1935 Social Security Act." *Social Security Bulletin* 70(4).

Dowd, Alicia C. 2003. "From Access to Outcome Equity: Revitalizing the Democratic Mission of the Community College." *Annals of the American Academy of Political and Social Science* 586(1): 92–119.

Draut, Tamara, and Javier Silva. 2003. "Borrowing to Make Ends Meet: The Growth of Credit Card Debt in the '90s." New York: Demos (September 8). Available at: http://www.demos.org/sites/default/files/publications/borrowing_to_make_ends_meet.pdf (accessed August 24, 2016).

Dynarski, Susan, and Judith Scott-Clayton. 2013. "Financial Aid Policy: Lessons from Research." Working Paper 18719. Cambridge, Mass.: National Bureau of Economic Research (January).

Edin, Kathryn, Melody Boyd, James Mabli, Jim Ohls, Julie Worthington, Sara Greene, Nicholas Redel, and Swetha Sridharan. 2013. "SNAP Food Security In-Depth Interview Study: Final Report." Washington, D.C.: Mathematica Policy Research.

Edin, Kathryn, and Maria Kefalas. 2005. *Promises I Can Keep: Why Poor Women Put Motherhood Before Marriage.* Berkeley: University of California Press.

Edin, Kathryn, and Laura Lein. 1997. *Making Ends Meet: How Single Moth-*

*ers Survive Welfare and Low-Wage Work.* New York: Russell Sage Foundation.

Edin, Kathryn J., and H. Luke Shaefer. 2015. *$2.00 a Day: Living on Almost Nothing in America.* Boston: Houghton Mifflin Harcourt.

Eisenson, Joshua L. 2014. "Exploring the Enforceability of Pre-Petition Hindrance Mechanisms to Prevent Bankruptcy." *American Bankruptcy Institute Law Review* 22: 247–66.

Essley Whyte, Liz. 2014. "Philanthropy Keeps the Lights on in Detroit." Washington, D.C.: Philanthropy Roundtable.

Faber, Jacob W. 2013. "Racial Dynamics of Subprime Mortgage Lending at the Peak." *Housing Policy Debate* 23(2): 328–49.

Fain, Paul. 2011. "Top of the Mountain?" *Inside Higher Ed,* December 21.

Farley, Reynolds, and William H. Frey. 1994. "Changes in the Segregation of Whites from Blacks During the 1980s: Small Steps Toward a More Integrated Society." *American Sociological Review* 59(1): 23–45.

Fry, Richard. 2014. "Cumulative Student Debt Among Recent College Graduates." Washington, D.C.: Pew Research Center.

Galster, George C. 2012. *Driving Detroit: The Quest for Respect in Motown.* Philadelphia: University of Pennsylvania Press.

Gilens, Martin. 1999. *Why Americans Hate Welfare: Race, Media, and the Politics of Anti-Poverty Policy.* Chicago: University of Chicago Press.

Giroux, Henry A. 2008. "Beyond the Biopolitics of Disposability: Rethinking Neoliberalism in the New Gilded Age." *Social Identities* 14(5): 587–620.

Gordon, Colin. 2014. "Racial Inequality." Washington, D.C.: Institute for Policy Studies.

Gould-Werth, Alix, and H. Luke Shaefer. 2012. "Unemployment Insurance Participation by Education and by Race and Ethnicity." *Monthly Labor Review* (October): 28–41.

———. 2013. "Do Alternative Base Periods Increase Unemployment Insurance Receipt Among Low-Educated Unemployed Workers?" *Journal of Policy Analysis and Management* 32(4): 835–52.

Granovetter, Mark S. 1995. *Getting a Job: A Study of Contacts and Careers.* Chicago: University of Chicago Press.

Gruber, Jonathan. 1997. "The Consumption Smoothing Benefits of Unemployment Insurance." *American Economic Review* 87(1): 192–205.

———. 2001. "Unemployment Insurance and Precautionary Savings." *Journal of Monetary Economics* 47(3): 545–79.

Halpern-Meekin, Sarah, Kathryn Edin, Laura Tach, and Jennifer Sykes.

# References

2015. *It's Not Like I'm Poor: How Working Families Make Ends Meet in a Post-Welfare World.* Berkeley: University of California Press.

Hamilton, Darrick, and William Darity Jr. 2010. "Can 'Baby Bonds' Eliminate the Racial Wealth Gap in Putative Post-Racial America?" *Review of Black Political Economy* 37(3-4): 207-16.

Hamilton, Darrick, William Darity Jr., Anne E. Price, Vishnu Sridharan, and Rebecca Tippett. 2015. "Umbrellas Don't Make It Rain: Why Studying and Working Hard Isn't Enough for Black Americans." Oakland, Calif.: Insight Center for Community Economic Development (April).

Hancock, Agne-Marie. 2004. *The Politics of Disgust: The Public Identity of the Welfare Queen.* New York: New York University Press.

Hart, Carolyn. 2012. "Factors Associated with Student Persistence in an Online Program of Study: A Review of the Literature." *Journal of Interactive Online Learning* 11(1): 19-42.

Harvey, Adia M. 2005. "Becoming Entrepreneurs: Intersections of Race, Class, and Gender at the Black Beauty Salon." *Gender and Society* 19(6): 789-808.

Haskins, Ron. 2016a. "TANF at Age 20: Work Still Works." *Journal of Policy Analysis and Management* 35(1): 224-31.

———. 2016b. "Supplementing TANF's Work Requirement: A Compromise." *Journal of Policy Analysis and Management* 35(1): 238-40.

Henly, Julia R., and Susan J. Lambert. 2014. "Unpredictable Work Timing in Retail Jobs: Implications for Employee Work-Life Conflict." *Industrial and Labor Relations Review* 67(3): 986-1016.

Hill, Alex B. 2013. "Map: Color Coded Detroit Growth by Annexation." DETROITography, November 2. Available at: http://detroitography .com/2013/11/02/map-color-coded-detroit-growth-by-annexation / (accessed August 24, 2016).

Hilton, Margaret. 2008. "Skills for Work in the 21st Century: What Does the Research Tell Us?" *Academy of Management Perspectives* 22(4): 63-78.

Hirsch, Paul, Peer Fiss, and Amanda Hoel-Green. 2008. "A Durkheimian Approach to Globalization." In *The Oxford Handbook of Sociology and Organization Studies: Classical Foundations,* edited by Paul Adler. New York: Oxford University Press.

Hodson, Randy. 2001. *Dignity at Work.* Cambridge: Cambridge University Press.

Holland, Peter A. 2011. "The One Hundred Billion Dollar Problem in Small Claims Court: Robo-Signing and Lack of Proof in Debt Buyer Cases." *Journal of Business Technology and Law* 259: 259-86.

Hummel, Daniel. 2014. "Traffic Tickets: Public Safety Concerns or Budget Building Tools." *Administration & Society* (March 25). doi:10.1177/0095399714528178.

Hyman, Louis. 2012. *Borrow: The American Way of Debt.* New York: Vintage Books.

Iloh, Constance, and Ivory A. Toldson. 2013. "Black Students in 21st Century Higher Education: A Closer Look at For-Profit and Community Colleges." *Journal of Negro Education* 82(3): 205–12.

Jaggars, Shanna Smith. 2011. "Online Learning: Does It Help Low-Income and Underprepared Students?" CCRC Working Paper 26: Assessment of Evidence Series. New York: Columbia University, Community College Research Center.

Jamieson, Dave. 2014. "A Landmark Retail Workers 'Bill of Rights' Passes Unanimously in San Francisco." *Huffington Post* (November 25, 2014). Available at: http://www.huffingtonpost.com/2014/11/25/retail-worker-bill-of-rights-san-francisco_n_6221642.html (accessed August 24, 2016).

Jargowsky, Paul. 2015. "The Architecture of Segregation: Civil Unrest, the Concentration of Poverty, and Public Policy." Washington, D.C.: Century Foundation (August 7).

Kahlenberg, Richard. 2015. "How Higher Education Funding Shortchanges Community Colleges." New York: Century Foundation.

Kalleberg, Arne. 2011. *Good Jobs, Bad Jobs: The Rise of Polarized and Precarious Employment Systems in the United States, 1970s to 2000s.* New York: Russell Sage Foundation.

Katz, Michael B. 1996. *In the Shadow of the Poorhouse: A Social History of Welfare in America.* New York: Basic Books.

Kerbow, David, Carlos Azcoitia, and Barbera Buell. 2003. "Student Mobility and Local School Improvement in Chicago." *Journal of Negro Education* 72(1): 158–64.

Kochhar, Rakesh, and Richard Fry. 2014. "Wealth Inequality Has Widened Along Racial, Ethnic Lines Since End of Great Recession." Washington, D.C.: Pew Research Center.

Kochhar, Rakesh, Ana Gonzalez-Barrera, and Daniel Dockterman. 2009. "Minorities, Immigrants, and Homeownership Through Boom and Bust." Washington, D.C.: Pew Research Center.

Lacy, Karyn R. 2007. *Blue-Chip Black: Race, Class, and Status in the New Black Middle Class.* Berkeley: University of California Press.

Lambert, Susan. 2008. "Passing the Buck: Labor Flexibility Practices That Transfer Risk onto Hourly Workers." *Human Relations* 61: 1203–27.

# References

Landry, Bart, and Kris Marsh. 2011. "The Evolution of the New Black Middle Class." *Annual Review of Sociology* 37(1): 373–94.

Lemann, Nicholas. 1991. *The Promised Land: The Great Black Migration and How It Changed America.* New York: Alfred A. Knopf.

Lens, Vicki. 2012. "Judge or Bureaucrat? How Administrative Law Judges Exercise Discretion in Welfare Bureaucracies." *Social Service Review* 86(2): 269–93.

Levine, Judith Adrienne. 2013. *Ain't No Trust: How Bosses, Boyfriends, and Bureaucrats Fail Low-Income Mothers and Why It Matters.* Berkeley: University of California Press.

Livingston, Gretchen. 2014. "Fewer Than Half of U.S. Kids Today Live in a 'Traditional' Family." Washington, D.C.: Pew Research Center.

Local Initiatives Support Corporation (LISC). 2007. "Concentrated Residential Foreclosure Risk Analysis." Washington, D.C.: LISC (December). Available at: http://docplayer.net/3601230-Local-initiatives-support-corporation-concentrated-residential-foreclosure-risk-analysis.html (accessed August 24, 2016).

Loprest, Pamela, and Sheila Zedlewski. 2002. "Making TANF Work for the Hard to Serve." Washington, D.C.: Urban Institute.

Luo, Tian, Amar Mann, and Richard Holden. 2010. "The Expanding Role of Temporary Help Services from 1990 to 2008." *Monthly Labor Review* (August): 3–16.

Mandle, Jay R. 1978. *The Roots of Black Poverty: The Southern Plantation Economy After the Civil War.* Durham, N.C.: Duke University Press.

Mann, Ronald. 2009. "Patterns of Credit Card Use Among Low and Moderate Income Households." In *Insufficient Funds: Savings, Assets, Credit, and Banking Among Low-Income Households,* edited by Rebecca M. Blank and Michael S. Barr. New York: Russell Sage Foundation.

Manning, Robert D. 2000. *Credit Card Nation: The Consequences of America's Addiction to Credit.* New York: Basic Books.

Manning, Robert D., and Anita C. Butera. 2010. "Consumer Credit and Household Debt." In *The Encyclopedia of Contemporary American Social Issues,* edited by Michael Shally-Jensen. Santa Barbara, Calif.: ABC-CLIO/Greenwood Press.

Marcus, Jon. 2012. "Student Advising Plays Key Role in College Success— Just as It's Being Cut." New York: Hechinger Report (November 13).

Martin, Andrew. 2010. "Automated Debt Collection Lawsuits Engulf Courts." *The New York Times,* July 13, 2010, p. B1.

Massey, Douglas S., and Nancy A. Denton. 1993. *American Apartheid: Seg-*

*regation and the Making of the Underclass.* Cambridge, Mass.: Harvard University Press.

Maynard, Melissa. 2013. "Michigan and Detroit: A Troubled Relationship." Washington, D.C.: Pew Charitable Trusts.

Mazumder, Bhashkar. 2014. "Black-White Differences in Intergenerational Economic Mobility in the United States." *Economic Perspectives* 38(1): 1–18.

McGuire, Matthew. 2012. "Subprime Education: For-Profit Colleges and the Problem with Title IV Federal Student Aid." Duke University Law Journal 62(119): 119–60.

McQuade, Barbara L. 2014. "Detroit One Collaboration Leads to Indictment of Two Additional Latin Count Gang Members on Racketeering Charges." Detroit: U.S. Department of Justice, U.S. Attorney's Office, Eastern District of Michigan (February 10).

Metzger, Kurt, and Jason Booza. 2002. "African Americans in the United States, Michigan and Metropolitan Detroit." Detroit: Wayne State University.

Meyers, Marcia, Bonnie Glaser, and Karin McDonald. 1998. "On the Front Lines of Welfare Delivery." *Journal of Policy Analysis and Management* 17(1): 1–22.

Michigan Department of Consumer and Industry Services. 2000. "An Overview of Worker's Compensation in Michigan." Lansing: Michigan Department of Consumer and Industry Services.

Miller, Ben. 2014. "The Student Debt Review: Analyzing the State of Undergraduate Student Borrowing." Washington, D.C.: New America Foundation.

Morduch, Jonathan. 1995. "Income Smoothing and Consumption Smoothing." *Journal of Economic Perspectives* 9(3): 103–14.

Murphy, Alexandra. Forthcoming. *Where the Sidewalk Ends: Poverty in an American Suburb.* New York: Oxford University Press.

National Center for Education Statistics. 2016. "The Condition of Education: Undergraduate Enrollment." Washington, D.C.: Institute of Education Sciences, National Center for Education Statistics. Available at: http://nces.ed.gov/programs/coe/indicator_cha.asp (last updated May 2016).

National Fair Housing Alliance. 2006. "Unequal Opportunity: Perpetuating Housing Segregation in America." Washington, D.C.: National Fair Housing Alliance.

Newman, Katherine S. 2008. *Laid Off, Laid Low: Political and Economic Con-*

*sequences of Employment Insecurity*. New York: Columbia University Press.

Nielsen, Marsha L., and Kristine M. Kuhn. 2009. "Late Payments and Leery Applicants: Credit Checks as a Selection Test." *Employee Responsibilities and Rights Journal* 21(2): 115–30.

O'Brien, Erin E. 2008. *The Politics of Identity: Solidarity Building Among America's Working Poor*. Albany: State University of New York Press.

Oliver, Melvin L., and Thomas M. Shapiro. 1995. *Black Wealth/White Wealth: A New Perspective on Racial Inequality*. New York: Routledge.

Pager, Devah. 2007. *Marked: Race, Crime, and Finding Work in an Era of Mass Incarceration*. Chicago: University of Chicago Press.

Pattillo, Mary E. 1999. *Black Picket Fences: Privilege and Peril Among the Black Middle Class*. Chicago: University of Chicago Press.

Pavetti, LaDonna. 2002. "Helping the Hard to Employ." In *Welfare Reform and Beyond: The Future of the Safety Net*, edited by Isabel V. Sawhill. Washington, D.C.: Brookings Institution.

———. 2014. "Subsidized Jobs; Providing Paid Employment Opportunities When the Labor Market Fails." Washington, D.C.: Center on Budget and Policy Priorities.

Pew Charitable Trust. 2015. "The Complex Story of American Debt." Philadelphia: Pew Charitable Trust.

Pew Research Center. 2012. "The Monetary Value of a College Education." Washington, D.C.: Pew Research Center.

Porter, Katherine, and Deborah Thorne. 2006. "The Failure of Bankruptcy's Fresh Start." *Cornell Law Review* 92: 67–128.

Raphael, Jody. 1999. "The Family Violence Option: An Early Assessment." *Violence Against Women* 5(4): 449–66.

Ratner, David D. 2013. "Unemployment Insurance Experience Rating and Labor Market Dynamics." Finance and Economics Discussion Series Working Paper 2013-86. Washington, D.C.: Federal Reserve Board.

Reardon, Sean F., Lindsay Fox, and Joseph Townsend. 2015. "Neighborhood Income Composition by Race and Income, 1990–2009." *Annals of the American Academy of Political and Social Science* 660(1): 78–97.

Reese, Ellen, Vincent Giedraitis, and Eric Vega. 2006. "Welfare Is Not for Sale: Campaigns Against Welfare Profiteers in Milwaukee." *Social Justice* 33(3): 38–53.

Reisch, Michael. 2009. "Social Workers, Unions, and Low Wage Workers: An Historical Perspective." *Journal of Community Practice* 17(1): 50–72.

Retsinas, Nicolas, and Eric Belsky. 2002. *Low-Income Homeownership: Examining the Unexamined Goal*. Washington, D.C.: Brookings Institution.

Richardson, Charley. 2008. "Working Alone: The Erosion of Solidarity in Today's Workplace." *New Labor Forum* 17(3): 68–78.

Romich, Jennifer L., Nicole Keenan, Jody Miesel, and Crystal C. Hall. 2013. "Income Tax Time as a Time to Build Financial Capability." In *Financial Capability and Asset Development*, edited by Julie Birkenmaier, Jami Curley, and Margaret Sherraden.

Rossi, Peter H. 1955. *Why Families Move: A Study in the Social Psychology of Urban Residential Mobility.* Conducted under the joint sponsorship of the Bureau of Applied Social Research and the Institute for Urban Land Use and Housing Studies of Columbia University. Glencoe, Ill.: Free Press.

Rugh, Jacob S., and Douglas S. Massey. 2010. "Racial Segregation and the American Foreclosure Crisis." *American Sociological Review* 75(5): 629–51.

Sampson, Robert. 2012. *Great American City: Chicago and the Enduring Neighborhood Effect.* Chicago: University of Chicago Press.

Sarkisian, Natalia, and Naomi Gerstel. 2004. "Kin Support Among Blacks and Whites: Race and Family Organization." *American Sociological Review* 69(6): 812–37.

Schott, Liz, LaDonna Pavetti, and Ife Floyd. 2015. "How States Use Federal and State Funds Under the TANF Block Grant." Washington, D.C.: Center for Budget and Policy Priorities.

Schram, Sanford F., Richard C. Fording, and Joe Soss. 2008. "Neoliberal Poverty Governance: Race, Place and the Punitive Turn in U.S. Welfare Policy." *Cambridge Journal of Regions, Economy, and Society* 1: 17–36.

Seefeldt, Kristin S. 2008. *Working After Welfare: How Women Balance Jobs and Family in the Wake of Welfare Reform.* Kalamazoo, Mich.: W. E. Upjohn Institute for Employment Research.

———. 2015. "Waiting It Out: Time, Action, and the Process of Securing Benefits." *Qualitative Social Work* (October 8). doi:10.1177/14733250 15606188.

Seefeldt, Kristin S., Sheldon Danziger, and Sandra K. Danziger. 2003. "Michigan's Welfare System," in Michigan at the Millennium: A Benchmark and Analysis of Its Fiscal and Economic Structure, edited by Charles L. Ballard, Paul N. Courrant, Douglas C. Drake, Ronald C. Fisher, and Elisabeth R. Gerber. East Lansing: Michigan State University Press.

Seefeldt, Kristin S., Shelly Ten Napel, Dana Hopings, and David Levy. 2001. "The Summer Project in Berrien and Kent Counties: Participation

# References

and Post-Program Experiences." Ann Arbor: University of Michigan (May).

Seefeldt, Kristin S., and Heather Sandstrom. 2015. "When There Is No Welfare: The Income Packaging Strategies of Mothers Without Earnings or Cash Assistance Following an Economic Downturn." *RSF: The Russell Sage Foundation Journal of the Social Sciences* 1(1): 139–58.

Segal, Lewis M., and Daniel G. Sullivan. 1998. "Trends in Homeownership: Race, Demographics, and Income." *Economic Perspectives* 22(2): 53–72.

Sharkey, Patrick. 2013. *Stuck in Place: Urban Neighborhoods and the End of Progress Toward Racial Equality.* Chicago: University of Chicago Press.

Small Business Administration. Office of Advocacy. 2014. "Frequently Asked Questions About Small Business." Washington, D.C.: Small Business Administration (March). Available at: https://www.sba.gov/sites/default/files/FAQ_March_2014_0.pdf (accessed August 24, 2016).

Small, Mario Luis. 2009. *Unanticipated Gains: Origins of Network Inequality in Everyday Life.* Oxford: Oxford University Press.

Smith, Sandra Susan. 2007. *Lone Pursuit: Distrust and Defensive Individualism Among the Black Poor.* New York: Russell Sage Foundation.

Social Security Administration (SSA). 2011. "Annual Statistical Report on the Social Security Disability Insurance Program, 2011." Washington: SSA (July). Available at: https://www.ssa.gov/policy/docs/statcomps/di_asr/2011/index.html (accessed August 24, 2016).

Spinuzzi, Clay. 2012. "Working Alone Together: Coworking as Emergent Collaborative Activity." *Journal of Business and Technical Communication* 26(4): 399–441.

Stacey, Clare L. 2011. *The Caring Self: The Work Experiences of Home Care Aides.* Ithaca, N.Y.: Cornell University Press.

Standaert, Diane. 2014. "Payday Loan Quick Facts: Debt Trap by Design." Washington, D.C.: Center for Responsible Lending (July). Available at: http://www.responsiblelending.org/payday-lending/payday_loans_quickfacts.pdf (accessed August 24, 2016).

St. Louis Federal Reserve Bank. 2013. "Economic Snapshot: Student Loan Debt." St. Louis: St. Louis Federal Reserve Bank.

Stevenson, Betsey. 2009. "The Internet and Job Search." In *Studies of Labor Market Intermediation,* edited by David Autor. Chicago: University of Chicago Press.

Stone, Chad, and William Chen. 2014. "Introduction to Unemployment Insurance." Washington, D.C.: Center on Budget and Policy Priorities.

Stone, Chad, Robert Greenstein, and Martha Coven. 2007. "Addressing Longstanding Gaps in Unemployment Insurance Coverage." Washington, D.C.: Center for Budget and Policy Priorities.

Sugrue, Thomas J. 2005. *The Origins of the Urban Crisis: Race and Inequality in Postwar Detroit*. With a new preface by the author. Princeton, N.J.: Princeton University Press. (Originally published in 1996.)

Sullivan, James X. 2008. "Borrowing During Unemployment: Unsecured Debt as a Safety Net." *Journal of Human Resources* 43(2): 383–412.

Sullivan, Teresa A., Elizabeth Warren, and Jay Lawrence Westbrook. 2000. *The Fragile Middle Class: Americans in Debt*. New Haven: Conn.: Yale University Press.

Tach, Laura, and Sarah Sternberg Greene. 2014. "'Robbing Peter to Pay Paul': Economic and Cultural Explanations for How Lower-Income Families Manage Debt." *Social Problems* 61(1): 1–21.

Thomas, June Manning. 1997. *Redevelopment and Race: Planning a Finer City in Postwar Detroit*. Baltimore: Johns Hopkins University Press.

Trisi, Danilo. 2012. "The Myth That Single Mothers Don't Work." Washington, D.C.: Center for Budget and Policy Priorities.

Tüzemen, Didem, and Jonathan Willis. 2013. "The Vanishing Middle: Job Polarization and Workers' Response to the Decline in Middle-Skill Jobs." Kansas City, Kans.: Kansas City Federal Reserve Bank.

U.S. Bureau of Labor Statistics. 2013. "Occupations with the Most Job Growth." Washington: U.S. Department of Labor.

———. 2015. "Occupational Outlook Handbook, 2016–17 Edition: Home Health Aides." Washington: U.S. Bureau of Labor Statistics.

———. 2016. "Unemployment Rates for the 50 Largest Cities." Washington: U.S. Bureau of Labor Statistics.

U.S. Department of Agriculture. 2016. "Supplemental Nutrition Assistance Program (SNAP): National Level Annual Summary." Washington: U.S. Department of Agriculture.

U.S. Department of Agriculture. Office of Policy Support. 2014. "Characteristics of Supplemental Nutrition Assistance Program Households: Fiscal Year 2012." Washington: U.S. Department of Agriculture.

U.S. Department of Health and Human Services. 1999. "Temporary Assistance for Needy Families: Average Monthly Number of Families and Recipients, 1999." Washington: U.S. Department of Health and Human Services.

———. 2004. "Caseload Data 1993 (AFDC Total)." Washington: U.S. Department of Health and Human Services.

# References

U.S. Department of Health and Human Services. Administration for Children and Families. 2012. "LIHEAP Q&As for Consumers." Washington: U.S. Department of Health and Human Services.

———. 2015. "Characteristics and Financial Circumstances of TANF Recipients, Fiscal Year 2013." Washington: U.S. Department of Health and Human Services

U.S. Department of Treasury, with U.S. Department of Education. 2012. "The Economics of Higher Education." Washington: U.S. Department of the Treasury (December). Available at: https://www.treasury.gov /connect/blog/Documents/20121212_Economics%20of%20Higher %20Ed_vFINAL.pdf (accessed August 24, 2016).

U.S. Government Accountability Office (GAO). 2008. "Bankruptcy Reform: Dollar Costs Associated with the Bankruptcy Abuse Prevention and Consumer Protection Act of 2005." Washington: GAO.

———. 2012. "Unemployment Insurance: Economic Circumstances of Individuals Who Exhausted Benefits." Washington: GAO.

U.S. House of Representatives. Committee on Ways and Means. 2012. *2012 Green Book.* Washington: U.S. Government Printing Office.

Watkins-Hayes, Celeste. 2009. *The New Welfare Bureaucrats: Entanglements of Race, Class, and Policy Reform.* Chicago: University of Chicago Press.

Weaver, R. Kent. 2000. *Ending Welfare as We Know It.* Washington, D.C.: Brookings Institution Press.

Werhane, Patricia Hogue, Tara J. Radin, and Norman E. Bowie. 2004. *Employment and Employee Rights.* Malden, Mass.: Blackwell Publishing.

Wilson, William J. 1987. *The Truly Disadvantaged: The Inner City, the Underclass, and Public Policy.* Chicago: University of Chicago Press.

Wilson, Robin. 2010. "For-Profit Colleges Change Higher Education's Landscape." *The Chronicle of Higher Education,* February 7, 2010.

Zuberi, Daniel. 2006. *Differences That Matter: Social Policy and the Working Poor in the United States and Canada.* Ithaca, N.Y.: Cornell University Press.

# INDEX

Boldface numbers refer to figures and tables.

# Index

certified nursing assistants (CNAs), 53–54

Chapter 7 and 13 bankruptcies, 175–176. *See also* bankruptcy

Charles Terrace, 21

Charmaz, Kathy, 207

check-cashing stores, 167

Chicago, Illinois, 1–2, 16, 48

Child Protective Services (CPS), 131, 137, 189–190

children: childcare for, 4–5, 59, 63; education and, 37–38, 85, 89–90; housing instability and, 40–41; juvenile facility costs, 159; parenting issues, 77, 82, 178–179; poverty and, 8, 35; savings accounts for, 198; welfare and, 114

child support payments, 132, 155, 162

citizen patrols, 28

civil rights movement, 2, 6

Clinton, Bill, 124

Coates, Ta-Nehisi, 110, 198–199

*Code of the Street* (Anderson), 3

collection agencies, 169–172

collective bargaining. *See* labor unions

community colleges, 6, 81–82, 90–91

community organizations, 196–197

computer maintenance jobs, 56–57, 64–65

concentrated poverty, 1–2, 6, 16. *See also* social isolation

Consumer Financial Protection Bureau, 95

consumption smoothing, 149–150, 154–157, 161–163

contract employees, 55–56, 118, 188–189

Corinthian Colleges, 95, 232*n*36

Corktown, Detroit, 23

counselors, academic, 83–85

coworkers, 58–61

Credit Card Accountability, Responsi-

bility, and Disclosure Act (CARD, 2009), 196, 236*n*12

credit cards: bankruptcy and, 181–183; interest rates and fees, 146, 151, 155–156, 164–165, 196, 235*n*9, 236*n*12; national average of debt, 153–154; payment plans, 147, 164–165, 172–175, 196; predatory lending and, 150–151, 197; unemployment and, 146–147

credit reports and scores: access to credit and, 7, 149, 196, 236*n*12; bankruptcy and, 182–183; employment and, 7, 149, 182–183; foreclosure and, 108; garnishments, predicting, 174–175; hardship payment plans and, 165; late payments and, 7; low scores, 149; mortgages and, 100, 104; renting housing and, 7, 182–183; student loans and, 91–92, 94

crime: arson, 31–32, 97; children and, 178–179; domestic violence, 131, 182; gangs and, 22; gun violence, 19, 25, 27–28; insurance fraud, 31–32, 97; normalcy of, 28; racial violence, 17, 98; robberies, 19–20, 27–28, 107–108

criminal records, 2, 49, 128–129, 149

cultural humility, 202

Darity, William, 198

Data Driven Detroit, 19

Dearborn, Michigan, 33

debt: bankruptcy and, 175–184; collection of, 169–172, 197; in Detroit, 151–154, **153**; national median amount of, 153; origins of, 154–160; overview of, 149–151; paying off, 160–164; principal vs. interest, 164–169; refusal to pay, 171–173; as sharecropping, 7, 147–149, 161, 168–169, 199; social abandonment and, 7–8, 147–148; unemployment and, 146; upward mobility and, 4, 7, 147, 149; voluntary vs. involuntary repayment, 169–175;

# Index

# Index

racism (*cont.*)
  reparations and, 198–200; violence and, 17, 98. *See also* residential segregation
real estate business, 71–72
real estate market: antidiscrimination legislation, 2, 3; housing crisis, 79; redlining, 97–98, 100; white flight, 2–3, 17
redlining, 97–98, 100
refinance of loans, 104, 109–110
rental properties: credit scores and, 7, 182–183; eviction from, 29, 40, 44, 228n38; rent-to-own arrangements, 97, 101–102, 167
reparations, 198–200
research methodology: data analysis, 206–208; focus of study and, 202–203, 207; interviews, 205–206; interview topics and questions, 216–223; overview of study, 9–12; participant characteristics, **209–215**; perspective of researcher, 201–202; sample for, 203–205
residential segregation: causes of, 5–6; in Detroit, 106; persistent patterns of, 33, 47, 198; redlining and, 97–98, 100; social abandonment and, 8–9; wealth-stripping and, 199; white flight and, 2–3, 17
restrictive covenants, 17, 98
retirement accounts, 108–109, 142
"right sizing" Detroit, 45–47
rights of employees, 63–67
right-to-work laws, 193
riots, 17
River Rouge, Michigan, 33
robberies, 19–20, 27–28, 107–108
Romney, Mitt, 140
Rossi, Peter, 228n40

safety net. *See* Unemployment Insurance; welfare

San Francisco, California, 193
savings: for children, 198; for consumption expenses, 150; for education expenses, 80; lack of, 108–109; priority of, 71; unemployment and, 146
scrapping, 26–27
secured debt, 157, 179. *See also* mortgages
segregation, 6, 66. *See also* residential segregation
self-employment, 55–57, 70–73. *See also* entrepreneurship
Shaefer, Luke, 121, 125
sharecropping, debt as, 7, 147–149, 161, 168–169, 199
single-parenting, 11–12, 50, 82–83, 114, 134
slavery, 148–149, 198–199
Small, Mario Luis, 59
small businesses. *See* entrepreneurship
small claims court, 172–173
Snyder, Rick, 18
social abandonment: African Americans and, 199–200; city revitalization and, 46–47; debt and, 7–8, 147–148; in Detroit, 15–18; in education, 13, 78–80, 89–90; in employment, 13, 51–53, 133–134; explanation of, 3–4, 13–14, 188–189; in homeownership, 13; new social transformation and, 4–9; policy and institutional changes and, 8–9; social isolation and, 3–4, 188; wealth accumulation and, 4, 111; in welfare and benefits, 13–14, 133–134, 142–144. *See also* policy prescriptions
social control, 137–138
social institutions, 1
social isolation: African Americans and, 1; causes of, 2–3; combating, 192; in education, 79, 87–88; employment and, 1, 5, 13, 53–61, 67–68,